W9-CLG-274

TAKING CARE OF MEN
Sexual Politics in the
Public Mind

The idea of the sensitive, post-feminist 'new man' has received great attention. This book sets out to determine how much of the hype is based on fact, and why such images have proliferated. McMahon focuses on the pivotal issue of men's relationship to the vital daily work of caring for people – both physically and emotionally – revealing much confusion about the extent and the interpretation of change. Using statistical data, as well as interview transcripts and media analysis, McMahon draws insightful distinctions between pleasure and performance, assistance and responsibility, gendered personality and gendered jobs, and – underlying all – between consumption and production. Incorporating social theory, psychology and popular culture, this book argues that the recent social conversation about men largely avoids the vital political point that men's material interests provide a major motivation for resistance to pro-equity change.

After an earlier career in physics and computer science, Anthony McMahon has since lectured in sociology at Deakin and Monash Universities, developing one of the first Australian university sociology courses on men. He has published articles in journals such as *Theory & Society* and the *Journal of Australian Studies*, and has contributed to edited collections and numerous conferences. This is his first book.

To B.E.

TAKING CARE OF MEN

Sexual Politics in the Public Mind

ANTHONY McMAHON

Monash University

CAMBRIDGE UNIVERSITY PRESS

PUBLISHED BY THE PRESS SYNDICATE OF THE UNIVERSITY OF CAMBRIDGE
The Pitt Building, Trumpington Street, Cambridge, United Kingdom

CAMBRIDGE UNIVERSITY PRESS
The Edinburgh Building, Cambridge CB2 2RU, UK   http://www.cup.cam.ac.uk
40 West 20th Street, New York, NY 10011–4211, USA   http://www.cup.org
10 Stamford Road, Oakleigh, Melbourne 3166, Australia

First published 1999

Printed in Singapore by Craft Print Pte Ltd

Typeset in New Baskerville 10/12 pt

A catalogue record for this book is available from the British Library

National Library of Australia Cataloguing in Publication data

McMahon, Anthony.
Taking care of men: sexual politics in the public mind.

Bibliography.
Includes index.
ISBN 0 521 58204 0.
ISBN 0 521 58820 0 (pbk.).
1. Men – Socialization. 2. Sexual division of labor.
3. Sex role. I. Title.

306.3615

ISBN 0 521 58204 0 hardback
ISBN 0 521 58820 0 paperback

Contents

Preface

Since the advent of second-wave feminism, sexual-political issues about men have come onto the public agenda. From some quarters we hear optimistic reports about the extent of change in men's lives, and even those who find actual change to be slow are inclined to stress the change in public rhetoric – 'at least we are talking about it'. But what are we saying?

I wrote this book because I felt something vital was missing from most discussions about men and social change: a serious recognition of the central role men's material interests play in their motivation to defend the gendered status quo. While at one level 'everyone knows' that men still benefit from various privileges, what initially surprised me as I surveyed the extensive public debate about men and change was the way this point is systematically obscured or marginalised in both popular and academic discussion. Slowly, though, surprise turned to understanding – after all, if the social conversation about men is blandly apolitical this is itself in the interests of men.

My analysis ranges broadly over social and psychological theory, feminist theory (especially the type most popular with men), empirical social science, the pop-sociology and pop-psychology of popular experts and media pundits, popular culture and popular ideologies. This is not quite such a huge and unmanageable range as might first appear, since social theory often turns out to be not very different from popular ideology. Perhaps this is particularly true in the case of gender, where tough truths about the social world seem to be particularly unpalatable. There is much at stake.

I have chosen one area of social life for detailed analysis – the vital routine daily work of physical and emotional care for human beings. My personal history has led me, since childhood, to be profoundly struck by the arbitrariness and injustice of the 'sexual division of domestic labour', to use the seemingly dull but highly suggestive jargon of sociology – not that sociology has always followed the logic of the language of labour as far as it should. However, the proper application of the materialist paradigm of labour to include the daily work of caring for people yields, I believe, a valuable new way of thinking about men's situation and men's interests in the gender order. In particular, it clarifies the crucial point that men constitute a social, not a biological, category, one based upon the appropriation of love.

This book therefore belongs to a genre which has been out of favour in the last two decades – the materialist political critique of ideology – though there are signs that this situation is changing and that it will again be intellectually respectable to interrogate systems of ideas in terms of the interests they serve. My principal conclusion is that just as women continue, on the whole, to take care of men body and soul, so does the new rhetoric about men and change. The cultural and political imperative to take care of men appears to remain strong.

Introduction:
Changing Men?

In September 1997, following the death of Diana, Princess of Wales, Prince Charles and his sons stood in front of the vast wall of flowers which the grieving public had placed outside Kensington Palace. This was a very public moment, and a very political one. Charles' reputation as a father had not been good. Two years earlier the popular commentator Polly Toynbee had described Charles as the 'archetypal father of his generation – the failed New Man':

> Philip was playing squash when Charles was born, but Charles was in at his son's birth, and it made him feel 'grown up', he told the cameras. Watching a birth is easy, it's the rest that eludes them. Charles, introspective, sensitive, yearning to do better than his own father, has failed too. Sons in boarding school, himself absent most of the time, he looks stiff and awkward with them in public (*Independent*, 10 June 1995).

With their mother gone the boys were in their father's care, at a time of extreme emotion, and under intense public scrutiny. The *Daily Mirror* told its readers that Charles must be a loving father, 'one in a million', its opinion based on a widely reproduced press photo that showed Charles and Harry holding hands as they gazed at the floral tributes to Harry's mother. After all, 'at 12, most boys would not have dreamed of holding their father's hand in public' (*Agence France Presse*, 9 September 1997). Explaining how the 'royals turned the tide' by their behaviour at the funeral, journalist Patt Morrison singled out another moment of physical intimacy between father and son: 'In the brief shade and presumed privacy of the Horse Guards passage, a camera-caught moment had shown a father, Prince Charles, leaning solicitously towards his small son' (*Los Angeles Times*, 8 September 1997). With such touches of

1

intimacy the royal family managed, according to Morrison, to overcome the 'venomous' public mood which had preceded the funeral.

Why must a prince show physical signs of being a loving father to counter an outbreak of republican sentiment? This was not just an exercise in the politics of class. Charles was caught up in the politics of gender: his masculinity was in question, and traditional signifiers of royal masculinity would not do. The moment called for a sensitive and caring father to fill, symbolically at least, the dangerous void created by the withdrawal of Diana's distinctly feminine care for her sons and for the people. The required image had to flirt with the feminine, and at the same time assert masculinity. This balancing act has often been required of men in recent decades – required of both 'real' men and of men as they are imagined in the public mind.

The issue of the feminisation of men arises in a variety of ways, but central to most is the 'sexual division of domestic labour', as sociologists put it. This may be an ugly phrase, but it is a very useful one, and certainly not narrow. Since it covers all the necessary elements of care and maintenance of people which occur in households, domestic labour ranges from cleaning the family's toilets to sensitively nurturing the family's psyches. It is labour because it requires effort and it must be done, continually; and it remains sexually divided – for whatever reason, the majority of domestic labour, whether toilet-cleaning or soul-soothing, is carried out by women.

The question about Charles was whether he could nurture his boys. He was, in effect, being asked to demonstrate that he was an adequate mother, physically intimate and caring. This would hardly have been possible without several decades of debate about the sexual division of domestic labour – in effect, a debate about sexual politics. Sometimes this was quite explicit: at the first British Women's Liberation Conference, in 1970, Rochelle Wortis presented a paper entitled 'Child-rearing and Women's Liberation', which placed the division of domestic labour at the centre of an analysis of women's oppression, and called for increased male involvement in housework and childcare: 'Men can and should take a more active part' (Wortis 1972: 129–30). In the early anthology *Radical Feminism* (Koedt et al. 1973), Judy Syfers listed the numerous ways in which wives lack the kinds of personal care given to husbands. Her article was titled 'Why I Want A Wife':

> I want a wife who will take care of my physical needs. I want a wife who will keep my house clean. A wife who will pick up after my children, a wife who will pick up after me ... I want a wife who is sensitive to my sexual needs, a wife who makes love passionately and eagerly when I feel like it, a wife who makes sure that I am satisfied (Syfers 1973: 61–2).

But it was not only radical feminists who argued for, or expected, a change in the division of domestic labour. Mainstream commentators and experts took it for granted that change was desirable, especially because of the increase in the employment of married women. The unfair double burden of paid and unpaid work for women with family responsibilities was widely discussed, and one obvious solution to the problem was an increase in the amount of domestic work done by men. By 1975 the International Labour Organisation was calling on husbands to alleviate the 'serious worldwide problem' of women's double burden (*New York Times*, 6 January 1975).

Change in men's domestic lives was nearly always constructed as complementary to change in women's lives in the public sphere – the 'revolving-door' theory that as women entered the paid public workforce men would perform unpaid domestic labour. As the British sociologists Young and Willmott put it: 'If women go out to work, and if in that way their roles are not different from those of men, so much more difficult is it to preserve segregation in their roles at home' (1973: 121). The result was the 'symmetrical family', as sociologists, following Young and Willmott, described the new model of marital equality. The symmetrical family became a thoroughly mainstream issue. Men were contributing more to home life, but 'nowhere near equity yet', the *Christian Science Monitor* (14 April 1983) told its readers. The question of how men would continue to change was, according to Diana Zuckerman, a social scientist interviewed for the article, the 'most interesting question of the 1980s'.

The extent to which men have changed is hotly disputed. In this supposedly post-feminist era, many take it for granted that everything about gender has changed: writing in the Melbourne *Age* (27 September 1989) well-known social commentator and gender expert Bettina Arndt informed us:

> The days when a man could expect to come home to a pipe and slippers and a snooze in the easy chair are well and truly over. Now, whether they like it or not, when the paid working day is over, the second shift awaits them. Cooking, cleaning, childcare, all manner of tedious tasks previously shouldered by willing wives, are now out for tender.

Indeed, everything must have changed, or the idea of post-feminism falls to the ground. In the *Independent* (11 April 1995) Sue Slipman argued that women are now so assertive that they simply won't put up with the double burden: 'Women will no longer take the lion's share of responsibility for making male/female relationships work and for nurturing the children. Even if women wanted to make the old compromises, the gap between being assertive at work and a doormat at home is too great for the modern female psyche.'

At the same time, old-fashioned feminist discontent persists, even in conservative sections of the media. Joan McAlpine's complaint that 'you can demand an orgasm. But you cannot demand that your man cleans the toilet' suggests that women's assertiveness may sometimes be more effective with the private than with the public aspects of domestic labour (*Sunday Times*, 16 June 1996). While some interesting changes have occurred, post-feminist rhetoric is overblown and feminist discontent persists for a very good reason: the symmetrical family has not become the norm, and the double burden of employed married women remains. Arlie Hochschild (1989) expressed the disappointment of many when she discussed the persistence of the sexual division of domestic work in terms of a 'stalled revolution'. I will argue that men have, on the whole, been the agents of this stalling; this prepares the ground for what strikes me as most interesting, an analysis of the ways in which men have been thought about in this period of sexual–political challenge.

This book is, therefore, about men, social change, sexual politics and ideology. In it I examine what happens when issues about men and social change come onto the public agenda, issues which are clearly matters of sexual politics. I have often heard it said that no matter how slow actual change might be, 'at least we are talking about it'. But what are we saying? The sexual division of domestic labour is a particularly useful focus for this examination. It is probably the area of men's lives in which the greatest change has been desired, anticipated and reported. Much of the analysis will concentrate on men's practices within marriage, but this limitation is not because of narrow vision on my part. It is the debates about men and domestic work which them-selves privilege marriage: indeed, it could be argued that much of the rhetoric I will explore constitutes an attempt to bolster and reaffirm marriage in the face of the threat posed by changes in women's lives, and the resulting dissatisfaction of many wives with the division of labour.

Since the issue clearly raises the question of the feminisation of men, it allows us to explore the negotiation of male identity in a particularly delicate situation. In his discussion of approaches to the study of men, David Morgan (1992) suggested that it is particularly useful to examine cases where masculinity is made problematic by men's entry into fields previously considered feminine, including occupations such as nursing. My approach is similar, examining how men are understood in the context of their (real or supposed) entry into the 'feminine' world of the domestic work. As we will see, tension surrounding the possible descent of men into 'wimpiness' (lack of 'manliness') is very evident.

How far can gender convergence proceed before precipitating a crisis in the gender order?

This book details what is known about the actual lives of men and women, how domestic labour of all kinds is organised, and what changes have (or have not) occurred. However, my main concern is with how we think and talk about this – the public conversations about the issues. How have the issues of men and change been represented, discussed and imagined? A large range of genres is examined, including social theory, empirical sociology and psychology, the pop-sociology of 'expert' commentators, the psychological advice literature, personal accounts of family life, popular ideologies, and mass-media representations. Interesting similarities will turn up: distinguished social theorists can sound like journalists, and journalists can reproduce social theory; some aspects of feminist difference theory bear a certain resemblance to older, more conservative ideas; psychoanalytic concepts have worked their way into popular consciousness, and so on.

There are many voices in the public conversation on these issues. I will not spend much time discussing overtly conservative voices, voices which are unashamedly opposed to change. Not because they are unimportant, but because their sexual politics are quite straightforward. The literature of the recent Christian movement for American men states that the trend towards gender convergence must be rolled back: 'I'm not suggesting that you ask for your role back, I'm urging you to take it back' (Promise Keepers 1994: 79–80). Rhetoric of this kind calls for an analysis in terms of a male backlash, as many writers have argued, but I think that optimistic and progressive voices about men and change also need close attention. Here the sexual politics are not always as clear as we might at first think; unravelling the politics of the rhetoric about gender convergence is my principal task. My main argument is that the rhetoric manages quite well to depoliticise the issues and is thus complicit in the maintenance of male privilege, whatever its intention may be.

By 'progressive' I mean rhetoric which apparently favours the convergence of men's and women's lives through weakening the sexual division of domestic labour; and by 'optimistic' I mean rhetoric which is impressed by the extent of change so far, or confidently expects change in the future. I do not necessarily use the terms to indicate approval. As I will show, the issues (not to mention the rhetoric about the issues) are extremely complex. To take the view that the symmetrical family is an obvious good would be naive; it would, among other things, take it for granted that heterosexual marriage is the most desirable context for personal life.

Because the book is about the social conversation, there are numerous direct quotations. There is no better way to indicate the tone of popular (or academic) thought: the texts themselves are, after all, the relevant data. Take, for example, the advice for new fathers by psychologist Bob Montgomery which appeared in *Australian Penthouse* (April 1990). The article was headed 'Cluck Cluck: Are You Ready for Fatherhood?', though the instanced cluckiness of fathers departed from the maternal model. No summary could do it justice: 'You will notice a sudden change in your lifestyle. You can't spontaneously decide to just go out, because you haven't lined up a babysitter. Some activities may be curtailed. Even before the baby arrives, you may find your sex life suffering.'

Not all references will be to such popular sources. I also make extensive reference to social theory, both because it is part of the social conversation I wish to discuss and to ground my analysis. Everyone, academic or not, has a theoretical position, and part of my project is to demonstrate how the social conversation about men, no matter where it appears, is always theoretical, whether explicitly or implicitly. My theoretical view of gender, like that of many male writers in this area, is drawn from French feminism, though, in my case, not from the work of Kristeva, Cixous and Irigaray. Other feminisms have originated in France and, as Christine Delphy argues, what is known as 'French feminism' in English-speaking countries is in fact an anglophone concoction, hardly recognisable as feminism within France itself (Delphy 1995). Much of the theoretical underpinning of my analysis is based on the work of Delphy and her colleagues, which recognises men's direct interest in the sexual division of domestic labour – something which stares us in the face when we look at life as it is actually lived. This is something which, in one sense, everyone knows, but it is also exactly the thing which nobody says. As we will see, the variety of ways in which it is not said are many.

Part I sets out the empirical and theoretical framework which informs the rest of the investigation. Chapter 1 shows that a marked sexual division of domestic work persists, with men typically acting as 'helpers' rather than sharers of equal responsibility. A general male right to superior personal service and to leisure is evident. This is a source of considerable tension between men and women, but men's self-interested resistance to change is usually quite effective. The chapter concludes with a critique of the current fashion in social theory of abandoning interest-based analysis.

Chapter 2 argues that the work of feminist materialists provides the best way to theorise the division of labour and men's interests in upholding it. Feminist materialism builds on the fundamental materialist analysis of labour, showing how the 'labour of love' can be exploited: the distinction between production and consumption –

'caring about' and 'caring for' – is crucial. It clarifies that men are not just beneficiaries as consumers, but are themselves produced through domestic work. The chapter traces the history of this analysis and the critiques which have been directed at it, which have much in common with popular ideology.

Part II shows how the social conversation of men and domestic labour produces a bland, optimistic and apolitical account of change. Chapter 3 outlines the many strategies, some quite remarkable, which mainstream sociology and its allies (including popular understandings) use to posit a plausible 'revolving door' account of change. The discussion is grounded empirically (for example, in evidence about the past), methodologically (for example, in a critique of the framing of research programs and the presentation of results) and theoretically. It is *not* argued that nothing at all has changed. The point is that most commentary interprets the evidence optimistically, whereas it should better be understood in terms of a largely successful male resistance.

Commentators who see little change in men's practices often take heart from certain cultural changes. Chapter 4 examines the way issues of men and domestic work have been represented in the mass media and popular culture. The New Man and the Sensitive New Age Guy are complex figures which often bear little resemblance to the men who share domestic work equally; when they do, it is more at the level of the satisfaction of female fantasy. The history of marketing to men shows that the construction of the male consumer is a major force behind the figures, and this helps to steer men in a feminine direction without undermining male privileges. However, there are many other images of masculinity on the agenda; the New Man is already out of date, and more robust images of men are on the rise.

By far the greatest optimism about change concerns fatherhood. This is the most significant area in which issues of men, domestic life and social change have been discussed. Chapter 5 explores the representation of fatherhood in many genres, including personal accounts of fatherhood, expert advice to fathers and the related research literature. Fatherhood offers many opportunities for apparently progressive accounts which reinstate gender difference and male privilege. Fatherhood very neatly signifies masculinity, which helps resolve any tensions about the New Man's 'wimpiness'. The new 'sharing' fatherhood also nicely disarms critiques of marriage: the blurring of the distinction between production and consumption is particularly important – men who love their children are assumed to be sharing equally in the work of the family.

Part III discusses a variant of the revolving-door thesis, which comes from commentators who concede that change is slow, and search for obstacles to change. Chapter 6 discusses a variety of such obstacles, all of which downplay the significance of men's pursuit of their self-interest. Some accounts are vague and general, attributing resistance to entities such as 'society' and 'tradition' and avoiding political analysis. Some argue that women are the main obstacle to change, while others target social 'structures' such as the nature of paid work, but in such a way that men's interest in these structures, and agency in their maintenance, is glossed over. Empirical evidence shows, in any case, that the 'obstacle' of paid employment does not prevent men pursuing their goals.

The obstacle to change which is most often cited, both by theorists and in popular understanding, is the male psyche. Chapter 7 discusses the paradigm that men's failure to be nurturing and caring results from the trauma of separation from their mother. The similarities with popular texts and common-sense understandings are striking. Such psychological accounts of men propose that men have a 'need to dominate' which arises from psychological flaws in their make-up, thus men are suffering victims forced to seek power over women. The wide success of the theory in fields from academic feminism to the mass media, and especially among men, is a key instance of the depoliticising of sexual politics.

The book finishes by reviewing the main conclusions of this study. The social conversation about men and the sexual-political issue of domestic work omits the most significant fact about male resistance to change – that it suits men. This seems to be too unpalatable to be made explicit – to say it about gender relations undermines the romantic ideology of modern sharing marriage. Meanwhile, men's interests continue to be served by the same discourses which deny them, and which continue to invite us to wait until men are ready to change.

PART I

The Interests of Men

CHAPTER 1

Having a Wife:
The Division of Labour and Male Right

The basic facts about the gendered division of domestic work, especially the double burden of employed wives and mothers, are hardly a secret. Qualitative sociological studies such as Arlie Hochschild's *The Second Shift* (1989) have been widely reported. News items based on quantitative data from large-scale studies also appear, often being contrasted with the 'myth' of the New Man:

> The survey exploded the myth of the New Man. While 90 per cent of men agreed that they should share the chores, less than a fifth ever helped with cooking, cleaning or laundry (*Daily Mail*, 31 August 1993).
>
> Couples who share these tasks number about 1 per cent, according to the market research organisation Mintel. The 'sharing couple', like the New Man, is a shattered myth (*Independent*, 21 December 1993).

Nevertheless, it is worth discussing carefully the empirical evidence of the division of domestic labour. Not to restate the obvious – that a broad sexual division of labour exists – but to explore in detail what is known about the organisation of domestic life, especially in connection with men's practices and attitudes. This sets the basis for the theoretical discussion in this chapter and chapter 2, and the subsequent analysis of the way men have figured in the public mind.

The example of married men in households where both spouses have paying jobs will be emphasised, since optimism about change is based on this case (though contrasts with other situations, within and outside marriage, prove very revealing). The revolving-door model, discussed more closely in chapter 3, is simple enough: as women take on more paid work, men will compensate by taking on more unpaid work. This chapter mostly discusses typical situations and partly relies on statistical averages. A study of the typical has its limitations, but it is the best place

11

to start. Atypical situations, such as role-reversed or egalitarian marriages, have been seized upon by optimistic commentators. In much of
the literature the typical is too hastily written off as a residue of tradition, and attention is given instead to those (few) men who comprise a
supposed vanguard of change. The complex question of the rate of
change must wait until chapter 3.

There are many quantitative studies of the division of domestic
labour, of widely varying quality. Chapter 3 shows how easy it is for
quantitative researchers to produce results which invite bland, apolitical
interpretations. I will cite the most reliable quantitative data, including
those which come from large-scale studies in which participants keep
detailed diaries of time-use. I will also report data from qualitative
studies which use techniques such as participant observation and open-
ended interviews. Qualitative studies can reveal the reality of daily life
in a way that quantitative studies simply cannot. Compare the following
two extracts from the same study. Each reports quantitative data, but the
second also has a qualitative aspect:

> Four out of 52 female respondents said that attempts to get their husbands to
> do more housework had any long-term success (Dempsey 1997: 178).
>   In the course of conducting interviews I have overheard husbands demand
> of their wives: 'Why are there no socks in the drawer?' 'Isn't dinner ready? I
> said I'd be home early tonight!' I have also heard them issue orders such as
> 'Clean up the family room. It looks like a pigsty!' In *every* instance the wife
> deferred (Dempsey 1997: 191, emphasis added).

Little will be said about variations associated with race or social class
differences, or differences between the various countries for which
substantial data are available – the industrialised countries of Europe,
North America, Asia and Oceania. This is not due to lack of interest or
lack of space, but because there is a great deal of evidence that these
matters are barely, if at all, relevant (Lupri & Symons 1982; Collins 1985;
Seccombe 1986; Andorka 1987; Coverman & Sheley 1986; Chambers-
Mulholland 1987; Dempsey 1988; Wright et al. 1992; Baxter 1993;
Sanchez 1993, 1994; Massey et al. 1995; Nakhaie 1995; Zhang & Farley
1995).

Men's performance of domestic labour is one of the few sociological
phenomena of which this can be said. It is certainly not the case for
many of the factors which are supposed to influence the level of men's
domestic work. For example, women's income levels clearly depend on
social class, and higher income is supposed to give women greater
bargaining power in terms of domestic arrangements. Similarly,
women's employment levels vary considerably between nations, and
employment of any kind is supposed to improve a woman's bargaining

position. However, there are no significant cross-cultural and cross-class differences in men's performance of domestic labour, which overturns a number of strongly held prejudices.

For example, the common belief that sharing domestic work is a phenomenon of the middle class in general or the new class of highly educated professionals (the 'chattering classes') is quite unsupported. Indeed, when small class differences are found, it usually turns out that working-class men perform slightly more domestic work than middle-class men (e.g. Hochschild 1989). American studies report that racial differences are small, and indeed sometimes report that white men perform less domestic work than African or Hispanic American men (e.g. John & Shelton 1997. See Lindsey 1997 for a literature review). Neither are stereotypical views about national differences borne out. The famously lazy men of Russia do about as much domestic work as American men, though the work patterns are different: American men spend more time shopping, and Russian men cook and care more for children (Cutler 1990). In the Scandinavian countries, where gender equality is usually accepted as the most advanced, the division of domestic work has resisted a wide variety of policy interventions: 'men still need a little push', according to the Norwegian delegate to the UN committee on discrimination against women (Inter Press Service, 4 February 1995). It seems that the division of labour is static even when family life in general is subject to extremely rapid change. Over the past few decades the birth-rate in the province of Quebec has changed from among the highest in the West to one of the lowest in the world, and marriage rates have also fallen dramatically. But Quebec women continue to perform much the same proportion of domestic work as women elsewhere (Descarries & Corbeil 1989).

'The overwhelming finding to emerge from these studies is that women are still responsible for most domestic labour' (Baxter 1993: 80). This is the monotonous refrain of the most reliable empirical sociology. Not that every household is identical – wide variations within each type of household do occur (as we will see, even this simple fact can be optimistically viewed as evidence of general change), and there is great variation between different household types, at least for women. For example, the arrival of the first child increases the average domestic work of a wife from about 25 hours per week to about 60 (Dempsey 1997). By contrast, the lack of significant variation in men's typical domestic workloads in differing situations is quite remarkable. For example, a review of 65 studies covering the period 1970–92 concluded that husbands performed an average of about 10 hours per week of domestic work, irrespective of the employment status of the wife (Kunzler 1994). The conclusion of a large body of well-conducted

research in many countries was that husbands do not perform substantially more domestic work in households where wives are employed.
The same striking result was found both in straightforward studies
which compared all households with and without employed wives, and
in more complex studies which controlled for variations in factors
affecting the household's domestic workload, such as the number and
age of dependent children (Meissner et al. 1975; Berk 1985; Nock &
Kingston 1988; Komter 1989; Shelton 1990; Baxter 1993; Sanchez 1993,
1994). When studies do find that wives' employment makes some
difference, the effects are small. Bittman and Pixley (1997) reported
1992 Australian data showing that husbands of employed wives perform
about two hours more unpaid work than husbands of unemployed
wives. Another study reported that husbands of employed women performed about one hour per week more domestic work than husbands of
unemployed women (Baxter 1993). This could be said to give some
support to the optimistic model of change, but a more honest assess-
ment would be that the evidence of such small differences in men's
domestic work is devastating for the revolving-door model, discussed in
detail in chapter 3.

Other elements which might be thought to influence male domestic
work turn out to be equally insignificant. Factors such as the relative
earning capacities of spouses, relative educational levels, and the number and ages of children have been thoroughly investigated. The usual
hypothesis is that such factors should alter the relative bargaining
position of spouses or the household domestic work requirements, and
thus affect men's domestic work contribution. At most, very modest
effects are reported; some studies find no significant effects at all, or
effects in the direction opposite to that expected. For example, Brines
(1994) reported that men did less domestic work as their wives' incomes
increased (chapter 6 discusses this in terms of a 'doing gender' model).
As one large and complex study concluded: 'very little could be found
that affected how much husbands did' (Berk 1985: 161). This is not, of
course, the case with women's domestic work, which is easily shown to
vary in response to children's needs and the availability of assistance
from family, friends, neighbours, market services and state services.

One general review of early research into factors related to men's
domestic work dubbed it 'much ado about nothing' (Miller & Garrison
1982: 242), but it is not exactly nothing to find that hypothesised
influences on men's domestic work are insignificant. That is itself a very
significant finding. Thus when a researcher reports that hypotheses
about influences on men's domestic work were untestable because so
few cases of men sharing the housework could be found (Dempsey
1997), I am inclined to differ. That so few men share housework speaks

loudly about the various hypothesised influences: their effect is mani-festly insignificant. If we repeatedly find that men's domestic work levels are insensitive to apparent demand, we should perhaps stop trying to explain variation and focus instead on the apparent constancy (Shelton 1990). Or, to be more accurate, we should focus on the constancy *within* marriage. The situations of men inside and outside marriage are sig-nificantly different, a matter often overlooked by researchers who investigate intact marriages only.

When men enter marriage their participation in housework falls, and leisure time increases to be greater than at any other life-stage except retirement (Bittman 1991; South & Spitze 1994). One Canadian wife observed, 'Before we married he lived on his own and his place was so clean and tidy. But as soon as we got married, he somehow never felt he could clean up. It was all up to me' (Luxton 1983: 34). By contrast, when women enter marriage their amount of unpaid labour increases sharply (South & Spitze 1994), with some studies reporting a two-fold increase (Bittman 1991). Interestingly, some studies find that the key factor is not the fact of cohabitation with a male partner (which produces only a modest increase in women's domestic work) but being legally married (Shelton & John 1993). This increase occurs immediately upon marriage, and the birth of children further increases women's domestic work dramatically. The unavoidable conclusion is that work which pre-viously had been done by men for themselves becomes, upon marriage, the responsibility of their wives. In other words, the *main influence on the amount of men's domestic work is the presence or absence of a wife*. This way of putting things seems to be too political for the bulk of mainstream sociology, but it adequately sums up the empirical evidence, if our view is broad enough to admit comparisons between marital and non-marital households. Confirmation comes from an interesting piece of research into heterosexual couples consciously trying to construct an equal division of labour, which concluded that the key to success was the conscious rejection by both partners of the concept of wifehood (VanEvery 1995).

The point is also confirmed by the fact that the men who do the greatest amount of domestic work are those who are retired and alone (Bittman & Lovejoy 1993), separated or divorced (South & Spitze 1994), carers for frail elderly wives (Arber & Gilbert 1989), and single fathers (Wilson 1990). In marriages where husbands and wives are employed on different shifts, shared childcare (or at least babysitting) may be undertaken simply because it is the only possible option (Bryson 1983; Dempsey 1997). Thus some time-diary studies find that men's time spent with their children increases modestly when their wives are employed, but only when wives are employed at night (Presser 1988).

Heidi Hartmann (1981b) calculated that the presence of a husband requires about eight hours of additional work per week. The absence of a husband significantly reduced the amount of housework performed by women, and did not markedly increase the amount of time spent on childcare. Hartmann expressed the point memorably: husbands are a 'net drain' on the family's resources of labour time. This puts the problem of 'sharing' domestic work particularly starkly – the help that husbands provide does not even cover the amount of work they create. As one Australian wife told a researcher, 'it's like having an extra child' (Dempsey 1997: 173). Confirmation comes from the fact that sole mothers actually perform less domestic work per week than married mothers with comparable childcare responsibilities. One Australian study estimated the difference to be nine hours per week (Bittman 1991).

Husbands are not the only source of 'help' with women's domestic work, and comparisons with other sources of assistance are very revealing. The work of friends, relatives and neighbours, especially with childcare, can be quite significant. Such work by 'others' may exceed that performed by husbands. For example, Bittman's (1991) data showed that unemployed women perform an average 1.4 hours per week unpaid care for children not their own, comparable with the 1.7 hours per week the average man cares for his own children. The most substantial help for employed women may come from kinship networks (Szirom 1988) or from kin plus friends and neighbours (Evetts 1988). The availability of such help, especially with childcare, can make it possible for women to undertake employment which would otherwise be infeasible (Ericksen et al. 1979). Such support networks are overwhelmingly female. A particularly telling instance of help from outside the household is seen in the well-documented phenomenon of female relatives cooking and cleaning for men when their wives are absent (Boulton 1983; Murcott 1983a; Dempsey 1988).

Some studies report that other family members perform more domestic work than do husbands, whether wives are employed or not (Berardo et al. 1987). The contribution of children to domestic work is particularly important. As Virginia Morrow (1996) remarks, children's domestic work has been invisible to most sociologists, but in fact children in the average household perform about as much domestic work as their fathers (Ferree 1989; Manke et al. 1994). For example, Australian adolescent girls perform a mean of 8.4 hours domestic work per week (Bittman 1991). Some studies report that any additional help with domestic work when women are employed comes from children just as much as from husbands (Hicks et al. 1983); others find that help tends to be asked of children before husbands in such circumstances

(Chambers-Mulholland 1987). Morrow's (1996: 73) large-scale study of English children's written accounts of daily life found many cases of children taking this work for granted: 'My mum and dad both work. When I get home I usually tidy the kitchen and living room, then cook dinner for mum and dad and then I sit down and do my homework until they get home.'

Not surprisingly, the domestic workload of children, girls especially, depends on the demand created by their mothers' employment (Manke et al. 1994). In fact very little research of this kind has been done; the question of husbands' domestic work fits the proposed model of social change, but the possible contribution from children does not. The same could be said of the other possible sources of help for women. The use of market commodities and services, and state-supported services, can also reduce women's domestic workloads. If this is overlooked, it is possible to put an optimistic gloss on the fact that husbands in dual-earner marriages perform about one-third of domestic work, while husbands whose wives are not employed perform about one-fifth. This is not because husbands of employed wives respond to the evident need to contribute more to the household total workload by performing a *greater* amount of domestic work. The fact is that employed women simply perform much less domestic work: employed wives use a host of means to reduce their average weekly domestic work load from 45 to 26 hours (Kunzler 1994). For example, many employed women manage the double burden by purchasing commodities that require less work before use, such as convenience foods and disposable nappies (Ross 1987; Nock & Kingston 1988; Gilding 1994). Bittman and Lovejoy (1993) found that one-third of Australian households with children used childcare services, and that 20 per cent of households used cleaning services. More than half of Scandinavian households have employed paid cleaners at some stage (Kallstrom 1995).

A British study of high-earning dual-career couples concluded that the most common pattern was not the widely predicted sharing between husband and wife, but the rise of a new domestic division of labour between women, with the load being shared between wives and their employed domestic (female) help (Gregson & Lowe 1994). Another British study of women in senior management positions found that waged domestic help was indispensable to avoid career disruption, though the women still experienced the double burden to a large extent. In all cases the women selected, managed ('The most stressful thing I found about having children is finding the right nanny') and arranged payment for the domestic help, though the actual cost was sometimes shared between husband and wife (Wajcman 1996). An interesting finding is that paid services more often perform the domestic

tasks for which men are 'traditionally' responsible, such as house maintenance and gardening, than housework and childcare (Bittman &
Lovejoy 1991: 15; Baxter 1993). Dempsey (1988: 432) reported that in
the community he studied it was more acceptable for market services to
substitute for the unpaid work of men than for that of women. Any
increase in the rate of male participation in housework and childcare
may be connected with a decline in men's performance of outdoor,
repair and maintenance tasks, with a consequent modest shift of effort
into housework and childcare (Game & Pringle 1983).

A study of American marriages in which both couples had highly
demanding careers found that while there was still a marked division of
domestic labour, the sexual difference in amounts of unpaid work was
much less than in typical marriages, because neither partner performed
a great deal of domestic labour. Instead, women of lower socio-
economic status were employed to undertake childcare and housework.
Nevertheless, the wives retained responsibility in that they were responsible for hiring the help, often had to use vacation time to train new
employees, and filled in when the employees were unable to work. A
revealing fact is that the expense of the hired help was usually costed
against the finances of the wife, though one of the husbands reported
that he did assist his wife with the management of domestic labour
by helping her 'think of somebody she can call' (Hertz 1986: 194).
Similarly thoughtful 'help' from husbands was reported in an Australian
study. One female interviewee stated that 'my husband understands –
he's also in computing. He insisted I had help in the house, so I don't
have to spend my weekends doing housework. I felt uneasy about this at
first but I've got used to it ... My husband helped me in that' (Game &
Pringle 1983: 136). Such husbands were at least aware that paid services
were being used, unlike some of the husbands reported in another
Australian study, who were blissfully unaware of details of the household
routine (Bittman & Lovejoy 1993).

Choosing to Help

Up to this point I have treated domestic work as an undifferentiated
whole, citing patterns of weekly time-use, but the kind of work performed varies greatly, as do the conditions under which domestic work
is performed. Having full responsibility for the household routine is
very different from doing work only when asked for help, or when in the
right mood. Also, some work is more or less constant, while other work
can be scheduled to suit. This is perfectly well understood: media
discussions of *The Second Shift* referred so frequently to Hochschild's
remarks about the world of difference between occasionally changing

the oil in the family car and cooking every night that we can be sure she had hit a nerve. However, much sociological data and analysis fails to address even this level of complexity: time-use in hours per week glosses over the difference between urgent and non-urgent work, and between providing help and taking responsibility. Other studies, though, have addressed these issues, using methods ranging from complex time-diary studies to qualitative interviews.

One study of 160 American households found that 94 per cent of men were responsible for no housework or childcare tasks whatsoever, responsibility being defined in terms of 'remembering, planning and scheduling' (Barnett & Baruch 1987). Instead, the husbands provided (varying amounts of) assistance. As we will see, the existence of such assistance (even in quite small amounts) is often taken to be sufficient proof that domestic work is 'shared'. The term used most often by both men and women to describe male participation in domestic work is 'help', a term which clearly denotes freedom from ultimate responsibility. Other common terms are even more revealing. It speaks volumes about male freedom from responsibility that a father's time with his offspring can be spoken of by both mothers and fathers as 'babysitting' (Luxton 1983).

Particularly important is the fact that in many cases male help is not obligatory and routine, but a matter of choice. For example, Collins (1985) found that when men choose to cook they do not commonly take over the main meals, however competent they might be in the kitchen. The phenomenon of men occasionally cooking their specialty, to high acclaim, is a cultural cliché. In Dempsey's (1988) rural Australian study, this most often occurred at a barbecue, for which wives were responsible for all food preparation while husbands simply cooked the meat. The difference between providing help and taking responsibility for tasks is neatly illustrated by the common necessity for help to be supervised. As one woman remarked to her husband during a joint interview, 'time after time you are opening the fridge and saying where is the butter ... bend down and look' (Gill & Hibbins 1996). In Berheide's (1984) study half the women subjects reported that their husbands required supervision with domestic tasks. Another study described the extensive efforts women may need to teach domestic practices to their husbands. After six months of 'careful, though unstated strategising' by one of the women studied, the husband was doing the laundry, having been patiently coaxed through the appropriate series of steps. The woman concluded: 'I think I will train him to do the dishes next' (Luxton 1983: 40).

In this and other ways male help can actually lead to more domestic work for women, as does 'help' from children. One woman interviewee found she saved only half the time her husband spent helping her with cooking, since she had to instruct him in the use of utensils and the interpretation of recipes, and find all the ingredients for him (Bittman & Lovejoy 1993). Childcare can have similar effects. For example, mothers returning home may encounter a house needing to be tidied and children who have been 'running wild' and now need comfort and pacification (Luxton 1983). Some of the women interviewed in a recent Australian study had grown so tired of coming home to 'tired, unbathed and unbedded children' that they had given up their night-time employment (Dempsey 1997). Some of Luxton's female interviewees stated that it took more work to get help from their husbands than it did to do the work themselves.

Domestic work often involves the simultaneous performance (or 'juggling') of several tasks. This is a complexity which simple time-use data cannot capture. Some studies record also 'secondary activities', reporting that such activities are disproportionately the lot of women (e.g. Bittman 1996). Women report that much of their domestic work involves performing two or three tasks at once: the combination of meal preparation, child supervision and laundry work is the most common (Berheide 1984; Sullivan 1997). Simultaneous performance is not just for the sake of efficiency; tasks of this kind usually cannot be rescheduled. As a result women's time is highly 'dense', interruptible and fragmented, and managing it requires considerable creativity (Sullivan 1997; Hessing 1994). By contrast, the role of the helper may be far less demanding. Luxton (1983) concluded that much male help consisted of doing one task so that women could get on with others; a typical situation consisted of men reading a bedtime story to their children, so 'freeing' women to wash the dishes and tidy the kitchen. Similarly, Berk and Berk (1979) found that in families with young children, husbands mostly did evening childcare while their wives were doing after-dinner chores; when their wives were again available for childcare, most husbands quit for the evening. The fact that mothers are mostly present or nearby during father–child interactions, whereas the reverse is not true, also strongly suggests that men help while women juggle other tasks (Baruch & Barnett 1986).

Another indication of the choice exercised by male helpers is that the tasks particularly avoided by men are those which women, too, most dislike, but perform anyway: ironing, cleaning and washing (Oakley 1974; Collins 1985). The forms of domestic labour for which men do often take responsibility, such as home maintenance and gardening, can often be scheduled at will and can in part 'approximate a state of leisure' (Meissner et al. 1975: 430). Men also disproportionately undertake the more pleasant, playful or leisure-like aspects of childcare. In the words of one English woman interviewee: 'He just likes to play with him – he doesn't like any of the work involved' (Oakley 1974: 155). An analysis of Australian time-use data concluded that fathers compete with mothers only for the pleasant 'tasks' of playing, reading or talking with their children. Nevertheless, women's total time spent with children is so much greater than that spent by men that more of children's play (for children of all ages) involves their mother than it does their father (Bittman 1991). Another study concluded that men select the less onerous and time-consuming tasks such as washing-up, and overall prefer to undertake 'the fun parts of childcare: playing with the children, taking them to sport etc.,' rather than helping them with homework or caring for sick children (Dempsey 1988: 428). Some writers have even concluded that men may experience more of the 'fun parts' than do women. For example, Komter (1989) found that fathers reported more pleasure from contact with their children than did mothers, as the fathers' contact often consisted of playful interaction during periods of leisure. Saraceno's (1987) qualitative study of Italian households concluded that husbands reject tasks which are least tied to gratification or relationship in favour of tasks which are richest in symbolic meaning, freely given or spontaneous, in a process she dubbed 'skimming off the cream'. The complaint of one woman interviewee may stand for that of many others:

> I'm really glad he's spending more time with the children. They really enjoy it. But it's beginning to make me look more like the meany. Daddy plays with them and tells them stories and other nice things while I do the disciplining, make them wash up, tidy their toys and never have time to play because I'm cooking supper (Luxton 1983: 37).

Work and Leisure

So far the attention has been on work, especially the time it occupies. If we instead attend to time not taken up in work, we see a new face of the general failure of husbands of employed wives (or husbands in families with higher domestic labour requirements) to do more domestic work. The evidence reported above is the statistical distillation of countless instances of women working while men are free to relax. An example is the one collected in Luxton's (1983: 34) study: 'I come home from work dead tired and I still have to cook and be with the kids and clean up. And he just lies around, drinking beer, watching TV and I get so mad, I could kill him.' This example is depressingly routine, and I will take it as a model for the theoretical analysis in the next chapter.

It is difficult, certainly, to draw a sharp line between work and leisure. Many domestic tasks have leisure-like aspects (chapter 2 discusses this issue in connection with confusion over the meaning of work). We have enough evidence, though, to cast doubt on the idea that the leisure aspect of domestic work is enjoyed more by women than by men, though men may think this is the case – when one husband was asked what his wife's leisure activities were he replied 'ironing, sewing, reading' (Pahl 1989: 148). A telling point is that when men have reduced paid work hours, most of the resulting 'free time' is spent in increased leisure. They do not significantly increase their amount of unpaid work: a man's domestic labour time is only a little more sensitive to his own paid work hours than it is to those of his wife (Shamir 1986; Antill & Cotton 1988; Nock & Kingston 1988; Bittman 1991). The extreme example of this involves unemployed married men with employed wives. Despite the obvious pressure on them to undertake the bulk of household work, most studies find that such men do little or no more domestic work than do employed married men (Shamir 1986; Morgan 1992). One study found that unemployed men do even less domestic work (Brines 1994). By contrast, however, Wheelock's (1990) sample of unemployed men showed an increase in the amount of domestic work performed.

When results of time-use studies are summarised in terms of leisure outcomes, the impact can be striking, especially for households with high domestic work demands. One large-scale Australian study found that men in dual-earner marriages with children under 10 had 16 more hours per week uncommitted time than did their wives. Even in marriages with no children under 10, the gap was seven hours per week (Baxter 1993). In close agreement, Hochschild's (1989) summary of American data led her to estimate the 'leisure gap' for high-demand households at 15 hours per week. Bittman (1998) speaks of sub-populations of 'time-rich' and 'time-poor': the extreme of time-poverty is found among older married women with young children and full-time employment; the extreme of time-wealth is found among younger, single unemployed men with no dependent children.

Leisure is often considered residual, the time left over when work responsibilities are discharged. Studies of leisure can report their findings with bland statements such as 'Both men and women have comparably less leisure to the extent they engage in housework. Since women do more housework, they will consequently have less leisure' (Nock & Kingston 1989). This takes it for granted that work demands (both paid and unpaid) simply have to be met. As the authors ex-plained, 'by framing the issue in this way we are asserting the primacy of work in people's lives'. However, the data suggests another possible interpretation: perhaps men do less housework because they have more leisure, their time away from paid work being driven more strongly by leisure priorities. The quantitative evidence about men's failure to meet the evident extra demand in dual-earner marriages strongly suggests that leisure takes priority for many men.

This issue can be studied much more directly. Many qualitative studies show the jealous guarding of various male leisure rights, such as the right to time in pubs, and the general right to freedom of movement. Most women lack a similar degree of freedom. Their schedules are largely dictated by their domestic responsibilities, and women's residual leisure-time may be subject to their partner's control (Chambers 1986; Dempsey 1997). More money is spent on male leisure activities, and men feel less need to justify their expenditure (Pahl 1989; Dempsey 1997). Male help may be conditional upon it not interfering with either paid work or leisure activities: 'He's happy to take the kids to their sporting fixtures provided they don't clash with one of his fishing trips or something else that comes up. Mum always has to be available as backstop' (Dempsey 1988: 428). By contrast, many married women feel that they do not have the right to leisure time (Deem 1982; Wearing & Wearing 1988). In any case, women's responsibility for the household can mean that relaxing at home is simply pointless: 'It's not that anyone's going to whip me if I don't do it – but I know there's going to be double the quantity tomorrow, so I'm really just beating my own brow' (Oakley 1974: 44). Male leisure can itself create more domestic work, sport being a good example. Clothes need cleaning and repair, team social functions need catering, there is money to be raised, and so on (Dempsey 1997). In a variation on the tired theme 'what would we do without the ladies, God bless them' one male Australian lawn bowler praised female organisational and fund-raising abilities: 'I think they do a fantastic job. Where there's a job to do they settle down and do it spot on ... men are more casual than women ... there's no doubt, if the women weren't supportive of the men's club, I just wonder' (Boyle & McKay 1995: 565).

The Male Right

In summary, then, the typical husband enjoys a privileged position, with a greater right to leisure and an associated greater right to having his personal needs met by another. A common argument is that these rights are balanced by men's greater contribution to bread-winning, but the evidence about the situation in dual-earner marriages suggests otherwise (these and related issues are discussed in chapter 2 and again in chapter 6, in connection with proposed 'obstacles' in the way of an egalitarian division of labour). There is further evidence to support the idea that husbands have a right to leisure and service.

No matter how widespread the new rhetoric of sharing may be, qualitative studies consistently show that there are few effective social sanctions to help enforce an egalitarian division of labour. For example, Dempsey's series of Australian studies found that women, employed or not, are held accountable for the smooth running of the household: 'In this community if a kid is in trouble or has just got untidy clothes the mother is always blamed. "It's her fault"' (Dempsey 1988: 429). Accordingly, women's complaints about husbands' domestic practices receive no community support: 'When Tom refuses my repeated requests for help I know he has the whole town behind him' (Dempsey 1997: 207). Blumstein and Schwartz's (1983) study of American marriages concluded that a wife who does less housework than her husband requires almost inevitably jeopardises the relationship. By contrast, a husband may often, though certainly not always, do less than his fair share without putting the relationship at risk. A British study drew a similar conclusion:

> To put the sharing ideology to the test by complaining about inequalities in the domestic division of labour in a society where there are no sanctions guarding against their infringement is likely to be regarded as too slight a cause on its own for threatening the marriage bond (Brannen & Moss 1987: 141).

Undoubtedly the husband's right is, in many cases, qualified: a degree of help may be expected. The details of the ways in which male help is evaluated against expectations are discussed in chapter 3. We can, however, note that the fulsome praise which 'helpful husbands' generally receive suggests that expectations are relatively low: 'He's marvellous. He's a very good cook. Sometimes he'll say "I'll see to the meal tonight" and when he does he always shows me up because it always turns out terribly exotic. He makes an awful mess, mind you, which I have to clear up. He can do the ironing, though he doesn't do it often' (Oakley 1974: 159–60). One American study found that men who help considerably with childcare were described by their wives' friends as 'wonderful', 'fantastic' and 'incredible' (Coltrane 1989). The fact that most women believe that their own husbands perform more unpaid work than the average husband (C. Lewis 1986) also suggests that such praise is relatively easily earned. So too is the way in which tokens of help from husbands can be construed by women as a 'gift of love' (Thagaard 1997). For some women adequate support from husbands may simply involve positive support for wives' careers: 'Both of you are professional and you understand it ... He's always very supportive, not the individual sort of day-to-day things but very supportive in what I want to do' (Wajcman 1996: 625).

This does not mean that most women express unalloyed satisfaction with the division of domestic work. Certainly, bald survey questions of the 'are you satisfied' kind tend to be answered in the affirmative. The common finding that about one-third of women express direct dissatisfaction with the division of domestic labour (e.g. Pleck 1985) is often cited as indicating a high level of female satisfaction (e.g. Benin & Agostinelli 1988; Thompson & Walker 1989). However, more subtle quantitative studies which test the degree of satisfaction tell a more complex story. Women express higher satisfaction if their amounts of domestic work are low and the burden is shared more equally with their husbands (Ross et al. 1983; Belsky & Lang 1986; Antill & Cotton 1988; Benin & Agostinelli 1988; Ferree 1989; Machung 1989; Thompson & Walker 1989). The cross-cultural study by Stockman et al. (1995) shows that women's dissatisfaction levels are similar in Japan, China, Britain and America. A Virginia Slims poll which asked American women to rank sources of resentment in order of importance found that 'how much my mate helps around the house' ranked second behind financial issues (Townsend & O'Neill 1990).

Quantitative methodologies are unlikely to adequately capture women's dissatisfaction. Qualitative studies show, after only a little probing, that it is common for women to reveal barely suppressed dissatisfaction. For example, one British woman who earned more than her husband initially expressed satisfaction with occasional help: 'I'm quite happy if he plays with the baby so I can do something else. Yes, I wouldn't expect him to do anything more.' The researcher pressed on:

Interviewer: What about the housework?
Respondent: Well, I would like him to do more.
Interviewer: Have you asked him?
Respondent: Yes, frequently!
Interviewer: What was his reaction?
Respondent: He said 'Yes' but he doesn't usually (Brannen & Moss 1987: 138).

Similarly, qualitative studies reveal that even women who 'complain vociferously' about the division of labour throughout an interview can respond affirmatively to a direct question about satisfaction (Ferree 1989: 179–80). Brannen and Moss (1987) concluded that women's criticisms of their husbands' levels of domestic work are evident, but 'muted', and suggested that women are reluctant to express the negative side of marriage, especially in unambiguous terms of dissatisfaction. The direct expression of dissatisfaction would suggest a marriage in serious jeopardy and is reserved, they argued, for issues involving more serious breaches of marital ideology, such as infidelity.

The greatest source of women's dissatisfaction seems to concern the division of responsibility for practices for which everyday language has no settled term. One study found that three months after marriage women's main complaint was that they were understanding, tender and reassuring to their husbands, but that they did not receive similar care (Mansfield & Collard 1988). Another study reported that married women felt 'psychically deserted' and that despite dissatisfaction with gender inequalities in domestic tasks and finance, the greatest unhappiness concerned men's failure to 'do the emotional intimacy' (Duncombe & Marsden 1993). Another found that wives' satisfaction with the division of labour correlated most strongly with the degree to which husbands confided their feelings and initiated 'talking things over' (Erickson 1993).

Neither has sociology a generally accepted term for such practices. Erickson used the term 'emotion work', and many other terms have been used; 'emotional labour' is the most common (e.g. Cline & Spender 1988; James 1989). Duncombe and Marsden (1995) spoke of the 'triple shift', arguing that in addition to the usual double shift, employed wives put much effort into maintaining the psychic well-being of partners, children and even themselves. Time-use studies can shed little light on gender gaps in such practices. Even the idea that emotional practices should be thought of as a form of work at all is anathema to many. The ideology is discussed in the next chapter, and emotional work is very significant in subsequent chapters – confusions about the nature of emotional work lie at the heart of much of the optimism about New Men.

Studies of the division of labour often speak of the way in which it is 'negotiated' by couples (McKee 1982; Backett 1987; Brannen & Moss 1987; Darque 1988). The term 'negotiate' implies some discussion and compromise, but in fact the issues are rarely discussed by couples, at least not in any spirit of compromise (Luxton 1983; Hertz 1986; Bittman & Lovejoy 1993). Two patterns are common. In one the division of domestic work is simply not discussed at all:

> Interviewer: How do you decide who will do the cooking?
> Husband: We don't. She does it (Dempsey 1997: 193).

Alternatively, the issues come up for 'negotiation' when women question the prevailing order. Women often cite housework as the most common source of marital conflict (Glezer 1983; Mackay 1989). Some researchers reported that such arguments broke out during interviews with couples about domestic work. One such study concluded that the issue is fraught with the potential for conflict: 'the domestic division of labour is a fight waiting to happen' (Bittman & Lovejoy

1993). Another reported that in most cases couples seemed locked in 'tension-generating, manipulative power struggles' (Luxton 1983: 34), and Gerson (1986: 629) spoke of employed women engaging in 'protracted struggles' to increase male participation. To limit the scope of conflict women may employ an 'indirect strategy of cautiousness', as one researcher put it. For example: 'I really proceed slowly. I want to change things in a gradual way ... I reckon a lot with his feelings and I don't want to jeopardise my marriage because of my own things and wishes. I believe if you are too radical you risk destroying a lot' (Komter 1989: 204).

Whatever the tactics employed, the outcomes of attempts to raise male domestic work levels usually vary from limited success to the (more common) abandonment of the struggle. Only 8 per cent of wives in an Australian study reported any lasting effect from their efforts to get husbands to do more housework, and these women had sought only modest amounts of help in the first place. One of the women reporting long-term change summed up the improved situation: 'I do not have to persist so much now to get him to do something.' One-third of the sample reported only short-term changes, varying from 'he agreed to do it but never got round to it' to 'he did it two or three times and never again' (Dempsey 1997: 178–80). The majority reported no change whatsoever.

Women may desist because more work is involved in struggling for increased male participation than is involved in doing the work themselves (Luxton 1983). As one wife put it: 'I don't bang my head against a brick wall anymore' (Bittman & Lovejoy 1993). Many women appear resigned, one study reporting as typical the following remark: 'What else can I do? If he won't take on the tasks I have to do them' (Dempsey 1997: 190). Consider the tone in the following, where we can almost hear the sigh: 'Things are as they are, aren't they? You can't have everything settled as you prefer it.' Compare the remarks of the husband in the same marriage: 'As long as I know that everything is running smoothly I don't have to worry about it. If things would run out of control, then I would have to interfere' (Komter 1989: 198). Here potential male help is construed as interference, a rather self-serving view.

This brings us to the standpoint of men. Here are two (not necessarily representative) interviewees:

> My wife just has to do it, that is what she's a wife for. Isn't she? That's the wife's task, although one doesn't seem to agree with that anymore, these times (Komter 1989: 210).
>   What you want is to marry a woman graduate who is intellectual enough to hold a conversation with you, and someone who is confident to help you with

your decision-making processes through life, but who is also inclined to family care and household care. If you can find a woman like that you know you've won (White 1984).

Qualitative studies of men and family life are uncommon, partly because men are much less likely to agree to participate (Schumm 1987). Interviews with married couples about domestic work also show that many men are particularly uncomfortable with the prospect that their wives will be interviewed separately (Bittman & Lovejoy 1993). That same study also reported male resistance within the interviews, for example by trivialisation:

> The basic thrust of this communication was an attempt to place all subsequent events within the frame of play ... Occasionally interviewer's questions about housework were treated with barely concealed irritation and as beneath contempt ... Short, factual-sounding responses to questions also increased the impression of someone with far more important things on their mind.

As we would expect from the general failure of women to get more help with domestic work, there is scant evidence that the majority of men wish to increase their level of domestic work. Certainly many men wish to spend more time at home, especially with their children; this is not the same thing. Backett (1987) found only two fathers who said they would like to engage in full-time childcare, but both indicated their fear that the strain would be oppressive. Men who do undertake full-time childcare demonstrate dissatisfaction, as Wilson (1990) found in his study of single fathers. Though these men were performing most or all of the housework and childcare in their households, their attitudes about the division of labour were decidedly traditional, and they exhibited considerable resentment at their role.

Men with employed wives experience lower levels of personal satisfaction than do men married to full-time housewives, and believe they receive less in the way of personal services from their wives (Stanley et al. 1986). The desirability of personal service from wives was memorably expressed by one husband interviewed by a journalist: speaking of a period when his wife was temporarily unemployed and able to devote herself to domestic work full-time: 'It was great, like pulling into a pitstop' (Melbourne *Age*, 27 September 1989). Not surprisingly, men support a 'traditional' division of labour much more than do women. A 1986 American survey found that 64 per cent of women, but only 32 per cent of men, disagreed with the statement: 'It is usually better for everyone involved if the man is the achiever outside the home and the woman takes care of the home and the family' (reported in Thornton 1989). Australian opinion research by Mackay (1991) found that male interviewees (particularly when in an all-male environment) were 'wistful' about their lack of a 'proper' full-time wife able to devote herself to caring for family members. Mackay also warned his marketing clients to be wary of the image of the domesticated New Man, since his sample of men found the image unappealing.

Women's reports of unsuccessful struggles to change the division of labour are supported by the (regrettably few) relevant studies of men. One man explained that his strategy of resistance was learned in his youth: 'When my mother was so angry, I did not say anything either. I just went my own way, and I do this with my wife in a similar way ... I don't want to hear it, and then I don't hear it' (Komter 1989: 205). Similarly, one of Luxton's (1983: 39) interviewees stated baldly that he had no desire or intention to do domestic work but that, when pressed: 'I say "Sure, I'll do it." It shuts her up for a while ... really I don't intend to do it, but it prevents a row if I don't say that.' A revealing point is that many men consider women's employment a matter of female 'choice', and so justify their resistance to performing domestic work on the grounds that women have chosen their extra burdens (Dempsey 1988; Mackay 1989). This is a particularly serious blow for the optimistic rhetoric of the symmetrical family.

Two specific resistance tactics illustrate the general process. The first is a staple of sitcoms, and will be familiar to all. This is, as one researcher put it, the conscious 'mucking up'of the task so as not to be asked again (Dempsey 1995: 8). One man explained that his incompetence at cooking was a 'good trick', since 'if you burn the frypan and smoke the place out it's amazing how she'll start cooking afterwards' (Bittman & Lovejoy 1993). Resistance of this kind is sometimes knowingly pursued even by men who are full-time 'househusbands', about whom many optimistic accounts of social change have been constructed. In a set of personal accounts by such men, which Harper (1980) collected for her very optimistic *Fathers at Home*, one man wrote: 'I have strenuously maintained ever since making the change that I was absolutely hopeless at housework. There is an element of truth in this but it has also been a remarkably effective ploy in obtaining some assistance around the place' (Stokes in Harper 1980: 47).

Such strategies are surprisingly effective, given their evident transparency. As one study noted, men effectively 'blow the myth' by revealing considerable knowledge while explaining their incompetence. Thus one man justified his lack of laundry work: 'Too much detergent, not enough detergent, separate the whites from the darks, when they use the Javex, when they use the bleach!' (Blain 1994: 520). It is clear that women do understand the strategic intent behind male excuses (Mackay 1991). Bittman and Lovejoy (1993) observed that strategies such as feigning incompetence are often seen by women as a 'transparent form of resisting demands'. During their interviews they observed that many women signalled amusement, irritation and even exasperation with the manoeuvres of their male partners. As a woman in another study exclaimed: 'He knows how to run the dishwasher, he knows how to run a radial-arm saw, but he doesn't [laughs] know the clothes washer!' That study concluded that humour was a mechanism for coping with a power imbalance. Since men can refuse, making a joke of it hides the fact that women cannot (Blain 1994: 520, 547).

The second tactic is less amusing. One survey concluded that men employ various combinations of avoidance, denial, intimidation and violence to avoid domestic work (Gilding 1994. For further accounts of male resistance tactics identified in qualitative studies see Luxton 1983; LaRossa 1988; Hochschild 1989; Komter 1989; Bittman & Lovejoy 1993). Duncombe and Marsden's (1993) study of the division of emotional labour found that women's requests for better communication were met with strategies such as incomprehension, violent anger, avoidance by moving to another room, or cool logic on immediate issues. Both lists include violence. The literature on domestic violence and domestic work is not large, but there is some suggestive evidence about the link between violence and the division of labour. In their victim survey, Dobash and Dobash (1979) asked their respondents about the incident which had triggered the most recent instance of violence, and found that one-third concerned expectations about domestic work, making this issue the most common precursor of domestic violence. Scutt's (1983) case histories included instances of women being kicked out of bed late at night, with demands that dinner be cooked, the kitchen be cleaned and the laundry be done. In a survey of perpetrators, Ptacek (1988) asked for explanations of violence, and found that 78 per cent of men who had beaten their wives gave explanations which could be characterised in terms of husbands' perceptions that their partners had failed to fulfil the 'obligations of a good wife'; many of these concerned the wife's performance of domestic work to an appropriate standard. Similarly, Ellis (1983) found that many domestic violence incidents were based on men's complaints about the conduct of housework, especially the preparation and service of food according to their personal tastes and schedules. Luxton (1983) reported that women often limit their complaints about the division of domestic labour because of fear of their husband's violence.

Many men are aware that their wives would prefer a redistribution of the division of labour. Hochschild observed that most of the men she had talked to about her book had 'squirmed', while acknowledging that it was an accurate account (*People*, 4 September 1989). Over half of the

American men studied by Pleck (1985) believed that their wives wanted them to do more domestic work, in close agreement with Berk's (1985) American study in which 43 per cent of men stated that domestic arrangements were less than fully fair. Similarly, an English study by Warde (1990) found that 42 per cent of men agreed that they did less than their fair share of domestic work. Warde told the *New Statesman & Society* (12 January 1990) that this showed that men have 'an ideology of sharing in marriage that is not borne out in practice', a theme we will meet frequently in chapter 3. The world, however, may be harsher than this. It is perfectly logical to acknowledge another's dissatisfaction without intending to rectify the situation, no matter what the ideology of sharing marriage might tell us. Accordingly, a study of the relation between happiness and perceptions of fairness in domestic work concluded 'fairness in the division of labour matters for wives. For husbands, however, fairness is not related to marital happiness' (Ward 1993: 436).

Perhaps such results would be less shocking if they concerned, say, fairness in the global economy. Most people realise that economics is a matter of advantage and disadvantage. Suppose we learn that the happiness of the wealthy is not related to perceptions of fairness in the economy, but that happiness among the poor is. A psycho-political interpretation springs to mind. For the poor to acknowledge unfairness is to admit their disadvantage; for the rich to acknowledge unfairness is to admit their advantage, a matter less likely to cause dissatisfaction. However, a similarly political analysis of marital happiness runs counter to deeply held ideologies.

Men, Interests and Social Theory

How should the sexual division of domestic work be understood? I believe that men, on the whole (an important qualification), perceive that their interests are best served by maintaining the sexual division of domestic work, and use considerable resources to defend it. This was not my view when I began to think sociologically about men. Initially I puzzled over questions such as 'why don't men treat women better?' However, the evidence about the division of labour soon suggested that there is little mystery about the advantages of being the dominant gender group, or why men would wish to remain in that position. The situation is not very different from other forms of domination which yield personal advantage.

This is not a particularly popular position to take up. The great majority of men (and many women) writing on gender issues are uncomfortable, to put it mildly, with the view that men's interests provide the key to understanding gender relations. Much theoretical subtlety, usually of a psychological kind, has been applied to the question of *why* men want to dominate women. Much less theoretical effort has been applied to the question which is much more pressing, namely *how* men manage to continue to dominate. The conceptual and ideological mystifications which help men in this regard form the principal topic of the following chapters.

My view runs counter to major trends in recent social theory. Many writers object to appeals to group interests to explain social arrangements of any kind, a position that is particularly pronounced in thinking about gender. A writer in the field of criminology would probably not feel obliged to defend the idea that organised crime is pursued for material gain; a writer in the field of imperial history would probably not have to defend the point that imperialist policies have been strongly connected with the pursuit of economic and political interests – though even in such cases, recent social thought might tell us that such phenomena are the effects of criminal and imperialist discourses, which make it possible to adopt criminal or imperial 'subject positions'. But there is something about gender which makes interest-based analyses particularly unacceptable, both to theorists and generally, and this is extremely important in the way gender relations work.

One male social theorist who does emphasise the advantages which accrue to men is Australian sociologist Bob Connell. In one of his first discussions of men and gender, Connell and his co-authors described the claim of male liberationists that men stand to gain from women's liberation as 'naive at best, and at worst dishonest' (Carrigan et al. 1985: 580–1). In an extended treatment in *Gender and Power* (1987) he emphasised the broad collective interest of men in hierarchical gender relations, while stressing that not all men have the same degree of investment in patriarchy. His position on interests is perhaps clearest in *Masculinities*:

> Interests are formed in any structure of inequality, which necessarily defines groups that will gain and lose differently by sustaining or by changing the structure. A gender order where men dominate women cannot avoid constituting men as an interest group concerned with defence, and women as an interest group concerned with change. This is a structural fact, independent of whether men as individuals love or hate women, or believe in equality or abjection (Connell 1995: 82).

This does not mean that identifying the interests at work in a specific situation is the end of the matter. To argue that men have an interest in patriarchy seems to be taken by some as indicating that change is impossible, and this gloomy conclusion can lead to a rejection of the premise. This is too pessimistic, however – to have an interest is one thing, to secure it is quite another. Similarly, some critics of interest-based analyses seem to think that such analyses assume situations of complete domination in which the winners take all and are totally in command, but this is not the case. No situation of domination is ever secure or total; all are fraught with contradictions and limitations, and produce resistance. Thus, defending analyses relying on interests, Connell noted: 'Of course such a claim is merely a starting point; one must then demonstrate how the job is done, examine countercurrents and contradictions, etc.' (Connell 1997: 704). It is, however, an important starting point. If interests are left out of analysis very different analyses tend to follow.

For Connell, structures of domination and inequality inevitably go hand in hand with the construction of group interests: in other words, domination is not an abstract matter, but is always about something. This will seem obvious to some readers. After all, how can we even begin to speak about situations of domination or inequality without making some reference to the interests involved? Take the example noted earlier, in which one (employed) wife described cooking, cleaning and childcare while 'he just lies around', drinking beer and watching TV. I propose that we can best understand this scene in terms of male power being exercised to pursue an interest in leisure and avoid work. This mode of understanding is hardly controversial within the sociological tradition, being precisely that found in Weber's celebrated definition of sociological understanding in terms of understanding the motive of an action. For his illustration, Weber chose the case of a man chopping wood. We understand this in terms of motive, he argued, once we can establish whether the woodchopper is working for a wage, or is chopping a supply of firewood for his own use, or is practising a form of recreation, or is working off a fit of rage, and so on (Weber 1968: 8). The implication is that we cannot avoid making assumptions about the range of interests which might motivate a human action. Campbell (1996) shows how, in much post-Weberian sociology, the concept of motive is restricted to actors' publicly articulated rationalisations of action, and restates the significance of motive in the more 'forceful' Weberian sense, which points out that attributing a motive inevitably involves making an interpretation based upon our understanding of the range of conscious or unconscious motives (or interests) relevant to the case.

If we used the case of the seated man watching TV and drinking beer to illustrate Weber's point about sociological understanding, we might say that we understand it in terms of the man's motive once we establish that the seated man is an honoured visitor who would breach rules of etiquette by offering assistance, or is exhausted or unwell and in need of care and rest, or is a dominant household member taking his ease while food is prepared and his dependants cared for (there are two actors, and we would need to discuss the woman's motives as well). If the scene is repeated year after year, and we have reason to believe that the man is no more exhausted or unwell than the woman, the last interpretation becomes most plausible. Moreover, if the man confides that he realises that the situation is unfair but that he enjoys it anyway, and the woman confides that she has exhausted all strategies to change the situation, we may feel surer about the matter. As we have seen, this is the kind of situation which does occur.

Of course, the wilfully naive 'anthropologist from Mars' who makes no assumptions about human culture might not concede male domination in the Canadian domestic scene, on grounds such as these: 'For all I know the man is performing the laborious and socially necessary work of consumption, while the woman is expressing her personality through the pursuit of a hobby – how can I assume that she is not exploiting him?' But we are not from Mars. We are not very likely to entertain such doubts, though Pahl's case of the man who described ironing as one of his wife's leisure activities calls this into question. May we not conclude that the beer-drinking/TV-watching husband is exercising the privilege of domination in order to pursue his interest in maintaining his leisure rights? No, we may not – or so I have heard from very earthly (male) social theorists who have taken the Martian position concerning this example when I have mentioned it in seminars. In that view, any link between domination and interests is quite out of the question, given the principled refusal to acknowledge domination in the first place.

More common than this is a view which acknowledges male domination, but denies its connection with interests. Consider the words of a male interviewee in a study of domestic violence, who explained his tendency to batter his wife in terms of the maintenance of, among other things, his right to have his food cooked the way he wanted: 'I don't know if I demanded respect as a person or a husband or anything like that, but I certainly, you know, didn't think I was wrong in asking not to be filled up with fatty foods' (in Ptacek 1988: 147). On the face of it this is a struggle over personal service which includes violent tactics, revealing behaviour and attitudes resembling those of a master towards an unsatisfactory servant. But I was told at another seminar that the man was in fact blindly expressing his tragically wounded masculinity. According to this view, male domination only *appears* to concern the pursuit of interests. The deeper truth is that domination is the result of a crippling psychological process which leads men to want domination over women in order to bolster their insecure identities. Psychological accounts of this kind have been highly influential, and are discussed in chapter 7. For the time being, I simply want to question the plausibility of such accounts when applied to the routine non-violent daily domination apparent in the sexual division of domestic labour.

For many theorists, any talk of interests raises the spectre of a fixed human nature. This is anathema to the contemporary school of thought which stresses the fluidity of all social phenomena, arguing that 'reality' is a discursive product. In their influential work *Hegemony and Socialist Strategy* (1985), Ernesto Laclau and Chantal Mouffe were scathing in their critique of political theorists who rely on the objective interests of particular social groups. Given the 'heterogeneity of positions' within the working class which yields a plurality of 'subject positions', any appeal to the idea that, for example, workers have objective interests in common, is inevitably 'essentialist' and 'little more than an arbitrary attribution' (83–4). Not that interests disappear completely from their analysis; rather, social interests are produced discursively, through politicising ideologies, for example. Thus, they argued, serfs and slaves can be said to be oppressed only when there is an appropriate 'discursive formation' such as that of human rights, which amounts to saying that no serf or slave could understand that they were oppressed without such a discourse (1985: 154). As Terry Eagleton pointed out in his passionate critique of Laclau and Mouffe, proletarians would have an interest in securing better living conditions only if they were already socialists – only because they have, to use the jargon, taken up a socialist 'subject position'. Eagleton and other critics, while accepting that no social or political interest group is ever completely unified in its members' positions or interests, argue that writers such as Laclau and Mouffe stress heterogeneity to the point of incoherence. If such analyses were consistently pursued, there could be no rational basis for any political practice: 'there would be no good reason why the struggle against patriarchy should not be spearheaded by men, or the fight against capitalism led by students', it would all be a matter of which discourses and subject positions were most prominent at the time (Eagleton 1991: 214, 218).

Interestingly, such consistency of rigorous analysis is apparently not easy to maintain. In their own political analyses Laclau and Mouffe readily rely on unspecified assumptions about interests, speaking un-problematically about imperialist exploitation and brutal centralised domination in the Third World, and advocating in the West a pluralist politics which, in effect, respects the various interests of women, ethnic groups, and so on. An interest-based analysis has not been transcended, and it is hard to see why these particular groups' interests are to be privileged. Similarly, in a passage which is extraordinary given their

avowed anti-essentialism, Laclau and Mouffe (1985: 184) take as their
guideline liberalism's commitment to the 'liberty of the individual to
fulfil his or her human capacities'. What, in their view, could such
capacities possibly be? How would they justify their implication that this
is in the interests of individuals? It is not easy to avoid assumptions about
interests (see also Geras' (1987, 1988) extended critique of Laclau and
Mouffe in *New Left Review,* and the reply by Laclau and Mouffe (1987)).

Similarly, Stewart Clegg's post-structuralist *Frameworks of Power* (1989)
criticised all theories which rely on 'fixed interests on the one hand and
definite discourses representing them on the other'. Rather, interests
are themselves 'discursively constructed'. Accordingly, he argued that it
is just as fruitless for feminist theorists to base their analyses on the
supposed real interests of men and women, as it is for Marxists to rely on
supposed real interests based on class. Again, Clegg's own work demonstrated how difficult it is to avoid making assumptions about interests in
sociological and historical explanation. His case studies of the exercise
of feudal power relied, at every turn, on assumptions about the interests
of social actors and of competing interest groups. Thus, he cited with
approval an analysis of the feudal system as a 'method for keeping the
stomachs of the barons and their retainers full', based upon the
extraction of surplus agricultural product (1989: 157). Clegg appeared
willing to take for granted the human interest in having a full stomach,
without considering himself obliged to show how that interest was
discursively constructed.

As I mentioned earlier, the real sticking-point for critics of interests is
the belief that any appeal to interests is an appeal to a fundamental
human nature, which transcends all societies and is knowable before any
particular historical or social analysis. Debates about human nature
form a vast literature, and I do not intend to add to it. It is clear that
there are great difficulties in any attempt to establish once and for all a
model of universal human nature from which we can read a complete
list of human needs and hence human interests. Such attempts must
yield models which express the psychological and philosophical assumptions of their home cultures. All the same, it may not be unreasonable to
argue that it is in our interests to have enough to eat, or to have freedom
from ceaseless back-breaking labour, in any social system. Of course, not
all examples are of this simple physiological kind, though perhaps this
is the case more often than some care to recognise.

In general, what is at stake are men's interests in the maintenance and
reproduction of their historically constructed patriarchal relations. It is
possible to speak about interests without invoking the spectre of a fixed
human nature. Terry Leahy's formulation is succinct: 'It is not males
as a biological category that oppress women but men as a socially

constructed gender group. It is only as a socially constructed gender group that men can have 'an interest' in oppressing women' (Leahy 1990: 25). This is the kind of analysis Connell proposed when he spoke of the organisation of men's and women's interests in particular historically produced gender orders, independent of individual attitudes and values. Specifically addressing the criticism that such arguments smack of a trans-historical functionalism, he discussed the male interest in preserving dominance in gender relations as 'not a universal functional requirement' but 'a historically produced strategy in gender practice' (Connell 1997: 704). This is similar to analyses of capitalist interests: capitalists are a historically and socially constructed group, with material interests in the maintenance of capitalism which are real, concrete, and objective but which do not imply any trans-historical assumptions. This hardly settles the matter, especially for those who reject the notion that men as a group resemble capitalists in being socially constructed, but instead are a biologically defined category. After all, a capitalist can become a worker, but a man is just a man. Not so, actually. In the next chapter, I will argue that men (real men, men as they are now) are themselves produced through domestic work – and in that very important sense men are not a biological category but a socially constructed gender group.

From the contradictions of contemporary theory I do not draw permission to cite a universal human nature on which to ground analysis. Rather I will pursue a middle way, discussing the social world in relation to struggles over interests which are historically and socially dependent, but no less real for all that. In this case, as so often, the question of interests revolves around who does the work, on and for whom, and to whose advantage.

CHAPTER 2

Producing Men:
The Labour of Love

The Materialist Paradigm

How is work organised – actual, physical, bodily work – work which makes you tired? The social theoretical perspective which has put the greatest stress on the centrality of work is the materialist perspective. Materialist analyses concern 'actual individuals, their work, their actual productive activities, and the material conditions produced by these activities' (Smith 1987: 88) and begin from the standpoint of those who actually do the work. The perspective was first clearly spelt out in *The German Ideology* by Marx and Engels (1845–46). Their starting point was that people must be able to live in order to make history, and that life involves 'before anything else eating and drinking, a habitation, clothing and many other things'. The first historical act is, therefore, the 'production of material life'. This act is necessarily social, always taking place within a social relationship, and always organised according to some mode of production. Interestingly, the earliest statements of the materialist view explicitly included the making of people as well as of things:

> The production of life, both of one's own by labour and of fresh life by procreation, appears at once as a double relationship, on the one hand as a natural, on the other as a social relationship. By social is meant the cooperation of several individuals, no matter under what conditions, in what manner or to what end (Marx & Engels in Bottomore & Rubel 1956: 75, 77).

The mode of organisation of cooperative human labour is the key, Marx and Engels believed, to understanding any particular social formation. Domination and oppression are built upon the interested appropriation and exploitation of labour by the ruling class(es) of the day.

This kind of grand theoretical vision is very unfashionable in social theory. We are, it is said, living at a time in which all grand narratives of this kind are thoroughly exhausted. Marxist views are one of the main targets of this attack on unifying social theories. The influential German theorist Zygmunt Bauman (1989: 53) spoke of 'the increasingly apparent plurality and heterogeneity of the socio-cultural world ... with no clear-cut distinction between order and abnormality, consensus and conflict', this being related to the dominance of market relations, which are the 'arch-enemy of uniformity'. There is much which could be said about this kind of analysis. We might wonder whether the claim that the market dominates social life is itself another grand narrative, and question the plausibility of the notion that the global market which delivers, for example, American baseball caps to Australian boys really is the enemy of uniformity. We could also question the implication that market relations dominate all social life, including life in the private sphere, and ask whether views such as Bauman's simply continue the long tradition in social theory which privileges the public sphere as *the* social sphere. These are important issues, and later in this chapter I will argue that non-market-based relations in the private sphere are very significant in understanding gender relations. For the moment the important point is simple: diagnoses of the end of grand narratives and the decline of uniformity have a hard time dealing with the obvious persistence of one grand narrative at least, namely that of gender. If there are no clear distinctions any longer, someone has forgotten to inform all those households which maintain the sexual division of labour in a depressingly uniform fashion, across classes, races and nations. If there are no clear distinctions any longer, why have the features pages of my daily newspaper been citing heart-warming examples of men doing housework and childcare as evidence of something new and remarkable – and doing this regularly for the last 25 years? The persistence of gender divisions in social life may, after all, require analysis on quite a broad scale. The same could be said for other social divisions, and in this period of increasing dominance of globalised corporate capital there are some signs of a revival in Marxist analyses.

Of course, in the analysis of capitalist societies by Marx, Engels and those who followed their lead, the materialist paradigm was applied to understanding the organisation of the labour of paid employees in the market economy. Eventually, second-wave feminists sympathetic to the Marxist tradition began to decry this limitation, arguing that a materialist analysis of unpaid domestic work was required to complete the analysis of the production of material life: materialist analysis can, and should, refer to the social relations involved in 'any task or activity which the society defines as necessary' (Young 1981: 52). It is not difficult to see that domestic labour is socially necessary labour. As Ann Oakley (1974) observed in her ground-breaking book *The Sociology of Housework*, much domestic labour is concerned with primary physical survival: it is not a matter of providing life's little luxuries but of providing basic necessities such as disease-free food and a clean, warm dwelling-place. In this vein, Carol Thomas (1995) argued strongly that the expansion of domestic work made a major contribution to falling mortality rates in late 19th and early 20th century Britain. Taking up the challenge, Wally Seccombe began his 1974 article on housewives and capitalism in *New Left Review* with a parody of traditional Marxist understandings:

> It is as if capital were directing a play entitled 'The Working Day'. The curtain rises to reveal a group of industrial labourers crowding around the gates of a factory preparing to be hired for a day in return for a wage. The audience finds the action on stage so absorbing that they accept the immediate appearance of the play as a reality. In doing so, they forget that the actors are not the sole agents of the onstage action. Backstage are a group of stage hands (housewives) who have been preparing the workers for the opening curtain for hours beforehand. Although these workers are out of sight and therefore out of mind, they are nonetheless indispensable to the entire production (Seccombe 1974: 14–15).

Indeed! However, while the backstage work may be indispensable, Seccombe's spatial metaphor suggested that the 'entire production' of main interest is still the frontstage work in the capitalist labour market. As with most materialist analyses of domestic labour in the 1970s, Seccombe remained within a conventional Marxist framework, adding domestic labour to the existing analysis.

Analysis centred on two ways in which domestic labour supposedly functioned in capitalism (representative articles include Seccombe 1974; Gardiner 1975; Coulson et al. 1975. See Molyneux 1979 for a summary of the debate. The following account partly relies on Barrett 1980). First, domestic labour reproduces labour power: the wage labourer appears at the workplace 'fed, clothed, laundered, soothed and untrammelled by responsibilities for childcare' (to use Barrett's words). The value of the sexual division of domestic labour for capitalism is that the labour cost of reproduction is reduced if performed by a housewife rather than by paid workers or the labourer himself. Second, domestic labour reproduces the relations of production: in particular, the housewife socialises children into the appropriate place in the division of labour, provides an incentive for her husband's breadwinning role and cushions him against the alienation of wage labour. It was argued that domestic labour performed for capitalism the two vital tasks of maintaining the workforce on a daily basis and producing appropriate work orientations in current and future workers: in the standard jargon, domestic labour was understood in terms of its 'reproductive functions' for capitalism, namely the reproduction of labour power and the reproduction of the relations of production at the level of ideology. This stress on reproduction rather than production is very telling. Since production took place in the labour market, domestic work logically had to be seen as other than productive. This was consistent with the standard historical acount, accepted by Marxists and non-Marxists alike, that industrialism had led to the decline of the household as a productive unit; it had become a site of consumption.

This research program generated a large and not particularly memorable body of work. However, by the beginning of the 1980s the limitations of the so-called 'domestic labour debate' were widely recognised by many Marxist feminists: 'By the end of the 1970s disillusionment – and sheer boredom – with the debate was widespread' (Jackson 1996: 57). As Michele Barrett (1980) argued in her influential review, while capitalism had certainly incorporated and entrenched existing gender divisions, it seemed impossible to prove that it could not survive without the sexual division of labour. There are, after all, other ways of maintaining the workforce and producing appropriate work orientations. Much daily maintenance of labour power can be performed, and indeed is performed, by the market (fast-food outlets, therapists, cleaners, sex workers etc.), with the advantage of monetary profit. Appropriate work orientations can be maintained through compulsory military service, the education system, religion, popular culture and so on.

So, if it could not be proven that capitalism required women's subordination, attention had to turn elsewhere. Men were presented for consideration and some Marxist feminists did discuss this possibility. The outcome proved to be a decisive moment in the theorisation of gender relations. For example, Barrett, having argued that it cannot be concluded that capitalism is the chief beneficiary of the division of domestic labour, very briefly considered the possibility that it might be men who benefit, before concluding that this was a dead end. Barrett's argument stressed the disadvantages of the male working-class breadwinner role, in an analysis very similar to that which was beginning to be made by many male critics of gender relations. First, the position of breadwinner locks men into wage labour, pressing them to remain docile workers in order to provide for their families. Second, the nature of breadwinning has deprived men of significant access to their children. Barrett conceded that men perceive the breadwinner role as more desirable than that of the dependant, given their tenacity in maintaining the division of labour, but overall the male breadwinner role has consequences that are, she said, 'not so desirable'. While acknowledging that the establishment of the working-class family-household system resulted from the struggle of male and female interests, Barrett argued that the results have not been of great benefit to the working class, and thus not ultimately beneficial to working-class men (Barrett 1980: 216–19).

This argument leads to the hardly remarkable point that working-class men's position is not ideal, which rather evades the sexual-political question of whether such men benefit overall from the present arrangements. To show that some disadvantages accrue to a certain social position is one thing; to conclude that this is not a position of overall advantage is another. It is striking that Barrett sees working-class men only in terms of their class position in capitalist relations: the nub of the argument is that working-class men are subordinate to capital, therefore nothing in the present arrangements can be said to be in their interests. Barrett appears to assume that interest-based analyses apply only in winner-takes-all situations but they are in fact more widely applicable – it is the balance of interests which matters.

The collapse of the domestic labour debate was an important moment in the development of feminist social theory, which involved turning away from the possibility of analysis in terms of men's interests. If gender relations could not be explained in terms of capitalist structures, nor in terms of any similar structuring of men's interests, then other structures had to be found. As Carole Pateman (1988) put it, the 'theoretical impasse' led to a renewal of interest in the concept of patriarchy. Though there are important exceptions, this renewed interest was not usually pursued within the materialist paradigm. For many, the failure of the domestic labour debate seems to show finally that the materialist paradigm is inapplicable to gender relations. Barrett, for example, argued that family life and women's position must be understood in terms which completely transcend the Marxist analysis (and, by implication, transcend materialism as well). While accepting that capitalism was historically gendered, with existing family forms influencing the historical development of capitalism, she stressed that the domestic sphere should be understood in terms of 'ideological processes and the familial construction of gendered subjects' (Barrett 1980: 173):

> 'The family' provides the nexus for the various themes – romantic love; feminine nurturance, maternalism, self-sacrifice; masculine protection and financial support – that characterise our conception of gender and sexuality. It is, however, an ideological nexus rather than any concrete family system which is involved here (1980: 205).

This was a very common move, and one with major implications. The domestic sphere was not to be analysed in the same way as the public sphere. Rather than being a site of productive labour, the domestic sphere is the site of ideology and subject construction. The concept of the family as producing gendered subjectivity is even stronger in Barrett's later work. Referring to feminist uses of Lacanian theory, she argued that contemporary feminist theory was well on the way to developing 'psychic' as opposed to 'social' explanations (Barrett 1988: xxx). By 1992 Barrett's position had moved even further away from materialism, rejecting its validity in all domains of social life. In this respect, and others, her intellectual journey is representative of the recent major shifts in social thought. According to Barrett, materialism had been 'decimated' by the post-structuralist stress on discourse, subjectivity and meaning so that the classical materialist presuppositions are inappropriate to the issues now 'at the top of the agenda', namely sexuality, subjectivity and textuality (Barrett 1992: 215).

Feminist Materialism

However, some feminist writers who were dissatisfied with the domestic labour debate drew the very different conclusion that the materialist paradigm had to be applied more imaginatively. Their work certainly breaks with orthodox Marxism but retains the spirit of the original Marxist concern with labour; in my opinion it gives new life to a paradigm often thought to be worn out, if not stone dead. In the rest of the chapter I discuss this revised materialism – first, because its coherent theorisation of men's interests in the division of labour is invaluable for the analysis in later chapters, and second, because the critiques to which it has been subjected provide a significant case study from within feminism about taking care of men.

Heidi Hartmann, in an article memorably titled 'The Unhappy Marriage of Marxism and Feminism: Towards a More Progressive Union', forcefully argued that materialist analysis should concern men's direct benefits from women's productive labour in the domestic sphere, including sexuality and child-rearing: 'The material base upon which patriarchy rests lies most fundamentally in men's control over women's labour power ... men control women's labour power, both for the purposes of serving men in many personal and sexual ways and for the purpose of rearing children' (Hartmann 1981a: 14–15). It is this male interest in the control of women's labour power which creates the solidarity men depend on to maintain their domination. This is the key to the social relations of patriarchy.

In this vein, Hartmann and other feminist social theorists have developed an extensive body of work, usually described as feminist materialism (for a valuable overview of French feminist materialism see

Leonard & Adkins 1996. Other tendencies in feminist thought have also considered themselves to be in the materialist tradition; see chapter 7). In what follows I will rely on various writers, but especially on the work of the French radical feminist Christine Delphy and her long-time English collaborator and translator Diana Leonard. Delphy began developing her distinctive materialist feminist position in the 1960s, and her work therefore precedes the domestic labour debate and its collapse. In *Familiar Exploitation* (1992) and elsewhere, Delphy and Leonard are particularly clear and deeply engaged with the criticisms which their work seems to attract. As a result it provides a very good ground for discussion (see Jackson 1996 for a discussion of the intellectual and political sources of Delphy's work and her collaboration with Leonard).

Delphy and Leonard argue that a materialist account of gender relations must begin from the insight that women are oppressed through their work, just as, they believe, Marx and Engels began from the insight that workers were oppressed through their work. Feminist theory does not posit women's oppression, but rather grows from women's hard-won knowledge that 'there is no mystery, we are oppressed because we are exploited. What we go through makes life easier for others' (Delphy 1979: 100; Delphy 1984: 150). Materialist analysis begins from the standpoint of those who do the work, since, as Dorothy Smith (1987: 80) put it in her discussion of the materialist tradition, the beneficiaries of a system of labour are not the ones most likely to understand it: 'From the standpoint of ruling, the actual practices, the labour, and the organisation of labour, which makes the existence of a ruling class and their ruling possible, are invisible. It is only possible to see how the whole thing is put together from a standpoint outside the ruling class.'

To begin with the public sphere: analysis along these lines shows how men's dominance in the public sphere is absolutely dependent upon women's domestic labour, and men's resultant privilege of being uninvolved in routine family responsibilities. Women's labour in the private sphere is a necessary condition for the organisation of the male-dominated primary labour market, the rhythms of which 'ignore the family needs of individuals, ignore their responsibility with regard to relationships and with regard to family labour ... and at the same time assume that they have a family, a woman (mother, sister, wife), who takes on these responsibilities' (Saraceno 1987: 195, 200). As Pateman (1988: 131) vividly put it, 'the sturdy figure of the "worker", the artisan, in clean overalls, with a bag of tools and his lunch-box, is always accompanied by the ghostly figure of his wife'. And it is not only male wage labourers who depend on female domestic labour: Delphy and Leonard noted the extent to which businessmen and professionals depend on their wives' unpaid labour. They relied extensively (though critically) on Janet Finch's (1983) *Married to the Job*, which detailed the myriad vital unpaid tasks performed by the wives of such men, ranging from moral support, secretarial services and employee relations to entertaining clients by handing out endless cups of tea. At one level, 'everyone knows' the extent to which men at the top of the social and political hierarchy depend on their wives. For example, a feature article on the then Australian Foreign Minister spoke of his 'best asset':

> According to his neighbours, his friends, his cabinet colleagues and his staff, Gareth Evan's best asset is his wife, Dr Merran Evans, an academic economic modeller with four university degrees and the mother of his teenage children. Graham Little [a political psychologist, and one of Evans' neighbours] says: 'Merran is a great, saintly person, a soothing, smoothing person. She helps make him sensitive to other people' (Buckley, Melbourne *Sunday Age*, 27 June 1993).

While this is everyday knowledge, it requires a leap of theoretical imagination to put it this way: 'as wives we have provided the bodily and emotional support for men who have been actors and movers in the ruling apparatus' (Smith 1987: 153). Nor does this apply only among the 'rulers': radical male politics has also depended on female domestic labour. Varda Burstyn (1985: 81) described the extent to which left-wing men need women's care so that they can go to meetings, organise campaigns and 'write complicated, demanding theory' rather than 'wash socks, cook meals, nurse sick relatives, do homework with the kids' and so on. However, something vital is missing. After all, Marxist feminists were perfectly aware of the way in which the capitalist working day, and men's role in it, depended upon women's 'backstage' work; as shown in chapter 6, liberal analyses of the sexual division of labour make much the same kind of argument in reference to the male model of work. If we stress men's benefits in the public sphere we overlook what is most novel about the feminist materialist position, and run the risk of confusing it with all the Marxist and liberal analyses which place priority on the organisation of the public sphere in their explanations of the sexual division of domestic labour. This risk disappears if we give equal (or greater) attention to the private-sphere benefits men receive from the division of labour. Accordingly, most feminist materialists go out of their way to stress that the organisation of domestic labour directly benefits men.

Here the question of whether the household is a site of production or consumption is particularly cogent. The view that household production is a thing of the past may be plausible from the standpoint of those for whom the household is principally an arena for recreation, leisure, succour and rest, but from the standpoint of those who do most of the work which supports these practices, the idea is absurd. As Hartmann pointed out, every aspect of routine household consumption involves productive labour: 'Sheets, for example, must be bought, put on beds, rearranged after every sleep, and washed, just as food must be bought, cleaned, cooked, and served to become a meal' (1981b: 373). Delphy and Leonard (1992: 86–7) make the same point: what is called household 'consumption' usually requires two stages – the purchase of raw materials, then the 'transformation of these raw materials into a directly consumable product via household work, sometimes performed by paid servants, but more commonly nowadays by unpaid family labour ... This constitutes a very substantial part of the household's standard of living'. Even that quintessentially consumerist activity – shopping for the raw materials – should be seen as a form of productive work which households must perform, work which was once often done by servants or by shopkeepers taking orders, boxing them up and delivering them.

Much domestic work can be performed, and often is performed, as paid labour. When this involves domestic servants or other paid services it is easy to understand the distinction between those who produce and those who consume. However, in the case of unpaid family work, the distinction has only been clarified as a result of a considerable struggle by feminists, taking the standpoint of the unpaid producers. The sexual division of labour and men's privilege of uninvolvement is not just a matter of advantage in the public sphere: men enjoy the immediate privileges of a consumer. This has been put in a host of ways. Burstyn spoke of the way in which relative freedom from domestic labour makes men the leisured gender class:

> Men's freedom from the necessity to care for their own bodies and those of children, the sick and the elderly, through men's appropriation of women's productive labour and men's access to women's bodies and control of their issue ... indicates that we are talking about class relations between men and women (Burstyn 1985: 54).

Similarly, Hartmann (1981a) discussed men's higher standard of living with respect to leisure time and personalised services. Delphy and Leonard (1992: 261) referred to the highly personalised and diverse range of services, the '57 varieties of unpaid services', which wives perform for husbands, resulting in men's singular privilege of 'having things done for you individually, in the comfort of your own home, with full attention to personal taste'. They used the example of meal preparation to illustrate the difference between men's and women's private lives: even though everyone may seem to share the moment of consumption, women experience a qualitatively different meal from their husbands and children if they are solely or principally in charge of purchasing, preparation and clearing up. Women do not consume meals in the same way as men – as work done by someone else – since they cannot both wait and be waited on. In addition, husbands' particular tastes are often catered to, and they may receive superior food while sitting at the same table, this being justified by the ideology of the self-sacrificing wife and mother (see also Murcott 1983a; Charles & Kerr 1987).

The advantages of this form of privileged consumption are not very different from the advantages experienced by other kinds of privileged groups. The privileges of the bourgeoisie include such intangibles as:

> a first-class seat on a train [which] not only ensure's one's body is moved from A to B, but assures that same body comfort and peace and quiet – and the respect of the second-class passengers. Having a house in Provence is, of course, a material possession, but it is also the enjoyment of a particularly beautiful landscape and spending the summer near to a number of people similar to oneself (Delphy & Leonard 1992: 41).

A husband's typical privileges include, for example:

> someone to look interested while he tells his stories over and over again, or to make sure the food he gets on holidays does not upset his stomach, or to keep the children quiet when he wants to catch up on his sleep, or to make sure all the trousers bought for him have back pockets for his golf tees (1992: 42).

In earlier work, Leonard compared marriage with colonial rule, when all domestic work was done by the colonised: 'Being provided with protection from pollution and disturbance, having clean, quiet rooms, punctual meals, warm, tidy houses, washed, ironed and mended clothes provided for one is a privilege of the powerful' (Leonard & Allen 1976: 10). The example of maintaining interest in a husband's boring stories illustrates that the privileges of domination include being on the receiving end of psychological and nurturing practices. A wider range of practices than just housework and the physical care of children and other dependants should be considered as labour – all the processes involved in the 'production and transformation of people' (Ferguson 1984: 158). There is no settled terminology among feminist materialists. Perhaps the term 'emotional labour' (which is also employed outside the materialist paradigm) is the most commonly used, but there are many forms. Delphy and Leonard called it 'relationship work', stressing that caring is not just a matter of feeling affection but an active process of observing and modifying emotions: 'It is not just a question of thinking about someone, but doing actual activities: talking to them about things that interest them, fetching them things that give them pleasure, smiling at them, cuddling them, and stroking their bodies and egos' (Delphy & Leonard 1992: 21, 232).

Patricia Lengermann and Jill Nieubrugge-Brantley (1990: 323) spoke of the sexual and emotional work involved in 'the creation and main-tenance of health, personality, prestige and meaning'. Ann Ferguson and Nancy Folbre (1981) called it sex-affective production, which en-compassed child-bearing, child-rearing and providing nurturance, affection and sexual satisfaction. To speak of matters such as sex in terms of work is hardly novel. This is another example of something which 'everyone knows': a 1961 sex manual advised women that 'sex is too important to give it less call upon your energy than cooking, laundry and a dozen other activities' (in Leonard 1984: 173). The innovation is in incorporating the knowledge in social theory.

If domestic labour involves the production of people, then, to the extent that domestic labour is performed more by women than by men, we can say that *men themselves are its products*. Later I will argue that this wonderfully clarifies the meaning of the category 'men', and so under-cuts many of the objections to interest-based theory. The insight has been put in various ways. Burstyn (1985: 54, 82) wrote of the way women's caring labour is 'embodied' in children and men, and stressed the indispensable work of maintaining family relationships, whereby women 'spend a lot of time figuring out how to mediate between the conflicting emotional and material needs of family members' (see also Lynch 1989). Similarly, Anna Jonasdottir discussed the interactions whereby women and men create each other: 'our bodies and souls are both means of production and producers in this life process'. Such processes, she claimed, can be exploitative. In the typical case:

> men can continually appropriate significantly more of women's life force and capacity than they themselves give back to women. Men can build themselves up as powerful social beings and continue to dominate women through their constant accumulation of the existential forces taken and received from women. If capital is accumulated alienated labour, male authority is accumulated alienated love (Jonasdottir 1988a: 165–7).

The claim, then, is that the paradigm of labour and its appropri-ation can be applied to love. This is difficult to write about without appearing ludicrous. Kathleen Lynch (1989) pointed out the lack of an adequate sociological vocabulary to conceptualise 'love labour'. Words such as 'love' and 'care' carry various meanings; concepts such as 'love labour' and 'caring work' (not to mention the exploitation thereof) may seem absurd when meanings connected with free, spontaneous or desire-driven activities are in mind. To speak of love as labour, I was told by one (sociological) reader of an early version of this work, is the 'sort of thing which gives sociology a bad name' and which would make sociology an even more dismal science than economics, reducing every precious human activity to the same dreary political–economic level. Related criticisms of materialist views have been made by many feminists, and these are discussed shortly. Already, though, the materialist reply may be clear enough: to speak of something as labour is really just to take it seriously, as a necessary (precious, skilful) human activity, which to some is valuable enough to be worth exploiting. It is not materialist theory which sullies love. I cannot think of a better way of respecting love than to see it as capable of exploitation.

The Critique of Feminist Materialism

A wide-ranging feminist critique has been directed at the work of Delphy, Leonard and similar writers. It is worth examining this critique carefully, partly to help clarify the feminist materialist position but mostly because the critique itself makes a very suitable first case study for my main project. Many of its themes recur in other genres.

Materialist analysis suggests to some a crass view of social life, in which motives and interests are all narrowly material or economic, but this is not necessarily so, even with analyses of capitalism. As we have seen, many of the benefits which the wealthy individual consumes are the kind of thing which can also be appropriated in other modes of pro-duction. This involves, in addition to material goods (in the narrow sense), 'non-tangible goods and services, and things used for display and pleasure rather than instrumentally' (Delphy & Leonard 1992: 41–2). The interest in any system of exploitation is often the acquisition of such privileges, and this is particularly the case with the exploitation of domestic labour.

A related criticism is that materialist analyses are grounded in calculations about exchange. Chris Beasley (1996) argued that analyses like those of Delphy are weakened because their measurement of exploitation is market-based and monetary. For example, exploitation is measured in terms of women's lack of remuneration in private labour against the wage they would earn if they undertook the same labour in the capitalist marketplace. Beasley acknowledged that Delphy made a 'profoundly disturbing' account of the exploitation of women's labour, but since the account was founded in the market standpoint of ex-change, which is not applicable to the private sphere, it was dependent on the Marxist model. Thus, she concluded, work such as Delphy's still 'belongs to Daddy'.

However, dollar calculations of the value of domestic work do not underlie the materialist critique. Certainly, even some male economists have drawn attention to the productiveness of households by quantifying the cost to households if all the unpaid work of housework and childcare were provided through the labour market, at the going rate. For example, Ironmonger (1989b) described Australian households as a $90 billion industry, whose product equals half of the gross national product (as conventionally understood). Such calculations may have a rhetorical value, drawing attention to the sheer amount of unpaid work in the private sphere. But, as Collete Guillaumin (1996: 80, 105) remarked, such analyses hide the fact that being 'non-paid' is the intrinsic character of domestic work: 'being non-paid for a job means that it is part of its character not to have any relation with any quantitative measure whatever'. Thus Delphy and Leonard (1992: 95) argued that campaigns for wages for housework miss the point that 'the only work which is "unpaid" is work done within particular social relations'.

To analyse these particular social relations, Delphy and Leonard introduced the domestic mode of production, which operates alongside the capitalist mode of production. It was not intended to explain the totality of gender relations, but should be an indispensable 'cornerstone' (Delphy 1984: 22, 26; see also Delphy & Leonard 1992: 24). This makes it clear that capitalism and patriarchy are being theorised at the same level of the social formation. Capitalism and patriarchy are two distinct and equally social systems, both concerning the appropriation of labour; the two systems are 'empirically and historically intertwined' and influence and structure each other (Delphy & Leonard 1992: 47, 66). This crucially distinguishes materialist feminism from other feminist theories which argue that gender relations and the domestic sphere should be analysed at a different (ideological, cultural or psychic) level from that appropriate for capitalism or the public sphere (see also Walby 1989: 16).

A very important point is that the domestic mode of production is not defined in terms of the tasks performed, since many domestic tasks (even some aspects of emotional labour) must also be performed in the capitalist mode of production (Delphy 1984). A vital distinction is made by Delphy and Leonard between *tasks* and *jobs*. This is a distinction which cannot be grasped by technical quantitative understandings of the division of labour in terms of, say, the relative time spent washing dishes. The division of labour in the domestic mode of production is not a technical division of tasks but a division of jobs, in which routine responsibility for maintaining the household and the family is usually assumed by women; male 'gifts' of help ritually confirm this division.

This distinction, which recalls that between responsibility and help, nicely cuts through many of the hackneyed responses to feminist critiques of the division of labour:

> It is not a question of women cooking and cleaning and caring for children and men never doing these things. Such tasks are 'women's work', are not valued highly, but men do them from time to time within family households – though it should be noted that they generally do the more prestigious and interesting varieties of them: for example, cooking for guests or taking children for walks. Rather, domestic work is women's work in the sense that the status, the conditions of doing it, the relations of production of this work, are specific to family subordinates ... What we have in the family is not a division of tasks but a division of jobs. 'Jobs' combine typical tasks plus their condition of performance and remuneration and status (in the case of family work, the obligation to do it within the home, unpaid, invisibly and poorly valued) (Delphy & Leonard 1992: 135–6).

A particularly forceful way of putting this analysis of the division of jobs is seen in the claim that marriage is a labour contract. Since a wife's obligations to perform domestic work are institutionalised in marriage, to enter marriage is to enter into a labour contract. This may seem an extreme view to many, but it is quite consistent with the evidence about the existence of husbands' rights (chapter 1). While the rights of husbands are no longer as extensive as when wives were legally considered property, they still include the right to their wives' unpaid work (Delphy & Leonard 1992: 119). The reason domestic work has traditionally been viewed by economic theorists as 'unproductive' is not because of the nature of the tasks involved, nor because domestic labour is largely women's work. When the same tasks are performed in the labour market by women (or men) the labour is considered productive. Rather, the notion that domestic labour is unproductive is an aspect of the labour contract whereby domestic work is done unpaid for the head of the household (Delphy 1984: 88).

Delphy and Leonard's insistence on the centrality of marriage has been widely criticised. For example, Walby (1990) argued that their position is partial, given that not all women are housewives (see also Maynard 1990). However, Delphy and Leonard made it clear that their analysis applied as much to employed wives as to housewives. They also argued that, despite the fashionable stress on the variety of household forms, most people living outside the framework of family relations have been, or will be in the future, part of a nuclear family. Moreover, all women are affected by the institution of marriage, through, for example, its interactions with the labour market: 'the super-exploitation of all women in wage-work is determined by the domestic situation of most women ... and constitutes an economic pressure towards marriage' (Delphy 1984: 169). It is unfair to attribute the privileging of marriage to Delphy and Leonard and similar writers. The criticism would better be directed at the institution of marriage itself.

Another aspect of the marriage contract concerns the husband's obligations to maintain his household. To many this is just the other side of a reasonable bargain, but Delphy and Leonard criticised the widespread assumption that women's domestic work is fairly exchanged for men's provision of maintenance. The existence of maintenance does not guarantee non-exploitation: 'even in systems of forced labour, the workers are fed and housed, however badly' (Delphy & Leonard 1992: 124). They stressed that since there is no evaluation, the unpaid work done by women and other subordinate family members is not a repayment for the head's maintenance, but rather demonstrates their dependence on the head of the family: 'The services which a married woman provides are not fixed. They depend on the will of the employer, her husband. And these services are not paid according to a fixed scale. Her keep does not depend on her work, but on the wealth and goodwill of her husband' (Delphy 1984: 70). In any case, the issue is rather out of date, given that women are significant breadwinners in the majority of even middle-class families. The fact that employed women still perform the bulk of household work, while not being as free as their husbands to spend the money they earn, makes the rhetoric of just exchange highly implausible (Delphy & Leonard 1992: 117; see also Edwards 1984: 131).

Another important point is that the domestic mode of production is not regulated by the laws of a market. This is not a peripheral matter. What is valued about many of the practices of domestic work is that they meet idiosyncratic requirements in a highly personal way rich in emotional and symbolic significance. Such practices simply cannot be provided in a rationalised form, whether through the market or through state provision (Delphy & Leonard 1992: 136; see also DeVault 1987). The lack of market mechanisms does not mean, as many seem to think, that exploitation is an inappropriate category of analysis. The capitalist mode of production is just one mode whereby it is possible to extort labour or gain profit from the labour of others; the exploitation of domestic labour is not mediated by instrumental exchange relations but takes place within a different mode, requiring face-to-face domination. Delphy and Leonard agreed that a materialist analysis of the family would be in danger of 'missing the whole point of the family' if it claimed, as its critics often assume that it does, that the family involves the same kind of impersonal and calculative transactions as those in the market. The absence of measured exchange does not mean that family transactions are not highly regulated and obligatory; like other non-market transactions, such as the exchange of gifts on various occasions, family transactions are reasoned and ordered. There can be exploitative relations without mediation by instrumental exchange relations; this is the point of theorising a separate domestic mode of production. The family is not a haven from exploitation: 'We do not say just what family relationships are *not* like: how they are different from (rotten old) wage labour. We also explore the real nature of family relationships – and some of this is less palatable' (Delphy & Leonard 1992: 110–11). An important source of misunderstanding deserves mention. Feminist materialist analyses seem to some readers to absurdly construct marriage in terms of utter female exploitation and degradation. This is not the case: the possibility that a particular husband may be highly benevolent is recognised, though benevolence is the privilege of one who is dominant, and is always subject to withdrawal (Delphy & Leonard 1986: 64). Further, individual women may be better off in marriage than outside it. Women who enter marriage are often 'economically, socially [and] sexually' advantaged. Thus, women may be, at least in the short term, 'arguably better off cooperating than kicking against the traces' (Delphy 1979: 64; see also Delphy & Leonard 1992: 19, 46). It may seem that it has been conceded that, after all, marriage serves women well. But this would be to ignore the interaction of the public and private spheres. If some women may be better off in marriage, it is because the organisation of the public sphere makes the alternatives unpalatable. Women's situation in the labour market constitutes an 'objective incentive to marry, and hence the labour market plays a role in the exploitation of their domestic work' (Delphy 1984: 20; see also Delphy & Leonard 1992: 64). Women's dependence is a matter of exploitation in both the public and private spheres.

Delphy and Leonard discuss the importance of the exchange of gifts in non-market transactions, referring to a study by Bell and Newby (1976) which showed how a gift is a valuable way of stabilising hierarchical face-to-face interactions. For example, the husband's 'gifts' (of his wages, of taking her out for a drink, of help in the house) place his wife in debt, so that women's unquantified domestic work is seen as a (freely given) counter-gift to the one received. This is starkly revealed by the fact that many married employed women feel obliged to earn enough to cover the cost of replacing their personal labour before they feel entitled to any income of their own (Delphy & Leonard 1992: 123, 141).

Gift exchange has been extensively studied by anthropologists. Pierre Bourdieu described a very similar situation of labour exploitation in which an ideology of freely given assistance masked the exploitation, though in his case the relations were those of class rather than gender. In the non-capitalist agrarian Kabyle society of North Africa the exchange of gifts is of central significance. If the recipient of a gift is unable to make a counter-gift, the obligation to honour the exchange may be discharged through labouring on the land of the gift-giver. The denial of the interested (and hierarchical) nature of such exchanges takes the form of rituals where the manner of giving is such that:

> the outward forms of the act present a practical denial of the content of the act, symbolically transmuting an interested exchange or a simple power relation into a relationship set up in due form for form's sake, i.e. inspired by pure respect for the customs and conventions recognized by the group ... But in reality such denials of interest are never more than *practical disclaimers* (Bourdieu 1972: 194, emphasis in original).

For the rich man, the collective misrecognition through the ethic of honour serves his interests in euphemistic form; for the poor man, nothing suits him better than 'to play his part in an interested fiction which offers him an honourable representation of his condition'. Bourdieu concluded that 'society cannot ask or expect of its members anything more or better than denial'. Neatly combining material and ideological levels, he argued that the labour required to conceal the significance of the exchange was just as important as the labour needed to fulfil the exchange. The parallels with Delphy and Leonard's analysis are strong, even up to their point that the effort put into making marriage appear equitable is another form of (exploited) work. Bourdieu's analysis has not been subject to the same scathing criticism, but his work does not touch upon the relations between men and women, perhaps the most complex of all social relationships.

I hesitate to rely on Bourdieu, for several reasons. His dismissal of feminist theory as unscientific is one. Another is his habit of publishing as his own, ideas produced by radical feminists, thus 'invisibilising' women researchers (some of whom are his colleagues; Armengaud 1993). One example will make the point: Bourdieu stated that women must 'make themselves seductive through cosmetic work' and that this constituted 'a very important part of their domestic labour' (Bourdieu 1990, my translation). However, citing this distinguished male theorist may help convince sceptical readers that exploitation and 'freely given' work are compatible, and can go together very well.

Many critics of feminist materialism argue that it represents a male-centred view. Perhaps because of its Marxist ancestry, it is often assumed that the point of the materialist critique of the sexual division of domestic labour is that women's domestic burdens restrict their participation on equal terms with men in the public sphere, in employment, politics and so on. However, feminist materialism does not privilege the public sphere in this way: this is clear, for example, in the way Delphy pointed out the limitations of the idea that it is '"the family situation" which influences the capacity of women to work "outside" ... The originality in my approach in this field has been to invert the direction of links' (Delphy 1984: 20). Making this inversion reveals that the situation of women in the labour market also influences women's situation within the family, providing the incentive to marry, noted earlier. The masculine/public sphere is not being valorised. On the contrary, the argument is that one significant aim of male domination in the public sphere is to produce wives, through maintaining a large pool of women needing to marry and thus enter into the domestic labour contract, so that men may receive the associated benefits of the private sphere.

In a widely read article, Jane Flax characterised feminist materialism's view of the family as a 'miniature political economy with its own division of labour, source of surplus (women's labour), and product (children and workers)', diagnosing this as an instance of traditional ways of thinking which embody the mindset of male domination. To search for the root or cause of gender relations and male domination is to adopt a mode of thinking which is itself grounded in domination:

> perhaps reality can have a structure only from the falsely universalising perspective of the dominant group. That is, only to the extent that one person or group can dominate the whole will reality appear to be governed by one set of rules or be constituted by one privileged set of social relations. Criteria of theory construction such as parsimony or simplicity may be attained only by the suppression or denial of the experiences of the other(s) (Flax 1987: 633–4).

The argument is that feminist materialism, while claiming to start from the standpoint of those who are dominated, has adopted the standpoint of the dominators. Feminist materialism has suppressed or denied the experiences of the very people whose standpoint it purports to represent, namely experiences such as pregnancy, child-rearing, sexuality, pleasure and desire – the 'complex fantasies and conflicting wishes and experiences women associate with family and home' (1987: 631). According to Flax, these cannot be theorised in the materialist paradigm of labour and production.

In this vein Sarah Gregory, in a critique of Rosemary Deem's (1982) analysis of women and leisure (which partly relied on Delphy to theorise the subordination of women's leisure-time in favour of their husbands' leisure), argued that the concept of leisure was not necessarily an appropriate category for women, and that the exploitation of women should not be overstated: 'What is known of women's pleasures in reproduction and child-rearing; in creating the home environment; in being at the centre of the intricate social web of a community' (Gregory 1982: 51). Such views reflect a key development in 1980s' feminist theory, namely the stress on gender difference, both in its constitutive role in gender subjectivity and more generally in a determination to counter the patriarchal devaluation of the feminine. In her preface to a re-issue of *Women's Oppression Today*, Barrett criticised the use of 'oppression' in the original title: 'Oppression' looks rather crude in terms of current feminist work: does sexual difference necessarily mean oppression? Are there no distinctive female moralities or vocations that we would want to value more positively?' (Barrett 1988: v). Barrett stated that formerly she had considered women as oppressed because their lives involve practices and attitudes of little worth; now, however, since women's 'moralities and vocations' should be seen as inherently valuable, oppression becomes an inappropriate concept.

Arguments of this kind have been widely used against feminist materialism (and other theorisations of male power, indeed hierarchical power of any kind). Beasley (1992: 5) argued that such views considered social life only in terms of domination, and thereby rendered women's experiences and their labour invisible by marginalising 'characteristics of embedded interaction and obligation'. Thus, 'docility, passivity, cooperation, self-sacrifice, the ethic of care, and connections with others are not attributed as a naturalised central dynamic in history'. As a result, she concluded, the 'narrative of the slave' is erased. This is rather contradictory, since we cannot speak of slaves without assuming the existence of domination and exploitation.

It is curious to attribute to feminist materialists a devaluation or invisibilisation of women's practices. After all, the basic point – that women are worthy of being exploited for themselves (Delphy 1984:134) – indicates a high valuation of women's work. Both feminist materialists and writers in the difference theory tradition deplore the devaluation of women's work and women's perspectives. But, in very significant contrast to difference theorists, Delphy and Leonard argued that this devaluation should not be thought of as the cause of women's oppression. The problem is not that men have failed to see the value of women's work. In a critique of Annie LeClerc, who discussed men's 'mistaken' belief that domestic work is not valuable, Delphy drew an analogy with class relations: 'Is it just a question of the ruling class having been "mistaken" – of their not having *noticed* the usefulness of the workers?' (Delphy 1984: 200). Instead of puzzling over why domestic work is devalued, Delphy and Leonard argued that devaluing ideologies always arise when labour is exploited: 'the existence of exploitation *requires* the constitution of an exploited population, which in turn requires the creation of a sexist or racist or classist ideology' (Delphy

1979: 98; see also Delphy 1984: 173, 206; Delphy & Leonard 1992:16).
The root problem is not the devaluation but the exploitation, and to
argue that women's labour is exploited is not to devalue it.

Certainly, to treat caring as a form of exploitable labour runs counter
to deeply held beliefs, according to which women care in the name of
love. Barrett and McIntosh (1979) took such a view when they argued
that Delphy's analysis absurdly requires us to believe that children
exploit their own mothers. Similar criticisms that it is difficult to see
women's nurturance of their children in terms of instrumental interests
and individual gain are made in Fox (1988) and Jonasdottir (1988b).
This argument has rhetorical force because of young children's manifest
helplessness and need for care, but it only makes sense if men are completely removed from consideration as potential caregivers: 'Clearly
services applied *to* children are not appropriated *by* them, but by the
person who would have to perform (half of) the work if his wife did not
provide the totality, i.e. the husband' (Delphy 1979: 93; see also Delphy
& Leonard 1992: 125).

While feminist difference theory stresses women's freely given work
of caring for helpless children (or other helpless dependants), feminist
materialists emphasise that much of women's care is directed to those,
such as husbands and older children, who are perfectly able to care for
themselves (and for others). In such ways husbands and certain other
privileged family members are both relieved from having to care for the
genuinely helpless, and themselves treated as though they were helpless.
As Wendy Hollway (1983) observed, men are often seen as 'little boys'
needing mothering, and this knowledge, which has often had conservative effects, should be reclaimed for feminist politics.

Critics of the concept that care is labour (exploited or otherwise)
often stress the pleasures of caring. The immediate result may be the
creation of a pleasurable social situation; if for example 'cooking and
serving a meal to husband and children increases the sex-affective
energy available to everyone ... how can one see it as work' (Ferguson
1984: 164). However, in no way does the materialist critique of the
organisation of domestic labour require that the tasks performed be
intrinsically unpleasant. Delphy and Leonard's distinction between tasks
and jobs is very useful here. They show how confusion about the
devaluation of domestic work can be cleared up by observing that it is
not the tasks themselves that are devalued, but the job of the person
responsible for domestic work under the relations of the domestic mode
of production, whereby routine domestic work is done 'in a subordinate position by people who have the general status of subordinates in
society' (Delphy & Leonard 1992: 136). Concentrating on tasks and
their supposed nature is a form of fetishism similar to that analysed by

Marx, in which relationships between people are disguised as relationships between or to things (Delphy 1984: 199. Delphy's discussion of fetishism was largely prompted by de Beauvoir's explanation of women's subordination in terms of the 'immanence' of their household work, as opposed to the 'transcendence' supposedly inherent in men's various public sphere projects: de Beauvoir 1960: esp. 175). Arguments about the interest or value of tasks completely miss the point:

> Debates about whether or not, say, cooking is 'really interesting' or 'really important' can remain endlessly unresolved. Some say it is, some say it is not, some men say they enjoy it. But people are usually talking about the tasks extracted from the relations of production within which they are typically done. (Men virtually never do cooking in the same conditions as women, that is routinely, for household consumption, as economically dependent housewives) (Delphy & Leonard 1992: 136).

There is nothing intrinsically unpleasant about the tasks of domestic labour; in particular the pleasures to be found in affection, sex and child-raising. Their point is that exploitation is not incompatible with a considerable degree of pleasure, in the domestic sphere and elsewhere:

> [we cannot] accept the argument that sex and reproduction are not work because women enter heterosexual relationships and bear children willingly and get pleasure from these activities. After all, most people could be said to enter paid employment willingly within our society, and some get considerable pleasure from it. Choosing to do something and benefiting from doing it does not preclude its being work; nor does it guarantee it is not work done for someone else, as part of an inequitable exchange (Delphy & Leonard 1992: 22).

Thus, despite the criticism that they ignore the love women feel for their husbands (e.g. Duncombe & Marsden 1995), Delphy and Leonard do accept that marital love is a reward in its own right. The point is that love and exploitation are not mutually exclusive. Rather, women's love for their husbands can be a source of satisfaction and at the same time the means by which men receive benefits such as 'more work from the wives in question, since the love, respect and identification veils the very fact that labour is being exploited'. Similarly, loving his wife does not prevent a man from exploiting her labour (Delphy & Leonard 1992: 17, 258).

In any case, caring work is not always performed with love. There are two common meanings of care, associated with caring 'about' and caring 'for':

> Caring about someone, in the sense of feeling affection for them, is based on spontaneous feeling of affinity, and as an emotion per se it has little implication for how people spend their time – except that they might want to spend it together. On the other hand, caring for someone, in the sense of servicing their needs, may have little or nothing to do with caring about someone. The basis for the provision of the services of caring may be based not on affection and affinity, but on other modes of obligation (Ungerson 1983: 31).

Confusion between these two forms of care lies at the root of much misunderstanding about the materialist analysis of caring work. Graham (1983: 16) discussed caring as a 'labour of love' where the 'labour must continue when the love falters'. Delphy and Leonard put the point forcefully:

> An individual woman may choose a particular man as her husband because she loves *him* (rather than the rest of the bunch); and working for him as a personal dependant will certainly encourage her to respect and identify with him. But the emotion and the work are separate, and familiarity can equally breed contempt. Some wives have a hearty disrespect for their husbands and distance themselves emotionally – but they still work for them (Delphy & Leonard 1992: 17, emphasis in original).

Equality and Sameness

The strongest way of stating the critique that feminist materialism is male-centred is to say that it proposes that women should become just like men. However, feminist materialism makes a fundamental critique of the categories 'man' and 'woman' which difference theory (and so much popular thought) relies upon. For example, the critique in terms of supposed maleness fails to see that the categories of men and women cannot be understood in isolation, but are mutually dependent:

> These two social groups are no more naturally based than any other power relations in society (they are no more natural than, for example, class or racial divisions) ... For us 'men' and 'women' are not two naturally given groups which at some point in history fell into a hierarchical relationship. Rather the reason the two groups are distinguished socially is because one dominates the other in order to use its labour. In other words, it is the relationship of production which produces the two classes 'men' and 'women' (Delphy & Leonard 1992: 258).

The insight that men *embody* female labour powerfully illustrates the point that 'men' make up a social category whose content would be quite different in a different gender regime. The fear that equality means that women would become like men is incomprehensible within a gender relations framework, since '*if women were the equals of men, men would no longer equal themselves*' (Delphy 1993: 7–8, emphasis in original). Women simply cannot become like men (as presently constituted) than all workers can become capitalists.

For example, the abstract agency required of dominant men in the public sphere is supported by personal female care, and is based on their liberation from having to attend to their needs (Smith 1987). The abstract mentality of male-stream thought, with its construction of the autonomous subject, should not be understood from a static perspective of difference; instead it is built on women's work in a structure of gender relations. Fears that equality for women means adopting all the disagreeable characteristics of dominant men and giving up the concrete, embedded and relational aspects of life are unfounded.

Equally unfounded are the fears that equality for women means losing all the virtues associated with, say, motherhood. Certainly, if women's care in the private sphere is seen as the only possible site for expressing the values of intimate human relatedness, then analyses of the exploitation of women's caring work may seem to be beside the point – yes, it may be exploited, but who else will care so well? The state? This can happen even in work which adopts the rhetoric of materialism. For example, Hilary Graham, in 'Caring: A Labour of Love', stressed the way women's caring work yields 'material benefits for the state', though the material benefits individual men receive were not mentioned. She discussed women's caring work as exploited by the state, but observed that the question nevertheless remains: 'would you put your sister into care?' (1983: 29). The absence of the possibility that men might care intimately for others is remarkable. As Chiara Saraceno (1987) observed, the dilemma between women's personal care and bureaucratic social services is empirically true but theoretically false. Theories based on this practical situation take for granted the institutionalisation of men's freedom from responsibility for care.

At bottom, fears that equality means that women will become like men seem to take for granted that men just are as they are. The view of gender is a static one, and we are tempted to wonder whether there are assumptions about innate biological tendencies. How else can we understand the curious fact that men are effectively absent from the critiques of the supposed maleness of feminist materialism – they are not a category to be problematised. Certainly the concept of maleness is present in those critiques, but the possibility that humans of the male sex could be different from what they are just does not arise. Indeed, perhaps it is not desired: in a recent discussion of difference Delphy (1993: 6) wondered 'in a mood of despair, if there is not a deep and unacknowledged desire not to change anything at work behind the intellectual haze'. Similarly, she has suggested that behind the defence of motherhood there lies 'a radical contesting' of men's right to look after children at all (1994: 198). The belief that men cannot change means abandoning the possibility of fundamental change in gender relations. As Carol Bacchi (1990: 244, 259) observed:

> Debates among feminists along sameness/difference lines surface in contexts where there appear to be only two options, joining the system on its own terms or staying out. The debate dissolves, or never even surfaces, when it is possible to expect humane living conditions for everyone ...
> ... The problems which women face are infinitely more complex than asking if they are the same as or different from men ... [This] avoids all the real issues, such as how families are to be cared for. This is why those in power wish to present it that way. It allows them to avoid responsibility for the human side of people's lives.

As long as most men successfully resist change, it may well be empiric- ally true that many women are forced to choose between competing with the boys on their own terms and adopting a less competitive, more caring 'feminine' life. But social theory should not take for granted the current gendered construction of these different alternatives. Indeed, taking difference for granted may be quite congenial to men, allowing them to continue to evade responsibility for the concrete daily care of human beings. In this sense the criticism that feminist materialism represents a male view is particularly poignant.

PART II

The Revolving Door

CHAPTER 3

Stalled Rhetoric:
The Optimistic Will

Anything Goes

The lives of the two sexes are rapidly converging. Or so the mass media keep telling us: 'The role models are changing before our eyes. Children think nothing of mum doing the house repairs while dad cooks the dinner' (*Glasgow Herald*, 28 March 1994). Introductory social science texts have been telling a similar optimistic story for the last two decades. *The Family: An Introduction* (Eshleman 1985) was typical in assuring its student readers that contemporary American marriage was shifting from the 'complementary' type where husbands were employed outside the home and wives did the domestic work, to the 'parallel' type where both spouses were employed and both were responsible for child-care and housework. Often such change is explained in terms of the inexorable flow of modernity. In *Sociology* (Hess et al. 1985: 265) we find:

> This trend, called egalitarianism, is largely the result of the many liberating currents in Western civilisation, stemming from the Enlightenment. It is difficult to maintain a commitment to freedom and equality in the general society while denying its exercise in the most intimate unit of the social system.

Enthusiasm about the direction of change can overwhelm the distinction between present and future: the future is right here. According to the then director of the Australian Institute of Family Studies: 'The family of the future is with us now. It is a family of partnership, of shared responsibility for earning a living, for caring for children and other (elder) dependants and for managing the home with all the housework, shopping and time arrangement that these demand' (Edgar 1990: 51).

Leading social theorists joined the chorus. Influential German sociologist Ulrich Beck explained that 'feudal gender roles', the last vestiges of the Middle Ages, were 'melting away' as modernisation finally penetrated the domestic sphere. Thus:

> With a bit of exaggeration one can say 'anything goes'. Who does the dishes, and when, who changes the nappies, does the shopping and pushes the vacuum cleaner is becoming just as unclear as who brings home the bacon, who decides whether to move and whether nocturnal delights in bed may only be enjoyed with the companion one duly wed to share daily life with (Beck in Beck & Beck-Gernsheim 1995: 34, 37).

This is an interesting passage, even if we leave to one side the quaintly coy conflation of gender convergence with sexual freedom, and the equivocation involved in 'with a bit of exaggeration'. Am I churlish in noting that the list of domestic tasks reflects the role of someone who 'helps' with domestic work? Why didn't such time-consuming and demanding activities as routine childcare and cooking spring to Beck's mind?

On the face of it, the 'anything goes' story of contemporary family life is at odds with the evidence about the sexual division of domestic labour reviewed in chapter 1, and I will not labour this point. Rather, this chapter explores the various ways in which accounts of social change manage to present an optimistic view of movement towards gender equity. The accounts are largely drawn from the social sciences and from the (often quite similar) pop-sociology of the mass media. The general public's understanding of social change will also be examined. This strongly resembles sociological and pop-sociological understanding: the same bland and liberal rhetoric about transition towards equity is seen everywhere, with the different genres supporting each other.

My intention is not to point knowingly at the contradictions between people's lives and the way they are represented in optimistic accounts. That would be all too easy. It is more interesting, and more politically worthwhile, to discover how such accounts manage to make themselves plausible. One point must be made straight away. My analysis is not based on the view that nothing whatsoever has changed, a view which would force me to the rather implausible conclusion that the optimistic accounts simply propagate lies. That view is incorrect: as the optimists constantly remind us, there is evidence of some change in the sexual division of domestic labour. What matters is how this evidence is interpreted. First, though, we must briefly review the evidence itself.

Diary-based time-use data indicate small increases in adult male domestic work over the last few decades. In the United States average male domestic work (housework and childcare) increased from 11.5 to 15.7 hours per week between 1965 and 1985 (Robinson & Godby 1997).

In Australia a similar increase occurred, from 12.3 to 15.9 hours per week between 1974 and 1992 (Bittman 1998) while in Britain male domestic work increased from 9 to 12.6 hours per week between 1961 and 1983–84 (Gershuny & Jones 1987). Interestingly, women's domestic work hours have decreased, and at a faster rate than the increase for men. While Australian men's unpaid work increased by an average 3.6 hours per week between 1974 and 1992, for women there was a fall of 6.5 hours per week, from 41.5 to 35 hours (Bittman 1998). In the United States, women's average domestic work fell by 9.3 hours per week between 1965 and 1985, compared with an increase of 4.2 hours for men (Robinson & Godby 1997).

Since men's domestic work has increased and women's decreased, presenting the data in proportional form leads to a strong appearance of increased male participation. Robinson and Godby (1997) cited as evidence of a trend towards androgyny the fact that the ratio of male to female housework increased from 0.18 to 0.50 between 1965 and 1985, while noting that the same degree of change was not evident with childcare (from 0.27 to 0.29). Commenting on similar data, Arlie Hochschild told *Time* magazine that 'the arrow is moving in the right direction, just too slowly' (*Time*, 7 August 1989), and the *Los Angeles Times* concluded that 'this represents significant progress in just 20 years' (2 December 1988). However, from the data we can calculate that almost two-thirds (64 per cent) of the reported change in the sex ratio is due to a decrease in women's housework. As Bittman (1996) pointed out, most of the adaptation to women's increasing labour force participation appears to have come from women reducing their unpaid work, rather than from men increasing their contribution.

Particularly impressive evidence of change appears to come from measures which are based not on time but on, for example, participation rates. These measure the proportion of men who participate in various domestic tasks. In a 1980 study, Lewis investigated male care of infants, replicating the procedures used in 1960 by Newson and Newson (1963) and using a sample matching the earlier one in terms of socio-economic status and family composition, from the same English city. In 1980 70 per cent of men gave some help to their wives in the period following birth, whereas in 1960 only 30 per cent of men had done so; in 1960 51 per cent of fathers never attended a baby at night, but in 1980 only 13 per cent never did so (C. Lewis 1986). Similarly, Gershuny and Jones (1987) reported that British men's rates of participation in a series of domestic tasks rose substantially between 1961 and 1983–84. The largest increase was for the category 'cooking/washing-up', with a rise in male participation rates from 38 to 86 per cent over the period. However, not all studies reported increases in male participation rates.

Dempsey's (1992) study of an Australian rural town showed no significant increase between 1974 and 1985–86, and indeed there was some indication of a hardening of the sexual division of labour over the period studied.

Men's repertoire of domestic tasks appears to have expanded somewhat, with more men doing a range of domestic tasks which might formerly have been considered unmasculine (Bittman 1989). However, such simple data does not indicate the frequency of participation: it is a dichotomous variable, the two possible values being 'never participates' and 'participates'. Neither is the distinction between help and responsibility, between task performance and job performance, measured, though we have already seen enough contemporary data to be sure that most male work takes the form of help. Overall, then, we can say there is evidence of a modest increase in the range of tasks with which husbands help their wives – if we assume that evidence based on self-reports is reliable.

Determined Optimism

The desire to demonstrate change is very strong. This can involve a rather casual attitude to empirical evidence, which is perhaps unsurprising in mass-media accounts: one journalist countered a report of low levels of male childcare with her own intuition: 'All right, so that is an average, but it still does not square with the evidence around us' (*Glasgow Herald*, 28 March 1994). Social scientists can be equally cavalier with the data: a Danish researcher into paternity leave remarked, 'Men are changing much more than is shown in the statistics' (Inter Press Service, 4 August 1994). An American expert on fatherhood who confidently asserted that 'co-parenting (fully shared caring for children) ... is becoming the most common pattern of dual-job marriages in the United States' made the interesting admission that 'unfortunately, most of the more exciting current descriptions of men's sex roles are, strangely ... not empirically derived' (R. Lewis 1986: 17, 20). An Australian researcher introduced her relatively optimistic account of change by remarking that the empirical evidence about the resilience of the sexual division of domestic work had 'a poor fit with what I observed around me. In daily life, as well as in the media, there appeared to be some softening of gender lines' (Goodnow 1989: 55).

When empirical evidence is appealed to, contemporary data is often regarded as sufficient to justify optimism, it being self-evident to many commentators that men did little or no domestic work in the past. If men's participation rate has been near-zero until recently, any sign at all of male participation is proof of change. Jump and Haas (1987: 110–11) were encouraged to find in their study of 'dual-career fathers' many cases of men performing tasks such as diapering, feeding and toileting which, they confidently claimed, had been 'unheard of in an earlier generation of fathers'. This kind of argument is not new. A generation earlier Young and Willmott, in their well-known study of working-class communities *Family and Kinship in East London* (1957), recorded an 'emerging partnership' between husbands and wives. For example: 'Of the 45 husbands 32 gave some regular help to their wives with the housework; 29 had, to take an index trivial enough in itself but perhaps significant, done the washing-up one or more times during the previous week' (Young & Willmott 1957: 12). This was the only information cited about male domestic labour. However, since Booth's (1902) study of a similar community more than 50 years earlier had made no reference to men washing the dishes, Young and Willmott felt entitled to conclude that much had changed.

Pop-sociological accounts employ similar rhetoric. The *Ladies Home Journal* (January 1984) was encouraged by the fact that 50 per cent of men perform at least some housework or childcare, considering the 'long-standing traditional division of roles'. A syndicated American report of research that found that 10 per cent of households showed considerable sharing of domestic work asserted 'that's a big increase from just about zippo 20 years ago' (Gannett News Service, 2 December 1992). The belief that until recently men's participation in domestic work was 'zippo' can be so strong that casual observation and anecdotes are considered sufficient evidence of change. *Time Australia* (22 August 1988) introduced a cover story on 'Dads: Picking Up the Challenge' with observations of 'men out with strollers' and fathers who are 'totally unselfconscious about dandling children on their knees'. This new involved fatherhood was compared with the 'traditional father' who, we were told, had little or nothing to do with the daily life of his children, except as a 'stern authoritarian'. Some textbook writers seem to believe that including even one photograph of a man performing non-traditional work is enough proof. One of the optimistic texts cited earlier contained – as its single piece of evidence about change – a photograph of two men chatting in a street, each pushing a baby-stroller. The photograph was captioned: 'Fathers' roles have changed considerably over the past twenty years' (Eshleman 1985: 23).

In fact, similar observations in the 1950s had impressed a previous generation of social observers. Young and Willmott (1957: 10) were struck by what they assumed to be the 'new sight of young fathers wheeling prams up Bethnal Green Road on a Saturday morning, taking their little daughters for a row on the lake or playing with their sons on the putting green in front of the Institute of Community Studies'. At the same time Titmuss (1958: 117) used his observations of men playing with children and 'unashamedly' pushing prams as evidence that 'family life in industrialised Britain is changing'. If observations like these impress optimistic commentators decade after decade, we must begin to wonder about the assumption of zero male participation in the past.

If we take a long view, general historical accounts indicate that men's domestic work may have been declining since the industrial revolution. Ruth Cowan (1983) reminded us that in pre-industrial America men were responsible for vital domestic work such as building houses, butchering animals, splitting wood for the stove and tanning leather for clothes and shoes. Cowan also pointed out the significance of children's domestic work in earlier eras. Her main argument was that women's domestic load has been largely untouched by industrialisation, while that of men and children has been largely replaced.

Of course, such accounts are not based on sociological surveys, but on a whole range of documentary evidence. Little survey data is available before the 1960s. One exception is the 1924 American community study *Middletown*, which found that 67 per cent of fathers spent more than one hour a day with their children, according to their wives' reports (Lynd & Lynd 1929). Interestingly, a repetition of this study in the same town in 1978 found that the percentage had only modestly increased, to 76 per cent, though it was dubbed a significant increase by the researchers (Caplow & Chadwick 1979; Caplow et al. 1982). Another American study (c. 1940) found 60 per cent of fathers reporting 'routine' participation in childcare, in terms such as:

> Did everything from changing diapers to singing them to sleep. It was fairly frequent.
> Took care of the middle child for first two years as wife was ill, almost all the care.
> Considerable care. Changed diapers, clothed and put to bed, fed. At least did my share of it.
> Gave baths, changed diapers, walked floor, gave night bottle.
> Changed pants, bathed, fed formula and amused baby (in LaRossa 1997: 83–4).

Other kinds of data lead to us to further question the idea that any sign of male domestic work is evidence of change. A study of male diarists of the 16th and following centuries found several cases of men nursing their children through illness (Pollock 1984). In *The Condition of the Working Class in England*, Engels ([1845] 1969: 173) described, with regret, large numbers of unemployed Manchester men 'condemned to domestic occupations'. While their employed wives were at the factories, 'the husband sits at home, tends the children, sweeps the room and cooks'. A study that questioned elderly members of English fishing families about their experiences as children or young adults between 1890 and 1914 found that 38 per cent of men had helped their wives in domestic work, and that this had not been regarded as in any way remarkable. One woman reported that once a week her husband: 'used to say to me and my dear old mother – go in the other room I'm going to clean through. And he'd clean through my kitchen. I had a big cooking stove in there, with big white plates at the back, and he'd make that shine like a plate of glass' (Lummis 1982: 47).

Some optimistic studies which do not state that in the past men were uninvolved in domestic work, nevertheless use rhetoric which makes that assumption. Quite often the existence of varying levels of male participation is used to develop a typology of men, for example 'traditional' and 'shared caregivers' (Russell 1983a). Applying the label 'traditional' to a low level of participation invites us to assume that such was the typical practice in the past, and since not all men are labelled 'traditional' we are invited to see change. Other writers use similar terms evoking change, such as 'developing', 'emergent' and 'transitional', to describe the practices of those men who do somewhat more domestic work, stating that they depart from a past characterised by rigid sexual distinctions. Examples are titles such as 'The Emergent Father Role' (Entwisle & Doering 1988), 'The Developing Father: Emerging Roles in Contemporary Society' (Robinson & Barret 1986) and 'Fathers in Transition' (Jump & Haas 1987).

In effect, any sign of variance in male domestic work can be used to identify a group which points the way to the future. One American study dubbed its 'sharing fathers' (according to the subjects' self-evaluation on a five-point scale) as 'pioneers' (Coltrane 1989: 480). An Australian study of such men argued that while it could be objected that the rarity of sharing fathers made them undeserving of sustained attention, 'they are the vanguard of social change. Their very presence represents a departure from even a decade ago' (Harper 1980: 3).

However, if the past was not quite so 'traditional' as we are asked to believe, it may well be that practices which are not really novel have become visible simply because they fit a contemporary agenda. What was unusual or overlooked yesterday may be today's 'vanguard'. A reporter for National Public Radio described as 'extraordinary' the early marriage of Supreme Court Judge Ruth Bader Ginsburg: 'In an era when men did not change diapers, Marty Ginsburg did much more. He was often the principal child caretaker, allowing his wife to go on long professional trips' (*All Things Considered*, 7 June 1993). Those events took place in the 1960s. Marty Ginsburg was considered exceptional, since at that time men supposedly did not change diapers; a similar contemporary husband would, we assume, be only one person in the growing vanguard.

As Gilding (1994) argued, researchers have, at least from a statistical point of view, given disproportionate attention to such exceptions as role-reversed families on the grounds that they embody expected trends. Leonard put the same point more caustically when she marvelled at the spate of researchers 'charging off looking for deliberately exceptional forms' (Leonard 1987: 410). There has been quite a lot of charging-off. One study of 255 households (Harper & Richards 1979) devoted a whole chapter to two households, one a case of role-reversal and the other a case of shared responsibilities. Russell (1983a: 17) was forced to recruit beyond his original quasi-random sample to obtain enough cases of shared caregiving, since from nearly 600 initial approaches only 10 such families were found. While acknowledging that the number of truly egalitarian families was small, Russell and his colleagues asserted that 'it could be argued that they represent a growing group of families who are exploring new ways of dividing up the responsibilities for family and work' (Russell et al. 1988: 258–9).

Other researchers stretch their interpretation of 'sharing' to find enough cases to study. Goodnow and Bowes' (1994) Australian study of 'innovative couples' was widely discussed in optimistic terms. A typical press report described it as a study of '50 couples who equally share the housework', and quoted Goodnow's quiet optimism 'there is more equality and sharing. Women are still doing more, but the averages of male/female workloads are changing' (*Toronto Sun*, 2 January 1995). The authors' low level of expectation of male domestic work is clear, however. The most common pattern in these 'sharing' couples was described as 'non-stereotypical specialties'; 56 per cent of couples fitted that category. Several case studies were presented. In couple number 1, Robert prepared breakfast, made the beds, did the vacuuming, cleaned the bathroom on Saturdays and otherwise 'helped' Leslie a lot. In couple number 2, Edward did the ironing.

Another study of factors related to sharing domestic labour between spouses used what the authors admitted was a loose definition of sharing: 'Husbands do not have to do exactly half the housework or childcare for us to call these tasks shared ... If we used such narrow definitions there would be few cases to examine' (Ericksen et al. 1979: 306). The authors conceded that with such a protocol they would lose all their cases; thus childcare was considered to be shared if the husband looked after the children without the wife present at least once a week. Similarly, the British market research firm Mintel, failing to find significant numbers of sharing New Men, relaxed their criteria and were thus able to find that 18 per cent of men belonged to a category they dubbed 'Newish Man': to qualify, a man needed to claim to be wholly or partly responsible for at least one of cooking, laundry or planning shopping (*Independent*, 25 February 1994).

Mass-media accounts give similar disproportionate attention (from a statistical point of view) to cases of role-reversal involving house-husbands who 'man the home front' (Melbourne *Age*, 3 February 1988; *Australian Women's Weekly*, May 1988; *Australian* 20 January 1990). Journalistic accounts often resemble social science for the simple reason that social scientists are frequently reported. Not a few stories on men and change are built around interviews with male social scientists who are researching the issues for personal reasons. Data about the resilience of the division of labour can be countered by an optimistic report on the practices of the social scientist as pioneer:

> Balanced against such evidence are people like Peter Moss, one of a new breed of job-sharing men with whom one is tempted to be impressed. After I spoke to Peter Moss about his research into the subject of fathers at London University,. he had to rush home to put his one-year-old to bed and to make tea for Andrew and Hannah, aged ten and eight (Melbourne *Age*, 14 January 1983).

The Revolving Door

Most optimistic commentators put their faith in the simple model of change mentioned in chapter 1: when women enter employment, men will reciprocate with increased unpaid work. This has motivated many studies of the marital division of labour. It is worth saying immediately that one of the main ideological achievements of this work is in diverting our attention from all other situations and sources of domestic work. In the literature on change, small increases by husbands are made much of, but they may be less significant than increases in, for example, paid services and unpaid help from others. So, when respondents indicate that children or hired help perform certain tasks, some researchers simply eliminate the answers from their analysis (Hiller & Philliber 1986).

When women enter paid employment increased male domestic work may result, but other outcomes, such as divorce or separation, are possible. The changes in women's economic position which form the base for the rhetoric of the symmetrical family also make it more possible for women to become heads of single-parent households (Gerson 1986). Rather than a convergence of sex roles, this trend suggests some divergence, with many women taking sole or principal responsibility for childcare and support. Such women may be just as much a vanguard of change as are shared caregiving fathers. There are, in fact, many more women totally responsible for routine childcare than there are men who share childcare equally (Russell 1983b: 191), and it is likely that there are many more men who have little or no contact with their children than men who share childcare equally, given that in Britain and Australia, for example, one-third of separated husbands lose all contact with their children, and that a further third have little contact (Ingham 1984; Funder et al. 1993). Such men are not written up as pioneers, though, since their practices are not in line with the optimism of symmetrical family rhetoric.

Often the logic of change towards symmetry is taken for granted, but some writers clarify its underlying assumptions. A paper from the Australian Institute of Family Studies explained that 'reality testing' will cause adjustment in traditional attitudes:

> It stands to reason that if both partners recognise the economic necessity for wives to work as well as husbands, they will also be more likely to acknowledge the necessity to share household chores, childcare and other joint family responsibilities. Reality testing shows the lack of validity of attitudes that no longer fit (Edgar & Glezer 1992: 38).

Another writer appealed to the 'sociological concept of reciprocal roles', which apparently involves principles of fair or rational role allocation, to argue that women's employment inevitably means that men will either be pressed into more unpaid work or volunteer willingly to take their fair share of combined family and outside work. Otherwise 'role conflicts will proliferate, with accompanying stresses, until separation, divorce or a system of complementary roles again prevails'. In other words, unequal marriages are simply not possible in the long term; some kind of natural correcting process will restore parity (R. Lewis 1986: 22).

The ideal final outcome is 'The Symmetrical Family', as Young and Willmott titled their influential 1973 study. While they conceded that temporarily the family system was somewhat unfair to women, the inevitable trend was to a new and fair equilibrium:

> By the next century – with the pioneers of 1970 already at the front of the column – society will have moved from (a) one demanding job for the wife and one for the husband, through (b) two demanding jobs for the wife and one for the husband, to (c) two demanding jobs for the wife and two for the husband. The symmetry will be complete (Young & Willmott 1973: 278).

The flexibility of the model is clear. Any evidence of an increase in male unpaid work can be said to show the emergence of the final, symmetrical state (c), and any evidence of the sluggishness of change can be said to show the temporary persistence of the intermediate, un-balanced state (b). These are fundamental rhetorical moves of many optimistic commentaries. For example, we are reassured in the anaes-thetising language of social psychology that while 'disjunctions' (i.e. the double burden) may be experienced by individuals as 'stressful and emotionally disturbing', they are merely 'temporary' because 'trans-ition' is not yet complete (Ross et al. 1983: 809).

Young and Willmott's data about male domestic labour was hardly superior to that of their 1957 study. They concluded that husbands 'do a lot of work in the house, including many jobs which are not at all traditional men's ones ... the extent of the sharing is probably still increasing' (Young & Willmott 1973: 94). However, their only data was the result of one question addressed to husbands and wives: 'Do you/does your husband help at least once a week with any household jobs like washing-up, making beds (helping with the children), ironing, cooking or cleaning?' Eighty-five per cent of men helped at least once a week with one or more of these tasks; 15 per cent of these men helped only with washing-up. As Ann Oakley (1974) remarked, a husband who ironed his own trousers on a Saturday afternoon would be included among the 85 per cent assigned to the higher category of participation. Reviewing this and other similar studies, Oakley concluded that reports of shared housework were based on data which included only occasional male participation or, sometimes, merely the belief of wives that their husbands would help under some circumstances. Reports of sharing really amounted to variations on the theme of a rigid gender division of labour, which provided the 'baseline from which questions are asked and assessments made'. This too is a fundamental rhetorical move in optimistic accounts. We have met it already, in the excitement about vanguards and pioneers, and we will meet it again.

Symmetrical family models conceal a social class bias. By the time Young and Willmott were writing, paid employment and the resulting double burden were not novel for working-class women. This is graphic-ally illustrated by the two 'Middletown' studies, conducted in 1924 and 1978 in Muncie, Indiana (Lynd & Lynd 1929; Caplow & Chadwick 1979). In 1924 the double burden was the lot of working-class women only. Middle-class women were not employed. In 1978 both groups of women experienced the double burden. Thus, generations of women had experienced the supposedly transitional double-burden state, with little or no sign of movement towards symmetry. However, much sym-metrical family rhetoric gives the impression that middle-class husbands are expected to do better than their working-class peers.

In addition to the military metaphor concerning advancing columns headed by pioneers, Young and Willmott employed a striking mechanical metaphor when they spoke of change in terms of a 'revolving door' with 'men coming in, women going out' (Young & Willmott 1973: 122). From now on I will, for simplicity, refer to symmetrical family models of this kind as revolving-door models. In mainstream sociology and pop-sociology the simple model of the revolving door has become the standard explanation of social change in private life. An article on multiple-role women stated that their problem was temporary and would be gradually ameliorated: 'women's expansion of their roles into the work world should gradually free men to invest some of their energies in the family system' (Locker 1984: 13). Introductory student texts base their optimism on the obvious logic of the revolving door: 'Given the trend toward wives' employment ... it is safe to predict more egalitarian relationships in marriage, with a more flexible division of labor both in and outside the home than in our recent past' (Hess et al. 1985: 284). Likewise, an article on 'megatrends' for women (which also predicted that by 2000 the average American would have a 30-hour working week) announced that: 'Dual careers will bring a further breakdown of traditional sex roles. The era of Supermom, when women tried to do everything, is vanishing. The future promises a more equal sharing of family responsibilities' (*Ladies Home Journal*, January 1984).

Statistical Niceties

The results of long-term studies which track change in domestic work over a decade or more were discussed above. Such studies are expensive, and sociologists more often rely on contemporary data about domestic work to investigate change. This need not require the kind of un-grounded assumptions about the past I have already criticised. It might seem impossible to demonstrate change using only current data, but in principle it is possible, as long as other kinds of relevant external data about long-term change are used as well. The trick is to test models of the symmetrical family by measuring the association between various proposed factors and men's level of domestic work. For example, if it can be shown that husbands of employed wives perform more domestic work and that the rate of employment of married women has increased, a plausible argument can be mounted for a general increase in male domestic work over time. Such arguments are plausible rather than convincing, since they rely on a series of (usually unstated) assumptions. For example, if we conduct a study of happiness and find that people who are wealthier tend to be happier than those who are not, and we know that the general level of wealth has increased, are we entitled to conclude that general happiness has increased? Perhaps the poor are now even less happy than before.

As shown in chapter 1, model testing of this kind hardly supports the optimistic view – the evidence for increased domestic work by husbands of employed wives is weak, at best. In that chapter I relied upon the best available data, based on carefully conducted time-use studies. However, these studies are also expensive and are less common than studies based on simple survey data in which subjects respond to questions inviting them to estimate their level of domestic work. Estimates of time per week spent in various tasks may be collected, but such estimates are notoriously suspect. More commonly subjects are simply asked to report their frequency of participation, typically using a five-point scale. For example, a given task may be recorded as (1) always performed by the husband, (2) usually performed by the husband, (3) shared equally, (4) usually performed by the wife, or (5) always performed by the wife. Of course, terms such as 'equally shared' can bear many different interpretations.

Not all studies of these less rigorous kinds report higher levels of husbands' participation when wives are employed (e.g. Berardo et al. 1987; Antill & Cotton 1988; Burns & Homel 1989; Douthitt 1989). Others do, however, report some association, with respect to women's paid work hours or occupational status (e.g. Beckett & Smith 1981; Coverman 1985; Shamir 1986; Barnett & Baruch 1987; Crouter et al. 1987; Ross 1987; Kamo 1988); these results appear to support the revolving-door model. The details of the way this works are revealing. The studies usually employ complex statistical methodologies and report their results in a form opaque to the general reader. Beneath the complex statistics lie rhetorical moves similar to those encountered already.

In typical studies women's employment is considered in one of two ways, depending on the model being tested (this description of the two models uses the terminology of a representative study, Coverman 1985).

The first way is in terms of hours of paid work. Symmetrical family models of the 'demand/response' or 'exchange' kind suggest that labour time (both paid and unpaid) is fairly or rationally allocated in order to meet household demands. They predict that when women have greater paid work hours their husbands will increase their unpaid work time to compensate. Other factors such as family size and composition are also relevant in this model: men are expected to do more domestic work if there is more to be done.

The second way is in terms of indicators of occupational status, such as income. Symmetrical family models of the 'resource' kind propose that access to resources such as education, income and occupational prestige increases power. They predict that women with higher income or occupational status are better able to demand assistance with unpaid work from husbands.

The distinction between the models is crucial. Resource models take account of the fact that the labour market remains highly stratified with respect to gender, a fact which many symmetrical family proponents ignore or conceal. A woman may be employed, but earn much less than her husband and have much lower occupational status. The revolving door does not place all women on the same job-market level as their husbands. It is important, therefore, to distinguish the effect of women's paid work hours from the effect of women's paid work resources. Neither factor is particularly salient.

The pursuit of statistical niceties often masks the point that the magnitude of the reported associations is remarkably low. Results are frequently reported and discussed in terms of their level of statistical significance, rather than their actual magnitude. For example, the report of a significant association between the employment hours of wives and the unpaid work hours of husbands may sound impressive to the uninitiated. But in statistical inference 'significant' simply means 'unlikely to have occurred by chance'; to learn that an association is significant is to learn nothing about its magnitude, it is simply to learn that there is plausible evidence for the existence of an association – in our case, plausible evidence that husbands of employed wives have a detectably higher level of domestic work. We look in vain in some studies for an indication of the magnitude of the reported significant association, and in other cases the fine print (if we can interpret it) shows that the magnitude is small. Moreover, when, as is most common, the data is in the form of participation rates based on five-point scales, magnitudes of associations are relatively meaningless. (Writing from the point of view of an experienced practitioner, Cohen (1994) made a provocative critique of the routine misuse of statistical methodology in the social sciences, discussing these points and many more. Agger (1989) also criticised the 'notoriously low' value of many reported associations in social science research.)

Certainly, not all authors couch their 'positive' findings in totally optimistic terms. Some authors stress that despite the confirmation of some or all hypothesised associations, their data hardly supports the idea that the division of labour is equitable (e.g. Ross 1987; Kamo 1988). Many others are not so cautious. Coverman (1985) stated that her data 'overwhelmingly support the demand/response capability hypothesis as the best explanation of domestic labour time', with the employment of women placing 'demands upon their husbands ... to help relieve the strain by increasing their involvement in domestic activities'. That study, typical of its kind, is worth examining carefully.

Coverman's study was based on self-estimates of time-use, so we can, for once, express the results in terms of actual time, though we should be somewhat sceptical of the self-reporting methodology. The basic finding was that for each hour wives spent in paid work, husbands' unpaid work time increased by five minutes (controlling for family size), acknowledged as only a 'slight increase' (Coverman 1985: 93). On a straightforward interpretation of the fair-allocation model we would expect that the wife's extra burden of an hour's paid employment would be shared with her husband by his doing 30 minutes more domestic labour, and she 30 minutes less. The data shows that an average husband performed only one-sixth of his share of the extra burden, leaving five-sixths of the marginal division of labour to be explained. If we include the fact that less domestic work overall is done in households where women are employed, it could be argued that fairness does not require a man to do an extra 30 minutes unpaid work for each hour his wife is in paid work. A calculation based on typical figures about the domestic work time of employed women (Bittman 1991: 21) showed that it can still be argued, with respect to Coverman's study, that approximately three-quarters of the marginal division of labour had to be explained. This accepts that the husband cannot be expected to help maintain the standards of domestic work which prevail in households with full-time housewives.

The statistically significant, albeit small, sensitivity of husbands' un-paid work to wives' employment was said by Coverman to confirm the model of fair allocation of labour. However, it seems more plausible to argue that the data does not support this model. Indeed, it looks suspiciously like another version of the net drain, in which husbands do *some* domestic work but not enough to meet the evident extra demand.

Coverman's basis for arguing that the demand/response hypothesis was supported was that the relevant variables (hours of paid work and family composition) had a higher association with male participation than did the variables (such as relative education levels, income and occupational status) suggested by the relative resources hypothesis. (Coverman also tested, and rejected, a hypothesis about sex role ideology.) In other words 'overwhelming support' for a model merely means that it is superior to the alternatives considered. However, the most obvious hypothesis of all – that the division of labour is determined by gender – was not formulated for direct comparison. Doing this would have involved taking gender to be an independent variable, measuring its association with domestic work levels, then comparing this with the associations of other variables. The result would have been overwhelming confirmation of the model that domestic work levels are determined by sex.

Such a methodology would have treated the population of men and women as a whole. Instead, the two sexes were treated separately from the start, thus taking for granted the basic sexual division. It distracts attention from the fact that sex is the 'overwhelming determinant of the division of labour' (Baxter 1988: 93), and instead focuses attention on small effects and changes consistent with the proposed model of change. Oakley's (1974) criticism of the earlier literature as basing assessments on the sexual division of labour also applies.

In studies which treat sex as an independent variable, it is always by far the most important predictor of domestic work time. For example, Baxter's (1988) data showed that sex alone accounted for 50 per cent of the variation in domestic labour time, and only 8 per cent of the variation was accounted for by factors such as income levels and employment hours. A review of studies of men's unpaid work concluded that most can only account for 15–20 per cent of the variation in husbands' household contributions (using variables such as family size and composition, spouse's employed hours and income, education and sex role attitudes; Benin & Agostinelli 1988). Nevertheless, much effort is put into measuring and reporting such small effects.

Another point must be made about Coverman's study. We know that studies using the most reliable data do not support revolving-door models. However, Coverman used rather doubtful data from a study based on men's self-estimates of domestic work (Quinn & Staines 1979). The average value reported – 25 hours per week – was remarkably high, and scepticism is in order. Studies which compare diary-data and subjects' time estimates show a great degree of unreliability. Both sexes consistently underestimate total household time spent on domestic tasks and both underestimate the gender gap, but males do so more than females (e.g. Komter 1989; Bittman & Lovejoy 1993). Researchers have differing attitudes to such issues, especially sex discrepancies. Some treat them simply as methodological problems to be solved (e.g. Antill & Cotton 1988). But perhaps this is, in the words of Bittman and Lovejoy, to put 'misplaced energy' into attempting to reconcile incon-sistencies in answers to questions about the performance of domestic labour, in order to find the 'objective harmonious family reality'.

Estimates of time spent on childcare are particularly unreliable. Women tend to markedly underestimate their childcare time by dis-counting time during which they are responsible for children's welfare but are also performing other domestic duties. Women's estimates may be as little as one-quarter of the time they are actually responsible for childcare (Australian Bureau of Statistics 1993). In contrast, men tend to exaggerate their childcare time. Pleck's (1985) study showed men estimating their childcare time at an average 11.3 hours per week, whereas their own time-use diary entries showed only 1.7 hours per week. Many men, as well as some social scientists, appear to believe that whenever men spend time with children (with or without the mother present), no matter what the activity, they are undertaking childcare. Barnett and Baruch (1987) found that a proposed question about the amount of time fathers were at home but not interacting with their children had to be abandoned, since in pilot interviews fathers saw themselves as continuously available to their children, when at home, 'almost by definition'. The authors accepted this definition of the situation and abandoned their initial distinction between intermittent and intensive interaction, thus yielding a mean total interaction time for fathers and children of 29.5 hours per week. In Booth and Edwards' (1980) study 'Fathers: The Invisible Parent', such was the determination to make fathers visible that the total amount of time fathers spent in the same room as their children was analysed, since 'No doubt some of the time was spent talking with the child, caring for it, and in other ways taking the offspring into account, thus indicating some degree of involvement with the child.'

In light of this, Coverman's remarkably high figure for male domestic work is understandable. In the original study, the questions addressed to men had aimed to 'minimise male underreporting due to the feminine connotation generally associated with housework'. Accordingly, men were asked about the amount of time they spent 'taking care of or doing things with' children (Quinn & Staines 1979). The combination of Coverman's statistical methodology with data of this dubious value provides a clear case of the sociological determination to report change.

Ideological Change

In the early 1980s a survey of American male college students reported that one-third said they would prefer to work part-time or stay at home while their children were young. One of the researchers observed: 'I don't expect they will actually do it. But it's surprising they even want to. Ten years ago you would never have found many men saying such a thing' (*Christian Science Monitor*, 14 April 1983).

Revolving-door models propose other motors of change besides women's employment. The most frequent alternative is ideological and cultural change; in fact, often this is considered to be the main motor. A 1990 article in the advertising journal *American Demographics* assured readers that:

> women's home life will become easier. Men's performance at home has failed to measure up to women's expectations. But the outlook is positive, because men know they will need to become more involved in household responsibilities. Look for beliefs to be translated into behaviour (Townsend & O'Neill 1990).

Commentators often assume that principles of sex equity are actively pursued by individuals. The following passage from a child psychology text favourably contrasted modern America with other societies: 'Many societies – in Arab countries and in Africa, for example – prescribe much more rigid roles for males and females than our own society does. Furthermore, in our own society there is now a very clear trend against distinctions based on sex' (Harris & Liebert 1984: 304). Similarly, *Domestic Revolutions: A Social History of American Life* (Mintz & Kellogg 1988: 236) stated that progress towards the symmetrical family is a cooperative struggle embodying an egalitarian ethic: 'Americans are struggling to find a fair way to juggle individual, familial and social demands', though the authors added, somewhat cryptically, that the ethic is 'honoured as much in the breach as in the observance'.

Faced with evidence of the resilience of the domestic labour division, commentators often express puzzlement about, for example, 'attitude–behaviour incongruence' (Araji 1977: 309) – the failure of attitude change to translate into behaviour change (Burns & Homel 1989: 114), or the 'clash between thought and deed' (Segal 1990: 35). I will argue in this section that it would be naive to conclude that most people (men, especially) are strongly committed to equity in the division of labour. The qualitative studies reported in chapter 1 tell a different story, about the operation of a male right to leisure and servicing, which is generally supported by men and grudgingly tolerated by many women. Those studies found few, if any, social sanctions to enforce an egalitarian division of labour. An ideology unsupported by sanctions is hardly operating as a social norm. Even when couples appear to seriously subscribe to egalitarian practices, the work of maintaining the sharing of domestic labour largely falls to women, who find that they are 'the enforcers of egalitarian standards' (Smith & Reid 1986: 399). Moreover, since men who give their wives a considerable degree of help receive high praise, we can conclude that general expectations are relatively low.

One difficulty for ideological revolving-door models is that it is not at all clear that attitudes are strongly related to practices. Many studies (usually based on self-reports) have investigated whether individuals with more egalitarian attitudes have practices which are more egalitarian. Some studies found no statistically significant association between attitudes and the division of domestic work (Coverman 1985; Pleck 1985; Crouter et al. 1987). Baxter (1988: 93) summed up her results with the stark observation that 'even the most feminist women still adopt traditional practices', bearing out Oakley's reports (1974) of couples with a marked 'general air of egalitarianism' who maintained a rigid division of labour. However, the negative findings about the significance of attitudes come from studies which measured only general attitudes to sex roles and the position of women. When attitudes specifically relating to the division of domestic work are measured, low but statistically significant associations between attitudes and practices are found (Hiller & Philliber 1986; Ross 1987; Antill & Cotton 1988; Kamo 1988). Interestingly, studies which do report a significant association between attitudes and practices find that men's attitudes are more significant than women's (Kamo 1988), or that only the attitudes of men are significant (Hiller & Philliber 1986; Ross 1987; Antill & Cotton 1988). In summary, the statistically most significant finding of such studies is that men who explicitly express egalitarian attitudes about domestic work tend to perform (in their own estimate) somewhat more domestic work than other men. This strongly suggests the existence of male choice discussed in chapter 1 or, as one study expressed in the euphemistic language of role theory, 'male prerogatives in marital role bargaining are still quite strong' (Hiller & Philliber 1986). Of course, such studies cannot determine the direction of causality, and we must consider the possibility that men who perform more domestic labour have, as a result, more egalitarian attitudes. Alternatively, the point might be that men with more egalitarian attitudes feel obliged to report higher levels of domestic work.

Some writers find grounds for optimism in the fact that men put a high value on their involvement in family life, as if this implies support for the symmetrical family. Certainly the evidence that men value family life is persuasive. A 1986 Australian survey of personal values found that 64 per cent of men ranked family as most important, and only 4 per cent ranked work that highly (Melbourne *Age* poll, cited in Throssell 1991). Another Australian study found that men rate marriage as the greatest source of happiness, whereas women rate friends, health and family support as most significant (Travers & Richardson 1993). An English study (Blackburn & Mann 1979) found that almost 90 per cent of male manual workers rated a good family life at home above enjoyment of their work life. Qualitative studies reported similar male priorities, and showed that men identify companionship as the most important aspect of marriage, identify their wives as their best friend and express a desire to become more involved in family life (Rubin 1985: 129; Weiss 1985; Cohen 1987: 69). Donaldson's (1987: 179) study of Australian working-class men led him to conclude that his subjects had 'intense emotional dependency' on the family–household, the family giving meaning to the drudgery of paid work.

Such high levels of male investment in family life are often described as encouraging, but counter-intuitive. Cohen (1987: 70) reported that men appear to be more affected by family life than they 'have been thought to be', and Pleck (1985: 135), after reviewing the literature, reached the conclusion, which he described as 'very difficult to accept', that most men are 'more psychologically involved in their families than their jobs'. Throssell (1991: 24) also considered that the high value men place on family life was somewhat surprising, and assumed that it indicated a welcome 'gradual change'. This implies a past in which men valued family life less, but that is hard to credit. In *The Secrets of Men's History*, Filene used the correspondence of prominent American men to demonstrate a high level of dependence upon the domestic sphere. In 1775 the future president John Adams wrote to his children: 'My dear Nabby, Johnny, Charly and Tommy, I long to see you and to share with your Mamma the Pleasures of your Conversation' (7 July 1775, in Filene 1987: 109). Another future president, Woodrow Wilson, wrote to his intended bride:

> My own darling, I suppose there never was a man more dependent than I on love and sympathy, more devoted to home and home life; and, my darling, my heart is overflowing with gratitude and gladness because of the assurance that it now has a new love to lean upon – a love which will some day be the centre of a new home and the joy of a new home life. I shall not begin to live a complete life, my love, until you are my wife (2 October 1883; in Filene 1987: 108).

Why does the evidence about men's commitment to family life strikes commentators as both surprising and suggestive of change? The evident assumption is that men's non-performance of domestic work results from a lack of interest in family life. So we hear of 'the discrepancy between theory and practice. The vast majority of men act as though their priorities were the other way around ... as though work-life, rather than family-life were their chief source of fulfilment' (Throssell 1991: 24). But is there a discrepancy between theory and practice? Being the principal or sole breadwinner does not require men to value work before family; on the contrary, people desire stable employment in order to have a family. One of the strengths of feminist materialism is that it makes particularly clear that men *are* involved in family life, but more as consumers than as producers. Given the benefits men receive from the sexual division of labour in the family, it would be odd if men did not value family life. So, while many men continue to see their breadwinning role as sufficient contribution to the support of their family (Brannen & Moss 1987; Livingstone & Luxton 1989), it is perfectly consistent for them to value the home very highly, though probably as a site of receiving care than as a site of caring for others. This is nicely demonstrated in Woodrow Wilson's love letter. In the sentence immediately following the passage quoted by Filene, Wilson (then a student at Johns Hopkins University) wrote: 'Who is more affected by the character of his home than a student, and who has sweeter opportunities of unselfish ministrations than a student's wife?' (in Wilson's collected papers, Link 1967: 449). Valuing involvement in family life, and believing one should do the family work, are different matters.

General shifts in attitude are often presented as the best support for optimistic symmetrical family accounts. Most of the relevant data concerns public life, and a general egalitarianism may be diagnosed on the basis of widespread support for matters such as women's paid employment or women's participation in political life, but to be in favour of women's employment is not necessarily to be opposed to the double burden. A Eurobarometer survey found two-thirds majority support for both working wives and for women retaining all or most of the domestic role (Hakim 1996). Mackay's (1991) qualitative Australian opinion research found support for the employment of women *and* for the idea that such employment causes families to suffer, since families need mother's exclusive attention. Certainly, some recent studies appear to show a high level of domestic egalitarianism in both sexes. Australian researchers found that 97 per cent of women and 89 per cent of men agreed that 'If both husband and wife work, they should share equally in the housework and childcare', and that 87 per cent of women and 84 per cent of men agreed with the more general proposition that 'Men and women should do an equal amount of work in the home'. The chief difference lay in the strength of expressed attitudes: fewer men than women strongly agreed with egalitarian propositions, and fewer men than women strongly disagreed with propositions affirming a traditional division of labour. However, it is worth noting that answers to other questions must throw doubt on exactly what pro-sharing respondents had in mind. Thirty-six per cent of women and 42 per cent of men agreed that 'It is better for the family if the husband is the principal breadwinner outside the home and the wife has primary responsibility for the children and the home' (Bittman & Lovejoy 1993).

We must question the assumption that terms such as 'sharing' and 'participation' (with or without the modifier 'equal') bear a strong relation to genuine equity. Since many social scientists have very elastic definitions of shared domestic work, it would be odd if the general public were more precise. Time-use studies show that equitable domestic work arrangements are rare, but one study found that 44 per cent of women in full-time paid employment claimed that housework was shared equally with their partner (Martin & Roberts 1984). Respondents often report equity even when its absence stares us in the face. One woman told researchers that tasks such as vacuuming were shared equally, but added that her husband performed such tasks 'maybe once a month'. In the same study, another woman claimed that all family members, including the children, participated equally in housework. However, when she was asked if she had ever refused to do the housework, she replied that she had – and that the domestic organisation had collapsed (Bittman & Lovejoy 1993). In fact, some quantitative studies suggest that perceived equity and actual quantitative equity are entirely unrelated, there being no detectable association between the division of labour and perceptions of equity (Berk 1985).

The main finding of qualitative studies into perceptions of equity is that the meaning of sharing is 'elastic and private', and understood and practised within a context where a basic division of labour is taken for granted (McKee 1982). Backett (1987) found that the crucial requirement for a belief in sharing seemed to be participation by the father sufficient to provide proof of involvement, a proof which did not have to be regularly demonstrated. Occasional male help was sufficient proof, as long as it was given when it is felt to be 'really needed'. Couples did not evaluate their practices against abstract sets of ideals, but in terms of their perceptions of what seemed appropriate in their specific context. In particular, it was important that the husband was able to deputise for the wife during occasional absences. In some cases belief in the mere possibility that the husband could take complete charge of the children was sufficient to be subjectively satisfactory. One of Oakley's (1974: 141) respondents was satisfied with such theoretical help: 'He doesn't do anything regularly, but he'll do anything occasionally. Well, in theory he will: in practice he doesn't usually do anything at all. But he's not one of these people who say "It's your job, get on with it."' Brannen and Moss (1987) presented a similar case study showing that what women value is the symbolic meaning of potential male support. They concluded that equality was supported, but as a very general ideal rather than an 'elaborated concept supported by an explicit role model'.

So far, this discussion of attitudes has tacitly treated domestic work as homogeneous, but domestic work includes activities as diverse as toilet-cleaning and soothing hurt children. When questions about attitudes allow respondents to distinguish between various aspects of domestic work, differences emerge. Many respondents distinguish between childcare and housework. One study found that more than 90 per cent of men and women were in favour of sharing childcare, but that 68 per cent of women, and only 51 per cent of men, were in favour of sharing housework (Hiller & Philliber 1986). Respondents were more likely to claim that childcare was shared than they were to report sharing housework (Araji 1977). Since men tend to opt for participation in pleasurable activities with children rather than routine childcare and housework, and tend to consider all their time with children as a form of childcare, ideas about the 'sharing' of childcare can be very flexible indeed. The blurring of the difficult but necessary distinction between consumption and production is particularly noticeable here, as the discussion of the new 'involved' fatherhood in chapter 5 will show.

Social scientists have also been inclined to confuse shared leisure and pleasure with shared participation in domestic work. In their 1957 study, Young and Willmott were impressed by men spending more time at home with wives and children. As one of their women informants explained: 'If they want a drink of beer now, they go and fetch a bottle in, so they can watch the tellie at the same time' (Young & Willmott 1957: 9). The authors concluded: 'When they watch the television instead of drinking beer in the pub, and weed the garden instead of going to a football match, the husbands of Greenleigh have taken a stage further the partnership mentioned earlier' (1957: 145). Young and Willmott elaborated the point in their 1973 study. Referring to changes over the century such as the increase in the size of houses, the reduction in family size, electric lighting (whereby 'at least husbands could see the faces of their wives after dark without too great an expense'), the gramophone and colour television, they argued: 'What kept people out of the home (and especially husbands with their superiority of command over money) was the absence of attraction within it ... We very much doubt whether, before homes became Home, men at any rate would have passed more than half their time there' (1973: 98–9). Accordingly, they diagnosed a 'partnership of leisure', and argued that the unity of the family rested on its function not as a unit of production, but of consumption. Much of the force of their argument about the developing gender symmetry of family life came from perceptions of shared pleasures rather than shared work (Boulton 1983). Perhaps this is why they described the revolving door as 'men coming in, women going out', when the general logic of their argument suggested that women 'going out' was the earlier moment in the dynamic.

The diagnosis of a partnership of leisure also relies on dubious assumptions about the past, and is perhaps specific to certain groups or classes. Shared leisure is hardly new among middle-class families. Consider this contemporary report of the Marseilles bourgeoisie in the 1820s:

Before the Revolution ... men spent much of their time in cafes, in discussion groups, and at entertainments. Today such meeting places are still frequented, but in general, family fathers only rarely attend ... The family father, obliged to occupy himself with difficult business problems during the day, can relax only when he goes home. Everyone crowds around him. He beams at the children's games; he prides himself on knowing them well and their accomplishments delight him. Family evenings are for him a time of the purest and most complete happiness (cited in Shorter 1976: 226–7).

The writer attributed this change to such attractions as homes being better furnished (perhaps with better lighting so that men could see their wives?), and children being more genteelly brought up.

Another difficulty with interpreting survey data is that questions about attitudes to the division of labour are likely to tap respondents' beliefs about social change. If expert commentators can be so convinced that until recently men did no domestic work at all that they can interpret anecdotal evidence of men changing diapers as proof of change, we would expect this idea of change to prevail more generally. Speaking at one public forum on men and change my presentation of data about the sexual division of domestic labour was interrupted by an irritated male listener: 'My father never cleaned the toilet, but I do!' This was loudly applauded by the audience. Others report the same experience: Game and Pringle (1983) described how their students frequently argued that women's oppression was a thing of the past, given that men now perform housework. Challenged for evidence, students offered anecdotes of men putting food in the microwave oven or shopping on Saturday morning. Similarly, Mackay's respondents frequently cited anecdotes of male help with childcare to show that, as one put it, 'fathers today do much more than what our fathers did'. Or, as another colourfully put it: 'If our fathers could see how involved we were around the house – especially bathing the kids and things like that – they would be horrified. If they had acted like we act, they would have been thought poofters' (Mackay 1989: 7).

Not surprisingly, the model of the revolving door is widely believed. Mackay's respondents explained that change resulted because men were increasingly drawn in to relieve the stress of busy wives. In an article on the 'Chore Wars' one male interviewee explained that it was a 1990s' thing: 'Since it's the 90s, men have probably leaned toward doing more chores than they did 20 years ago. It's just a fact of life with both people working' (Florida *St Petersburg Times*, 26 May 1993). Apparently only in the 1990s have women entered the paid workforce. Interestingly, the speaker was co-owner with his wife of a cleaning company 'Man Maids'. Of the 12 men contacted by the journalist, he was the only one willing to be interviewed (perhaps the other 11 relied on Man Maids to do their share).

Reviewing the evidence, LaRossa (1988) identified a widespread folk belief that men are relieving women's double burden by performing much greater amounts of domestic work. The following extract from a judgment in an Australian court shows this folk wisdom in action:

> Of the seven wives of the seven judges of the Court of Appeal, three are in full-time professions or occupations, two are in part-time professions or occupations, one was in full-time employment before marriage, and the remaining one in part-time employment before marriage. I would think therefore that all of us have experience of what might be regarded as a more modern way of life, in which household tasks are shared (cited in Graycar 1989: 173).

It is confidently assumed that men who have working wives (actually, men whose wives have ever had any employment at all) are modern enough to share the performance of household tasks. The Australian High Court made such an assumption in its 1979 argument against the view that women have, in principle, a stronger claim to custody of their children than do men: 'As frequently as not, the mother works, thereby reducing the time she can devote to her children. A corresponding development has been that the father gives more of his time to the household and to the family' (cited in Graycar 1989: 162). Similarly, Australian courts have employed the rhetoric of equality when considering claims for accident compensation. On occasions, an employed woman's loss of the ability to perform domestic work has been treated less seriously by the courts than a similar loss suffered by a full-time housewife, on the grounds that the employed woman's husband would have been sharing the domestic work already (Graycar 1985).

So, as Pleck (1985: 75) suggested, those who give egalitarian answers to questions about sex roles may well be indicating their rejection of extreme traditionalism. If it is popularly believed that a 'traditional' rigid division of labour has been superseded and that male help proves that in modern families domestic work is now shared, then anyone who opposes the sharing of domestic work is identifying themselves as old-fashioned, by aligning themselves with an imagined past in which men either did no domestic work or performed only traditionally masculine tasks. Responses which supposedly indicate egalitarianism may simply indicate the desire to identify with what is believed to be the current typical practice, by giving acceptable answers. In this way, even where the sexual division of domestic work is evident it is possible to consider household organisation as progressive. Qualitative researchers have found that even couples with typical divisions of labour describe themselves (at least in interviews) as though they were 'children of the revolution in intimate life' (Bittman & Pixley 1997: 170). Consider the following male interviewee, who described his practices as modern and superior to traditional practices, but at the same time honestly demonstrated the narrowness of his vision of the modern:

> I did all the usual things that a modern father does, as opposed to my father. But still and all, I was not comfortable taking the kid for a day. That's the kind of thing I would have liked to have done. When I say that I'd like to have done it, I would not like to have done it at all, but intellectually I would like to have done it (Weiss 1985: 53).

This may help explain why Goodnow and Bowes (1994) found it easy to locate the 50 'innovative' couples mentioned earlier. They obtained their sample by asking everyone they knew for introductions to couples who 'did things differently'. In other words, they put their confidence in the general public's understanding of what is emergent and what is traditional. As a result, they felt entitled to report optimistically from the coal-face of social change. Their willingness to put the best face on their data is nowhere better demonstrated than in their discussion of the term 'chauvinist': 'How's that for a chauvinist statement', one of their male respondents said, of his propensity to avoid domestic work. The authors argued that this showed that the women's movement had at least led men to recognise that resistance to change is unjustifiable: 'With "chauvinism" as something to be avoided, the way is then opened for recognising the absurdity of arguing for the assignment of unpaid jobs on the basis only of gender.' We must wonder, though, if the man in question was not perfectly pleased with himself. In the 35 Up series of life-history documentaries, Tony the cockney taxi-driver and failed jockey was shown being happily treated like a lord by his wife. 'I sound like a real chauvinist, don't I', Tony said with a winning grin, when he explained the justice of this situation. We know he was not criticising himself; he was simply showing his awareness that the issue has been debated. Nevertheless, Goodnow and Bowes (1994) optimistically cited Tony, and this remark in particular, as evidence that the vocabulary of the women's movement has percolated to all levels.

Optimistic Gradualism

The rhetoric of change is dominant in the sociology and pop-sociology of family and household. Often it is described as gradual change, but the fact of change is always constructed as logical and inevitable. We have seen some of the rhetorical supports for the optimistic view. We do not need to criticise authors and texts as contradictory, or just plain wrong, though this does apply in some cases. Usually the rhetoric of change works in more subtle ways.

In his critique of American introductory sociology texts *Socio(onto)logy* (1989), Ben Agger documented the hegemony of an optimistic liberal discourse of social improvement, tracing this current of 'optimistic gradualism' back to its Judeo–Christian heritage. Agger's general critique matched the optimistic literature reviewed above only too well. Mainstream sociology, he said, 'gilds the iron cage of the present, making it bearable and thereby bearing it', explaining away contemporary inequality as a 'vestige of the pre-modern' and thus as a 'progressive, if ephemeral, "stage"'. Through its stress on the present moment as transitional, the discipline 'condemns us to an eternal present', thus glossing over the deep historical continuities (Agger 1989: 12, 17). This applies just as well to the quasi-sociological accounts of experts, commentators and journalists – to pop-sociology. While researching this and later chapters I read several hundred academic accounts of change and many more in the mass media, covering the last three decades. The sense of the 'eternal present' becomes quite disorienting. Much of the time it is hard to tell which decade we are in. Change is always just starting, and yet things are already different from the past! The present is forever transitional: there are vanguards, trends are *emerging*, much is yet to be done, but there are reasons for hope. And this persists from decade to decade:

> The housewife's lament has gone unisex. As inflation creeps skyward and two salaries are becoming essential, working men are filling in as part-time househusbands (*Washington Post*, 29 September 1981).
> Career women are waking up to the fact that their husbands can run the home and bring up the children ... In the first of a series of special reports on how we live today, Cassandra Jardine talks to men who do the ironing and cook the fish-fingers (*Daily Telegraph*, 27 December 1994).

Use of the present continuous tense – 'are filling in', 'are waking up' – invites us to view a revolution in progress before our very eyes. But it is a stalled revolution, and it breeds stalled rhetoric.

CHAPTER 4

It's on the Agenda:
Optimism over Images

In 1984 American journalist Bob Greene published *Good Morning, Merry Sunshine: A Father's Journal of His Child's First Year*. A celebrity endorsement on the book's cover nominated Greene for honorary membership in the company of mothers. Another, by talk-show host Phil Donahue, described the book as 'the most honest and personal account of the first year of fatherhood'. In the book, Greene described 'magical days' with his baby, Amanda, and returning home at night to his sleeping wife and baby: 'All that matters is that when you come home, this is waiting. It's a notion as old as mankind, and yet on nights like this it strikes me like the newest and clearest vision on earth.' But in fact Greene spent very little time with his baby, and much time on the road for journalistic assignments. He seemed never to have changed a diaper, and ate 'adult' meals alone in one room while his wife fed the baby and herself 'mushed-up fish' in another. As one reviewer observed, Greene, for an experienced reporter, had spent little time with the 'subject of his book contract' (Owen 1984).

New Father accounts of this kind were neatly satirised by Gary Trudeau in his cartoon strip *Doonesbury* in March 1985. One frame showed a man seated at his computer. A child has come into the room and is standing behind him. In earlier frames readers had learnt that the man was a journalist recording his experiences for a column on 'the new breed of involved, hands-on fathers'. Father says, without looking up, 'Not now son. Daddy's busy' (*Washington Post*, 25 March 1985).

How could Greene's account, written by a man who seemed to be less involved in housework and childcare than the average father of a young family, be regarded as a model for the new fatherhood? Not everybody was favourably impressed. Deborah Fallows (1985) commented that Greene's book exhibited a 'stylish attitude' rather than any commitment to parenting, and that it, and other popular personal accounts of the experience of fatherhood, represented a 'wave of sensitive-father chic'. Other examples were 'Fatherhood and My Rebirth as a Man' (Danzig 1981), and 'Daddy's Home: The Personal Story of a Modern Father who Opted to Raise the Baby and Master the Craft of Motherhood' (Clary 1982). An exasperated Barbara Ehrenreich remarked that, like many other women, 'I could not understand why every man who has changed a diaper has felt impelled, in recent years, to write a book about it' (Ehrenreich 1990: 140). Cowan (1987) observed that most of these accounts were not by men who were particularly innovative in their fathering practices, but by journalists who had discovered that a diary of their first year as a father could be turned into a book.

For several years after its release, popular discussions of fatherhood referred to the hugely successful 1987 Hollywood comedy *Three Men and a Baby*, directed by L. Nimoy. In the film, through a creaky plot contrivance, three single men who share an apartment find themselves responsible for the care of a baby girl whom one has fathered. The resulting battles with diapers provided much of the humour. A feature article about the new fatherhood cited, as its first example of the 'rediscovery' of fatherhood, the 'enchantment' experienced by the three fictional characters once they become accustomed to what is initially a 'nightmare world of dirty bottoms and midnight feeds' (*Time Australia*, 22 August 1988). Another article stated that the film indicated that the 'ultimate nod of approval comes, inevitably, from Hollywood'. Referring to the way in which the characters 'discover diapers' and 'paternal knowhow', the writer described the film as 'not so much the beginning of a trend as a reflection of change' (Melbourne *Age*, 3 February 1988). In fact the film was a standard comedy of role-reversal. The only way the intimate fathering experience could be made plausible was by the (implausible) removal of the mother, and indeed any woman who might have taken over. Following the conventions of the genre, traditional order was restored at the end. The baby's mother returned and moved in with the three men, who appeared destined to be her helpers. As one of the baby's 'fathers' said, 'She needs a full-time mother.' The men could thus resume the hedonistic lifestyles which had been so humorously interrupted and at the same time experience their new-found quasi-mystical joy in the baby's company.

When pressed for evidence of change, the rhetoric of optimistic gradualism has a useful trump card – it can always point to itself. Its very existence can be taken as evidence (perhaps even the best evidence) for optimism: 'Although few "new" men and shared caregiving fathers ... are out there in the streets, they are beginning to emerge, as evidenced by their being given increasing attention by the media and researchers'

(Russell et al. 1988: 258). Similarly, in the introduction to *The Father: Mythology and Changing Roles* we read that 'the changes [are] all around us. There has been a proliferation of books' (Colman & Colman 1988: xvi) and in *The Male Experience* we find: 'If one uses the growing number of books, journal articles, and other media presentations about increased father involvement with children, we could suggest that more and more men are increasingly motivated to become active fathers' (Doyle 1995). However, Greene's book suggests that we should be a little sceptical – not all the new rhetoric supports this simple optimism.

Of course, the point can be made more plausibly. In *Slow Motion: Changing Masculinities, Changing Men*, Lynne Segal was rightly sceptical about overly optimistic diagnoses of change in men's practices, but she found reason for qualified optimism in that issues about men and change had been widely canvassed. She referred, among other things, to the publication of personal accounts of fatherhood, magazine articles extolling 'loving dads', babywear catalogues 'where father stands proudly beside mother, with his own babysling and baby', and films such as *Three Men and a Baby*. This, she argued, indicated a significant shift since the 1950s, when 'questions of men's relationship to childcare, housework, violence in the home, were not yet on the conceptual, let alone the political agenda' (Segal 1990: 32–3, 93). The next two chapters explore what happens when issues about men and domestic work (sometimes this means issues which *appear* to be about the topic) join the public agenda. There is less basis for optimism than we might have expected, something which Segal (1993) herself has come to acknowledge. In this chapter I am concerned with the generally domesticated New Man, and his allies. Fatherhood, the source of the greatest amount of optimism, needs a chapter to itself.

The Domestic(ated) New Man

This is not the first era to see favourable images of domesticated men. A study of the American popular press since 1900 showed that images of fathering have alternated between father as provider and father as nurturer, the nurturer role being most pronounced in the 1940s and 1970s (Atkinson & Blackwelder 1993). For a period in the 1950s American readers were treated to what Cowan (1983: 200) called a 'hullabaloo' about 'new husbands' who diapered babies, dried dishes and were generally 'feminised'. But it would be silly to deny that issues about men and domestic work have been more prominent in recent decades than ever before. However, the issues are more prominent in some sites than others, and the treatment varies greatly. One of the most obvious reasons for caution about the significance of the new agenda is that the political question of inequity in domestic work is most apparent in sites addressed to women, and even there the sexual politics is, on the whole, very muted.

Certainly, men are directly challenged from time to time. For example, in 1993 American Catholic bishops gently reminded men in a pastoral letter that 'particularly when both spouses are employed, household duties need to be shared in a spirit of mutuality' (Reuters, 17 November 1993). Occasionally, hard data on the double burden appears in the news pages, especially when presented by a newsworthy public figure. This was the case, for example, when British MP Harriet Harman (later Minister for Social Security) tabled time-use data in parliament (*Glasgow Herald*, 16 March 1994). But such reports are often tempered by optimistic gradualism. Shere Hite concluded a fairly tough article on the sexual division of domestic work with a sweetener, 'Yet a lot of authentic sharing is starting to take place' (*Chicago Tribune*, 20 October 1987). More commonly, though, tough accounts of the division of domestic work appear in women's pages and female-identified lifestyle sections, women's magazines and talk-shows with a largely female audience. Within such sites women's complaints certainly are voiced: on its relaunch, *Ms* magazine dubbed the notion that men now do their share of housework as one the 10 biggest lies of the 1980s (PR Newswire, 29 July 1990). The first episode of the TV show *Roseanne* reached its climax with Roseanne Barr's character bellowing at John Goodman's, 'I put in eight hours a day at the factory, and then I come home and put in another eight hours, and you don't do nothin'' (*Christian Science Monitor*, 18 July 1989). When readers of the women's section of the San Diego *Union Tribune* were asked for reactions to the debates about women's status which followed the publication of Susan Faludi's *Backlash*, a letter writer who called herself 'Almost 50' exclaimed 'Equality – baloney! What I have in 1992 is a necessary full-time teaching job. I do over 80 per cent of the housework, and if I ask for help more than once I am told to stop complaining' (8 March 1992). The headline of an article on the double burden put it this way: 'They don't feel that men will either help or care. That's why many women say they harbour heavy-duty anger' (*Los Angeles Times*, 23 September 1990).

Talk-show host Sally Jessy Raphael told a seminar on Women in the 1990s, organised by *Ladies Home Journal* (November 1989), that women had won the right to be 'terminally exhausted'. On a positive note, however, she predicted that women could achieve whatever they desired, 'as long as we teach men to do the housework'. In this vein, accounts of inequity in domestic work spend much time outlining teaching strategies. An article titled 'How to Get Your Man to Help in the House' (*Australian Women's Weekly*, May 1988) recommended careful manipulation including praise for any help received, avoidance of criticism, the provision of appropriate information, giving him responsibility (implausibly, women are advised to simply 'put him in charge of supplies') and above all, patience. Alice Miller, director of Brooklyn College Women's Center, told women to give their men small manageable tasks: 'Take the least odious chore – grocery shopping for instance – and share that. Then tackle other chores in small gradual increments' (*Newsday*, 26 September 1992). *Ladies Home Journal* (April 1985) suggested to readers that if their man leaves odds and ends all over the house, they should ask him to put it in corners where 'it will be less visible, less of a traffic hazard', nicely combining the indulgence due to a child with the deference due to a superior.

We have seen that 'helpful husbands' receive glowing praise. Thus women are reminded that a man who helps with housework is a godsend, and much else can be forgiven. A 60-year-old widow wrote to the syndicated advice column of Dr Ruth Westheimer about her eight-year relationship with a widowed man. On his twice-weekly visits he 'helped with the driving, washing and some housework', but the relationship was draining her financially. He had expensive tastes and she paid all the bills, 'he saves for his old age and I am always broke'. Dr Ruth's advice was that the questioner should remind herself that she had 'decided to spend ... money on enjoying ... life with this man ... even if he is a little cheap when it comes to money, a man who is willing to do housework and drive you around is certainly not a selfish person' (*Chicago Tribune*, 18 August 1995).

Reason and negotiation are often recommended, on the assumption that change is inevitable and absent-minded men simply need to be reminded to catch up. The authors of *The Three Career Couple: His Job, Her Job and Their Job Together* told *Executive Female* (July 1993) that women should try an 'it's the 90s approach', by pointing out that respecting women as equals is 'today's definition of masculine. Macho has gone the way of the Bee Gees, junk bonds and rotary phones'. The following blandly optimistic remarks, in which women's 'resentment' makes a brief appearance, are typical in the advice literature for women: 'A discussion about the division of labour is in order. If he admits his reluctance and she, her growing resentment, they could begin to clear the air. She could give him some initial pointers where he feels ignorant, and they could agree on specific areas of responsibility for each – renegotiable at any time' (Delliquadri & Breckenridge 1980: 156). Even where the male interest in work avoidance, and the strategies men adopt in this respect, seem to be acknowledged, 'cooperation' and 'shared responsibility' can easily be achieved:

> Learned helplessness [is] a very special talent perfected by generations of fathers. This selective childcare is a great skill when it comes to changing a

nappy, preparing food and working the night shift. The strange thing is that the more enjoyable tasks are often learned with consummate ease. Usually this learned helplessness can be prevented by getting things off to the right start and working out the ground rules of cooperation from the very beginning (Green 1988: 38–9).

Supposedly, men simply need understanding. In a feature titled 'What to do if New Dad is Feeling Neglected', the *Toronto Sun* (8 April 1996) relayed a psychologist's advice to women to be 'sensitive to the man's mood' during pregnancy. After all, it is easy for men to 'feel nervous and insecure by [sic] a third presence, and look elsewhere for comfort'. In the large number of popular books explaining men to women, one stands out: John Gray's remarkably successful work on the sexes and relationships, *Men Are from Mars – Women Are from Venus* (1993). Gray's book was based on a myth about the origins of the sexes on two planets. The myth is simply a pedagogic device, Gray stressed, though we cannot be sure all his readers understood it that way. His point is that the sexes are as different 'as if' they had originated on different planets.

In synopsis: on Mars, men's culture was concerned with power, competence, achievement, problem-solving and efficiency. Meanwhile on Venus women's culture valued love, communication, beauty and relationships. The initial discovery of Venus by the Martians led to a harmonious order based on the complementarity of the sexes: Martians got things done and Venusians made the world beautiful. Sadly, after migration to earth, the sexes forgot their different origins, and from that flows the problems of married life. Martians forgot that Venusians need to feel loved, and Venusians forgot that Martians need to feel competent – this led, finally, to the division of emotional labour. Women want more from men emotionally and men pull away, because to have demands placed upon them is to question their competence – 'she's unhappy, so she's blaming me'. Gray's neat solution is for men to grasp that they can listen to their wives without feeling they have to fix their problems, and for women to understand that their men need to retreat into their own worlds from time to time (women, by the way, do not seem to need such time). For example, when men come home from a hard day at work they need a period of time 'solving easy problems' like reading the news and watching TV (this is called 'going into their caves') to recover their sense of competence, before they can turn their attention to the family. Women mistakenly see this as hurtful selfishness. It would be funny if it were not taken so seriously.

Some of the advice is so unrealistic as to be fantasy; magical solutions promising a better life. 'Amanda's' agony column in *New Woman* (May 1994) dealt with the issue of the unemployed husband who refused to do domestic work even though his wife was working:

It's time to help him separate the issues ... Help him schedule his day so he is involved in a productive job-search for the first two hours of his working day – say 9am to 11am – then having a coffee break and doing the chores until lunch. Then back to the employer attack until 5pm ... You may choose to prepare dinner together.

This was in reply to a woman who had written that any requests for help were bluntly refused. In other genres, the quality of fantasy is even more clear. The American kitsch painter Kata Billups has had considerable success with a series of Elvis Presley paintings, all of which pay reverent homage to the star. One, titled 'Elvis was a Real Man', shows Elvis doing housework. Billups told a reporter that the image came to mind one day when she felt bogged down by housework. 'Since I wasn't expecting any help from my husband, I decided to cheer myself up by painting Elvis doing the dishes' (Charleston *Post and Courier*, 29 July 1995). In her very interesting reading of Harlequin romance novels, Angela Miles (1991) uncovered a pervasive myth of 'male mothers'. While the male hero is independent and resourceful, he is also sensitive and considerate. His behaviour often recalls the mother–child relation: hero and heroine go shopping for clothes together, he tucks her into bed and gives her medicine, he comforts her when she has bad dreams. Miles argued that the fantasy addressed women's desires to escape from the duty to care for and comfort men, and to have access to care and comfort for themselves. Some of the advice for women does much the same thing, powerfully speaking to such desires but offering little to help them come true.

So far, the discussion has concerned treatments about men relieving women's domestic burdens in some way, but there are many other ways of discussing domesticated men. Jokes are one – a humorous, resigned, 'battle of the sexes' approach is much favoured: 'My mother-in-law-to-be did warn me of her son's mental deficiency when it came to things domestic. I nodded, secure in the knowledge that I would change things. Seven years later, he still hasn't worked out what the big white machine in the laundry, which fills with water, is for' (*Australian Women's Weekly*, March 1990). Erma Bombeck (Universal Press Syndicate, 28 July 1992) pursued a similar line: 'I have a fantasy where men and women change roles. It is not a pretty sight ... Basically they are warlike people who are happy only when they sharpen knives and meat cleavers that can cut paper. When was the last time you cooked paper?'

On and on it went – men are a hoot: rather than getting on with the job, they tinker with the domestic technology, while 'women know better ... we just do it'. Whole books of jokes about men appear: for example, 'What's a man's idea of helping with the housework? Lifting his legs so you can vacuum.' A newspaper interview with that joke's author Cindy Garner reassured us, though, that she is 'happily married' to Alan, a writer of psychology texts and her business partner, whose habits provide much of the source material, and that the Garners 'insist that even at their most pointed, the gibes are meant in fun' (San Diego *Union-Tribune*, 5 March 1992; PR Newswire, 22 October 1991).

Despite occasional eruptions of excitement about the possibility of new men and new fathers, magazines and books for women mostly continue to construct housework and childcare as the business of mothers. Here is *Cosmopolitan* on how to feel good about yourself when you return to the workforce after having a baby: 'Throw out all your old worn underwear. Then leave the kids with a sitter or have your husband watch them while you stock up on a whole new wardrobe of feminine underthings at a local lingerie store' (October 1995).

A telling sign is the persistence of the image of the destructive working mother. In the 1997 furore over the death of an American baby in the care of an English au pair, it was very easy to mobilise substantial opinion about the evils of working mothers. Much ink and airtime was spent stating that the baby's mother should never have left him. As Wendy Kaminer wrote in *Atlantic* (October 1993), women with strong careers, such as Hillary Clinton, still have a hard time convincing the public that they are nurturant as well. Compare this with the ease with which public men such as Prince Charles can demonstrate sensitive nurturant fatherhood simply by putting a hand on a son's shoulder.

Just as telling is the fact that popular discussions of employed mothers' problems with childcare only occasionally mention the possibility that male childcare might alleviate the problem. Probably the most common practical advice in the case of recalcitrant husbands is simply to pay someone else. A marriage and family therapist explained to the *Chicago Tribune* (12 November 1989) that when negotiation (characterised as saying 'please help lighten my load') fails to work, 'the concerned spouse might try to hire a service'. Another article agreed, though reminded women that children could also be useful: 'If you can't reason with him and you can't force him, you may as well leave him alone. Which is not to say that your overworked position can't be improved. You can use part of your salaries to pay for help ... There is also a point at which you tell your children they have to do more' (*Australian Women's Weekly*, May 1988). Child labour and paid services can be combined, of course. The Cleveland *Plain Dealer* (12 May 1996) consulted a husband and wife team of psychologists, authors of *Work Won't Love You Back*. 'Purchase labour from your children' was their first suggestion.

In the early 1990s the hot topic in American discussions of the work–family balancing problem for women was the 'mommy track', concerning the agonising trade-off for women between flexible work conditions to facilitate motherhood and the consequent downgrading of career opportunities. Similarly, the British debates which raged after the release of Catherine Hakim's 'Five Feminist Myths about Women's Employment' (1995) concentrated, as did Hakim herself, on the choice women face between career and motherhood. According to Hakim (1996), most women prefer to be supported financially, by a husband or by the state, while they produce and rear children; the sexual division of labour is efficient and advantageous to both sexes. Critics identified many weaknesses in Hakim's argument, but the obvious absence of husbands from her analysis (except as financial providers) was not often mentioned.

Thus, in article after article with titles such as 'Who Cares for our Children' (Melbourne *Age*, 5 August 1992), the issues are framed in terms of stay-at-home mother versus childcare. The new domesticated husband fails to appear where he might logically have been expected, something noted in chapter 1 in connection with aspects of feminist difference theory. The superwoman ideal is not dead; a *Cosmopolitan* feature 'Can You Be Somebody and a Mommy Too?' (October 1994) contained a brief phrase about the usefulness of a supportive husband, but the remaining 2600 words concerned complex strategies of juggling time and the construction of a 'reliable support system' (be careful that your nanny is not on drugs). A *Guardian* (18 August 1992) piece whose headline focused on the issue of who does the dishes in dual-job households briefly toyed with the issue of sexual equality – but this was in relation to the fact that despite lip service to equality, men still do not recruit, supervise or pay their household employees. In Teri Apter's *Why Women Don't Have Wives: Professional Success and Motherhood* (1985) we might have expected a discussion of the possibility of help from men. But this was not the case, since 'most women would not expect a husband to live as they could not happily live'. Why men do have wives was not discussed.

Neither, despite the great enthusiasm about the new involved father, is this figure prominent in material purportedly addressed to all parents – the literature on 'parenting', a wonderfully mystifying term. The great bulk of the literature is addressed, in effect, to women. In the very popular advice book *Babies: A Parents' Guide to Surviving (and Enjoying!) Baby's First Year* (Green 1988), despite the androgynous title, 'you', the reader, are female: 'If approached in the right way there is hardly anything that fathers will not do for their offspring. If you get things off on the wrong footing, you have only yourself to blame when later he refuses to wipe a bottom.' In any case, in some women's sites the New Father is explicitly unwelcome. The editor of American *Family Circle* rejected a feature on men's competence as caregivers: 'You mean you want me to tell our readers that everything we've been telling them all these years isn't true?' (in Margolis 1984: 99). Women who complain about lack of help from their men can get a sharp rap over the knuckles. Writing in the *Sunday Times* (25 October 1992), Anne Smith reminded young women that rather than loading their men with guilt about 'sleeping through the three o'clock feed' they should be glad that their children's fathers are around at all: 'The relentless emphasis on sharing has made young men very wary of assuming any sort of paternal commitment: fear drives them away as soon as they know their girlfriends are pregnant.'

The Sensitive New Man

The term 'New Woman' has appeared in every recent generation in connection with desired or supposed changes in women's lives, sometimes in connection with a New Man (Lee 1988). For example, in 1911 Olive Schreiner wrote passionately about the New Man as the New Woman's necessary spiritual and intellectual companion and source of inspiration (in Brandon 1991: 91). On occasions second-wave feminist writers have used the term to express their goals (e.g. Friedan 1981), and some optimistic social scientific analyses of change have also adopted the term, in studies with titles such as 'Reproduction and the New Man' (James & Russell 1987). However, the New Man's real home has been the mass media, with some overflow into everyday speech.

By the early 1980s the term was so commonly used that when *Ladies Home Journal* chose 'The Men in Your Life' as the topic for a 1984 survey, readers could be asked whether they would describe their husband as (a) A 'new man' who helps with the housework, (b) a traditional family man or (c) a real 'macho' man (June 1984, quotation marks in original). Many descriptions of the New Man have stressed men's performance of housework and childcare:

> Above all, the New Man is a doer in the home. He thinks nothing of polishing the floor or cleaning the toilet. As far as he is concerned there are no boundaries, no rules. If his partner is working late, he cooks dinner without a second thought. Sick of being the helpless bystander in the parenting game, the New Man takes to childcare with gusto (Melbourne *Age*, 9 September 1987).

However, it is significant that most discussions of the New Man refer not only to the performance of housework and childcare, but also to his 'feminine' qualities of sensitivity and nurturance. This is often the dominant theme, and will be discussed in later chapters. Revolving-door theory is given a psychological spin: 'While women are becoming more assertive, men are becoming more receptive. While women are discovering new dimensions of their sexuality, men are learning to be more sensual. Women are exercising their intellects, men discovering their emotions' (Baumli 1985: preface).

Early accounts of the New Man often took their cue from Betty Friedan's (1981) *The Second Stage*:

> 'I see a completely new man evolving', she predicted hopefully. 'The old man has been so grey, so abstract, so linear, so full of macho but shivering underneath. Now there'll be a man who has feelings, doesn't try to suppress them, doesn't have to be all that strong. The New Man is going to be a little richer, more vibrant, a more interesting man' (*National Times*, 2 May 1982).

Thus Franz Alt, a German writer and TV presenter, justified the significance of the title of his bestseller *Jesus: The First New Man*, 'Jesus did not repress the feminine side of his nature, that is why women 2000 years ago were crazy about him' (London *Times*, 14 December 1990).

The psychological traits of the New Man crystallised around the term 'sensitivity', a usefully ambiguous term with great potential for blurring the distinction between production and consumption. New Man excitement was probably at its peak between 1985 and 1987 (Moore 1989; Connell 1993; Mort 1996). For a brief period the New Man was flavour-of-the-month with feature writers, though the image of the domestic New Man was always something of a media sideshow, outweighed by more traditional representations of men as, for example, politicians, soldiers, businessmen, professionals, sportsmen, workers, criminals, husbands and lovers. Given the logic of media discourse, which must constantly seek or produce images of latest trends, the rise of the New Man in the 1980s was probably inevitable, given the 1970s media attention to the New Woman (Ash 1989). So was his decline.

By the time New Man fever reached its peak, references to the Sensitive New Man were becoming relatively common, and since the start of the 1990s the term favoured by the media has been Sensitive New Age Guy (often simply SNAG). The New Age connotations tend to psychologise the image, and the shortened version has mildly derogatory and humorous overtones (in Australian slang sausages are called 'snags', so the term is a doubly humorous label for sensitive men). As we will see, this is no accident. The term appeared in a much wider range of media, and entered everyday speech to a much greater degree than had the New Man. In 1998 it was still being used by my students as a term for gentle young men.

Initially SNAG retained its association with the domesticated New Man, and it was in that sense that Australian politicians briefly struggled to be known as SNAGs. During 1992 spin-doctors for the ruling Labor Party, including Anne Summers, ex-editor of *Ms* magazine, became concerned about women voters' negative perceptions of the prime minister, Paul Keating. The resulting image management included an appearance on a national radio program devoted to family and relationship issues, and a press release to the effect that the prime minister had taken time away from his duties to care for a sick child at home. Introducing sex-discrimination and affirmative-action legislation, Keating assured his audience that he was a 'sensitive new-age guy' (Melbourne *Age*, 1 July 1992, 20 September 1992). The leader of the opposition Liberal Party, John Hewson, joked about Keating's new image, adding that, unlike the prime minister, he ironed his own shirts and that he had come to the realisation that men and women were equal while performing this humble task (Melbourne *Age*, 3 July 1992; *Australian*, 4 July 1992). Indeed the ironing of shirts was, for Hewson, the epitome of New Manhood. When a journalist asked if he was a Sensitive New Age Guy, Hewson pointed to the ironing-board in his office: 'Does that mean I iron my own shirts?' (Melbourne *Age*, 19 September 1992). Although these interchanges were reported in newspaper pages dedicated to political news, they were treated as a deviation from normal politics. One national political correspondent concluded his story by remarking that the unemployed would be 'appalled' by such irrelevant posturings (*Australian*, 4 July 1992).

Over time, the 'sensitive' aspect of the SNAG has become paramount. The term has come to indicate varieties of male softness and/or emotional expressiveness. Often the intention is to denigrate. Cartoonist Doug Marlette explained why Bill Clinton was so easy to caricature: 'Bill is kind of a sensitive new age guy, the SNAG, and Hillary is the counterpoint to that. It's the gelded male and the Yoko Ono thing' (Fort Lauderdale *Sun-Sentinel*, 17 March 1996), though later revelations may have persuaded Marlette to a different view. Since the term is overloaded with meaning (soft *and/or* expressive), SNAGs can turn up where we least expect them. An article on American generals Norman Schwartzkopf and Colin Powell began by dubbing them Sensitive New Age Guys. The evidence? Schwartzkopf's autobiography revealed his distress at an incident in his childhood, when he killed a bird with his bow and arrow, and Powell, in his own words, feels 'the emotional power of this place begin to affect me' whenever he visits the Vietnam Veterans Memorial in Washington (Florida *St Petersburg Times*, 8 November 1992).

The term SNAG did not completely replace the New Man, who remained useful to journalists writing up new survey data on domestic work: 'the average British man seems to be more old boy than New Man when it comes to housework' (*Glasgow Herald*, 25 January 1996). A crucial point is that the drift towards psychological feminisation indicated by the stress on sensitivity does not necessarily imply a break from the issue of the labour division. Sensitivity engages with the desire of some women for change in the division of domestic labour. New Men and SNAGs may appear, at least at first, to promise male emotional support to women and children. Revolving-door accounts of men and change often make such links: 'We now live in a society in which ... men are expected to possess the emotional capacities that will enable them to tenderly nurture their children, and sympathetically listen to the frustrations and hurts of their wives, as well as share their own feelings of love, joy, disappointment and sorrow' (Balswick 1988: 197). The way this plays out in New Man imagery in women's magazines was traced by Rowena Chapman (1988) in 'The Great Pretender: Variations on the New Man Theme'. One of her examples was *Cosmopolitan*'s hymn to New Men: 'men who'll listen and be there at the end of the day, men who'll soothe, cherish, share the chores, as well as the social and sexual pleasures'.

But there is a more general, though related, way in which male sensitivity and emotional expression connect with women's desires. A very strong cultural theme is that sensitive men will not just be more caring, but will feel no need to dominate women in any way. Or, putting it the other way around, it is widely believed that men's need to dominate flows from psychological wounds, especially the inability to express emotions. This theme is traced in chapter 7, which argues that such psychological understandings give men a particularly useful and subtle ideological justification for dominating. Here we can observe that expressiveness and domination can quite happily coexist, and that expressiveness might have quite a different significance.

In his analysis of shifts in American masculinity, Michael Messner (1993) cast a critical eye on the widespread excitement about recent cases of great men crying in public. Ronald Reagan, Michael Jordan and General Schwartzkopf were examples. When Schwartzkopf shed a public tear for the Americans killed, wounded and captured in the 1990–91 Gulf War, he was roundly praised as a New Man. Messner pointed out, however, that at the same time the general was urging the president not to stop the war: 'We had them in a rout ... we could have made it a battle of annihilation.' An earlier historical phase of patriarchy may have required a stoic, instrumental and emotionally inexpressive masculinity, but now men can be emotionally expressive (or at least be perceived that way) and retain an old-fashioned style of violent dominating masculinity: Schwartzkopf remained Stormin' Norman. If there is a change, it is that certain situationally appropriate displays of sensitivity have entered the masculine style repertoire, or 'masculine gender display', as Messner put it. Crying in public may not indicate a relinquishment of power; rather, certain powerful individuals may possess the power to cry in public. In less dominant individuals crying in public is viewed very differently.

Displays of sensitivity such as public tears do not necessarily connote any kind of gender convergence or feminisation of men. Indeed, such displays (when carried off correctly) can underline difference – in Schwartzkopf's case the difference between a man strong enough to get away with it, and weaker men. And if sensitivity can mark one kind of status difference, what about others? Barbara Ehrenreich argued that the new male sensitivity was highly suitable as a marker of a superior position in the class system, relying on old prejudices about the lack of intellectual and emotional development in working-class men. In *The Hearts of Men* (1983) Ehrenreich pursued this point with perceptive analyses of machismo in movies, noting how machismo was linked to arrested growth and the lower class. Tony, the character played by John Travolta in *Saturday Night Fever*, rejected the macho Italian culture of his suburb after meeting Stephanie, who had true 'culture' and a city apartment. On the face of it, Tony came under the influence of a woman: she remade his style and made the rules about their sex-life, but the real message was, Ehrenreich said, that upward mobility equalled personal growth. Insensitive 'physical' masculinity may be acceptable in Brooklyn, but not in Manhattan.

Popular understandings of the New Man rely on a host of assumptions based upon status distinctions. Social class is one, race is another. Hondagneu-Sotelo and Messner (1994) began their valuable analysis of masculine gender displays by noting that their own students, mostly white and in higher socioeconomic groups, operated on the assumption that black, Latino, immigrant and working-class men were traditional, while middle-class educated men were forging a new sensitive egalitarian role for men. It is now widely recognised that the general category 'man' is projected against a female 'other'. The analysis of Hondagneu-Sotelo and Messner suggested, however, that the 'other' of the New Man is another *man*, the man of a supposedly inferior class or ethnic group. They argued that the image of the sensitive New Man is only sustainable if it carries a counterimage against which it may be compared, and this counterimage is 'traditional' masculinity – physical, stoic, inexpressive and misogynist – which supposedly resides among less privileged men. In chapter 3 I showed how optimistic rhetoric about new men involves assumptions about the traditional man of earlier decades. This idea can be expanded: the image of traditional man, the necessary other to the new man, is constructed as belonging both to the past *and* to the lower classes. As Messner (1993) powerfully put it, traditional men are constructed as survivors from an earlier era.

Readers may be inclined to demur, thinking that lower-class men really are more misogynist and less progressive. This is too large a question for a proper treatment here, but recall that there simply is no evidence of significant national, social class or race differences in the sexual division of domestic labour. Certainly there are stylistic differences in masculine presentation. Subordinate men often adopt a public aggressive posture, having few resources beyond their own bodies, while dominant men may have less need of such overtly physical display. There are many ways of signifying power; the sensitivity of the New Man may reflect his dominant status position, rather than any amelioration of male dominance. Hondagneu-Sotelo and Messner noted that the literature on masculinity among subordinated men assumed that the public faces of such men were 'personally and collectively constructed performances of masculine gender display'. However, they argued, this insight is often lacking in discussions of the New Man: 'the public face of the New Man (his "sensitivity", etc.) is often assumed to be one and the same with who he "is", rather than being seen as situationally constructed public gender display' (1994: 208).

The Consuming New Man

In 1983 a new line of (French) men's sportswear was launched in America – under the label New Man (*Daily News Record*, 10 November 1986). If sensitive New Man style can mark status differences between men, we would expect it to be strongly associated with styles of consumption, which are key markers of status difference. This is a field which has been extensively researched and theorised. In recent social theory Bourdieu's work has been particularly influential, especially in extending the understanding of consumption beyond the realm of material goods. In *Distinction* (1984) he showed how taste in various cultural and symbolic goods marks class position just as usefully as does taste in material goods. Featherstone elaborated Bourdieu's work in connection with the rise of the discourse of 'lifestyle', which, he argued, is based on the experience of the new *petit bourgeoisie* of cultural producers (including those in advertising and journalism), which aims to expand and legitimate its focus by building on its cultural capital – the manipulation of ideas and images. Thus, lifestyle becomes a 'life project', whereby individuality and a sense of style is displayed through 'the particularity of the assemblage of goods, clothes, practices, experiences, appearances and bodily dispositions' (Featherstone 1987: 56, 59;

see also Neveu's 1990 analysis of lifestyles as landmarks of social stratification). As a writer in the British advertising trade journal *Campaign* explained: 'Lifestyle advertising is about differentiating oneself from the Joneses, not ... keeping up with them' (Bell 1987).

Almost any kind of status difference can be assimilated by marketing's rhetoric of lifestyle. It should be no surprise, then, to find that the sensitive New Man has figured extensively in both the theory and the practice of marketing, and that lifestyle sections of newspapers provide a cosy home for New Man features. Indeed, some commentators believe that the term New Man achieved wide currency only when taken up by the world of fashion, advertising and marketing, rather than in any wider discourse about changes in gender relations (e.g. Reed 1990). The earliest published critical analyses of the phenomenon of the New Man (Chapman 1988; Rutherford 1988; Moore 1989; Ehrenreich 1990; Reed 1990) were largely analyses of the construction of the male consumer – Moore described the New Man as 'the available man with his available money'. In 'Tarting Up Men' Ash (1989) suggested that the term New Man arose in the British fashion media about 1984 to label shifts in designs for men (and the supposed related shifts in consciousness) associated with the arrival of a new wave of young female designers. As one of them put it: 'Where else was there to go? It's all been done before in women's wear.'

Of course the domesticated male consumer had been of interest to marketers before this. Marketers read sociology and conduct their own research, and the sexual division of domestic labour was discussed by marketers in the optimistic gradualist tones already familiar to us. The agency Cunningham & Walsh reported in 1980:

> Three years ago everyone was interested in the working woman; she represented a huge market. Now agencies are realising that the lives of husbands had to change too. Ads for beer have always been telecast during ballgames, maybe we should be showing soap flake commercials during those times ... We predict that what is now a small nucleus of homemaking husbands will grow into a significant segment, demanding the attention of marketers (*New York Times*, 1 November 1980).

What is important is the way the rhetoric of the sensitive domesticated New Man was drawn into marketing discourse. A 1983 marketing article by Eileen Prescott, president of a New York public relations firm, provides an interesting case study of the appropriation of New Man rhetoric. The title was simple – 'New Men': 'What are the characteristics of these "new" men? Can they be segmented easily by age, income, education and lifestyle? What products are they likely to buy?' Prescott began by noting with approval the degree of change suggested by the fact that advertisements were beginning to show men doing such things as baking cakes, feeding babies and discussing the merits of various toilet papers (this being particularly significant, since 'a man in a toilet paper commercial was once unthinkable'). Prescott suggested that such ads simply acknowledged that the world had changed, making the familiar exaggerated comparisons between traditional men and men in a 'post-feminist' world: 'Today, men are wearing aprons, cooking dinner, washing dishes, going shopping, and taking care of the children – with major consequences for American business … in this post-feminist era, a fellow certainly dares not ask his girlfriend for help'. Parallel psychological changes were also noted: 'more men showing emotion, caring, concern, tenderness – traditionally female attitudes', so that it is now 'acceptably masculine to care about one's house'. Accordingly, advertisers and marketers were advised to wake up to the new trend of men as all-purpose consumers; men buy 'not only cars, beer and stereo equipment but [also] coffee, cereal and soup'.

However, these remarks merely provided a gloss of optimistic post-feminist rhetoric to cover advertisers' intent to intervene in the world, rather than respond to it. Left to their own devices men might not change, since they 'need direction' if they are to extend their habits of consumption into such 'feminine' areas as cosmetics, fashion and home decoration. Prescott aimed to encourage the industry to widen its horizons and develop new market segments in the conditions of increased competitiveness. Particular attention was given to single affluent men, signified by the otherwise curious reference to 'a fellow's girlfriend'. Thus when Prescott advocated innovative marketing to match 'the remarkable new demographics of men', her evidence detailed the increase in the proportion of men living outside marriage (given the rising age of marriage and rising divorce rate). The growth of the gay male subculture was a very obvious subtext. As with so many other style innovations, it is likely that aspects of what was to be New Man style were pioneered in gay culture (see Mort 1996).

Frank Mort's (1996) analysis of recent marketing to men in Britain described the figure of the New Man as a hybrid, a condensation of multiple concerns, which knitted together masculine consumerism and other supposed trends in men's lives. Market researchers examined their data and came up with such images as the progressive and caring father and the fashion-conscious city-dweller, memorably described by Moorcock (1988) as 'the sensitive, caring, nurturing, fathering, slightly narcissistic, fashion-conscious politically aware New Man'. Chapman (1988) spoke of the way in which New Man imagery contained elements of both the man who performs domestic work and the male narcissist: 'the post-modern dandy worrying about the cut of his strides and fretting about the knots in his shoelaces'. Thus, she concluded, the New Man combined 'nurturer and narcissist' in uneasy tension, with the narcissist element becoming increasingly dominant. She traced the process of change through the evolution of the British magazine *Cosmo Man*, a stablemate of the women's magazine *Cosmopolitan*, which first appeared in 1984. *Cosmo Man* set out to appeal to the 'emotionally literate man' but soon changed to focus on the narcissistic status-preoccupied yuppie male. *Arena* followed two years later but experienced no such crisis of identity, emphasising from the outset conspicuous male consumption, employing intelligent and knowing prose to delineate a 'precise hedonistic etiquette'. Rutherford (1988) made a broadly similar analysis of the narcissistic New Man in magazines such as *Arena* and *The Face*.

Observing similar American trends, Ehrenreich caustically suggested that sensitivity, initially the most promising of new male traits, really signified 'the heightened receptivity associated with consumerism: a vague appreciation that lends itself to endless shopping'. The apparent feminisation of men was not as agreeable as had been hoped:

> We even welcomed the feminisation of male tastes, expecting that the man who was a good cook and tasteful decorator at 25 would be a devoted father and partner in midlife. We did not understand that men were changing along a trajectory of their own … It is the marketplace that calls most clearly for men to be softer, more narcissistic and receptive, and the new man is the result (Ehrenreich 1990: 136–7).

As New Man rhetoric moved out from the women's pages and began to address men, the sensitive New Man transformed, more or less smoothly, into a narcissistic consumer. The domesticated New Man moved backstage and was largely frozen into a caricature, marked by a few tokens of modernity such as diaper-changing and birth-attending – the same two practices which obsess commentators on the New Father (e.g. Melbourne *Sunday Age*, 21 November 1993). By the 1990s it was feasible to speak of the New Man entirely in terms of the feminised narcissistic male consumer. Reporting the launch of a £15 million British ad campaign for Gillette grooming gels, the *Independent* (1 March 1993) explained the company view: 'In the 90s every man is a New Man, ready to pamper himself with new shaving gels, aftershave gels, and clear gel anti-perspirants'. Even this could be couched in the rhetoric of liberation – men catching up with women. As a skincare ad put it: 'The gender walls are down – there is a new spirit of freedom in the air. Beauty is no longer the exclusive preserve of women' (*Weekend Australian*, 8 January 1994). An advertising executive, introducing his latest New Man fashion campaign, explained: 'The individual at the heart of this brand is in his early 20s, is discovering himself – discovering what women discovered years ago – that the mirror is perhaps more important than the other person' (quoted in Moore 1988: 58). In the *Independent* David Cook (25 July 1993) issued this rallying cry: 'Consumerism has given women a voice. Now men need to get more involved.' But, as Moore remarked in *New Statesman and Society* (2 March 1990): 'Did anyone seriously think that a few skincare products were going to cause the collapse of patriarchy?'

Steering Around the Wimp

As David Morgan (1992: 204) observed, journalistic treatments of the New Man often have a 'silly season' aspect, resembling such older journalistic stand-bys as sightings of escaped emus in the English countryside. The reference to odd animals is very apt: one Australian search for the New Man was framed in terms of a hunt for a new subspecies: 'We had heard that he was extremely rare, with only two or three reported sightings, mostly in Fitzroy' (Melbourne *Age*, 20 May 1988. Fitzroy is an inner Melbourne suburb favoured by the avant garde). The hunt was finally successful, with the discovery of a New Man who was mocked as a counter-culture stereotype, with his 'army surplus overalls and leather sandals', and his skilled preparation of drinks made from soy milk and carob.

'How many women would really prefer Tony Blair to Humphrey Bogart?' asked Margaret Morrison in the *Daily Mail* (11 April 1995). Any process of change concerning men which can, rightly or wrongly, be interpreted as a form of feminisation must inevitably negotiate tensions surrounding masculinity. Unless their goal is the unashamed elimination of gender difference, those who attempt to steer masculinity in an apparently feminine direction need to find ways of maintaining difference. If inspiration fails, the most obvious of devices comes in handy: when *Cleo* magazine (August 1990) gave leading Australian advertising agencies the unexpected task of producing mockup ads for a hypothetical campaign to encourage 'househusbandry', three of the six responses directly referred to testicles. There was 'Have you got the balls to be a mother?' boldly written across the crotch area of a jeans-clad male cradling a baby. Perhaps the fear of emasculation which the advertising agencies purported to allay was really their own. One agency simply gave it all up as a bad job, and showed a sad middle-aged man, with rubber gloves and apron, battling with a stack of dishes, who looked at readers plaintively. Again, the text concerned balls: 'They geld horses, don't they? Become a house husband. She'll hate you. You'll hate you. At least you will have something in common'. That effort came from the

John Singleton agency: Singleton is well-known in Australia for his opposition to political correctness.

The ease with which vitriolic counter-attacks can be made on anything smacking of feminisation is quite remarkable. The New Man and the SNAG have provided a field day for humorists and conservatives (often one and the same). My extensive file of derogatory descriptions of New Men and SNAGs includes the following gems of wit:

> The new man is a 'a fop, or flop ... a fish–fowl that nobody wants' (William Raspberry, *Washington Post*, 1 May 1985).
> We ceded our self-respect to the judgement of women, hence that 'lugubrious specimen' the 'trend-whipped post-feminist man' (Curt Suplee, *Washington Post*, 3 May 1987).
> The frozen yoghurt and save-the-whales type of squishy modern man ... in California these are known as SNAGs (John Lichfield, *Independent*, 2 June 1991).
> The horrible wimpish reality behind the fantasy of New Man ... high-fibre diets and sandals ... a disgrace to his gender ... the creature at the vegetable counter in Sainsbury's with a baby strapped to his back, looking like a squaw with its [sic] papoose as he sniffs the broccoli (Tony Parsons, *Daily Mail*, 11 February 1993).
> The toxic waste of feminism ... you've seen him out shopping, wearing bristly mud-coloured jumpers knitted by Peruvian lesbians, his offspring slung round his neck in an ethnic papoose ... he doesn't even walk properly ... he's probably forgotten what an erection is for (Jo-Anne Goodwin, *Guardian*, 14 February 1993).
> SNAGs are 'so, well, moist' (Sean Piccoli, *Washington Times*, 8 June 1993).
> We are therefore lobbying the Government to introduce legislation requiring the displaying of a British Safety Standard 'Wet Lettuce' sticker on any men unable to pass stringent testing to ensure that they are cryer-proof (David Thomas, *Sunday Telegraph*, 13 February 1994).

Enough. There are strong signs here of masculine hysteria. The New Man is horribly 'other', a moist soft limp sandal-wearing woman–man with baby in an ethnic sling. Worst of all, it would seem from the surprising repetition, a vegetarian health nut – he can 'whip up a nut roast at a moment's notice' (*Sunday Times*, 30 July 1995) – at best, a fish-eater, 'does he invariably order poached salmon?' (Suplee, *Washington Post*, 10 September 1984). This is a paradise for cultural anthropologists.

A key image in the derogatory rhetoric about sensitive New Men was that of the wimp. The term came from the language of adolescent boys: the wimp was the boy who was mild-mannered, unsuccessful at sports. At least, that was Suplee's story in his 1984 *Washington Post* piece 'Dawn of the Wimp' (10 September), in which he performed the nice trick of writing a semi-scholarly 'objective' account of the term's revival while at the same time making a very good job of reviving it himself. Usage of the term spread far beyond the sensitive New Man. Wimp rapidly became an all-purpose form of abuse for any man who could be construed as less than thoroughly masculine.

Earlier periods provide some interesting examples of the tricky task of renegotiating masculinity in a seemingly feminised direction, while avoiding wimpishness. In a survey of *Esquire* magazine in the 1930s and 1940s, Breazedale (1994) described one solution to this problem. It was a highly misogynist mixture: wordy analyses which derisively compared women's inferior tastes as consumers with the superior masculine taste which the magazine was in fact trying to produce appeared alongside the now famous stylised sexy female pictorials. These were crucial to the reassurance of the reader's masculinity but were rendered 'invisible', Breazedale argued, by occupying a trivialised 'bimbo zone', making the magazine fit for the coffee table rather than the sock drawer. Interestingly enough, *Esquire's* founders intended to produce a vehicle for ads for men's clothing; editorial content was, at first, almost an afterthought. Similarly, in her analysis of the birth of *Playboy* in the 1950s, Ehrenreich (1983) challenged the usual understanding that the magazine's chief purpose was to purvey soft porn, legitimated by the inclusion of serious writing. Rather, the porn legitimated what was really subversive – the advertising and lifestyle material (the bachelor apartment and the hi-fi) whose message was that to be a real man, men didn't have to be a husband. Hedonistic signs of status success could prove masculinity just as well, if not better.

How are tensions about wimpiness played out in the case of the sensitive New Male consumer? Some treatments give the game away by trying too hard. An article on marketing groceries to men begins: 'They are weekend warriors, male contestants in a supposedly non-contact event played with grocery carts in supermarkets. But when the aisles are crowded the course can be as risky as a roller derby oval' (*Chicago Tribune*, 1 September 1994). Key signifiers of masculinity are routinely added, so that in a special issue on women and change, *Time Australia* (Summer 1990) defined the New Man as '*strong*, gentle, caring, sharing' (emphasis added). 'Strong but sensitive' became a cliché in connection with discussions of SNAGs: 'You know, the strong but sensitive type. The kind of guy who can fix cars and change diapers' (Florida *St Petersburg Times*, 14 February 1990). At times the balancing act is so difficult that we can almost hear the patriarchal gears grinding. This is particularly clear in advertising, where many things must be said very quickly. An ad for male perfume read: 'For the 90s' man, this sophisticated scent is masculine, but not macho. Hero – with a warm, woody and spiced citrus fragrance – appeals to the man who is strong, confident, self-reliant and rugged – but also caring' (*Australian Women's Weekly*, August 1990). Read aloud this is laughable, but it is not meant to be read aloud – rather, we rapidly read the little collection of signifiers. In another ad, for toilet water, the balance is just as tense: 'Cool Water is power tempered by sensitivity. Intensely male with a gentle nature; sensuality tamed by a sense of civility' (*HQ*, Winter 1993).

In such ways dangerously feminine products can be marketed as highly masculine. In a 1987 discussion of perfumes and toiletries for men, *Campaign* explained that the era of the wimp which feminism had created was over, and that the new male commodities promised a more masculine future (in Mort 1996: 63) However, while cosmetics have been a great success for marketers, some other commodities have proved more diffult to masculinise. A 1990 British campaign for Electrolux vacuum cleaners was targeted at men; this was claimed as the first such attempt (*Marketing*, 8 March 1980). Men appear to need careful handling in this area. Miele's luxury vacuum cleaner Silverstar was written up in the London *Times* (7 September 1991) as one of the few designs which encourage men to do housework, 'with its beautifully designed silver contours and five-gear action' it would appeal to male 'technophiles'. It seems easier to convince men to care for their appearance than for their carpets.

The work of negotiating a masculine form of narcissism seems, on the whole, to have succeeded, and tensions about the male consumer's masculinity have eased. The rhetoric of the new male consumer took the risky but necessary course of riding on the back of ideas about changes in gender relations. This occurred somewhat differently in Britain and America. The British rhetoric went out of its way to avoid tying New Man imagery to changes wrought by feminism, while the American rhetoric was more relaxed about making the connection (Mort 1996). Either way, the construction of the male consumer had raised the dangerous possibility that narcissistic men might also be feminine men, but once the difference between these two was firmly established it became possible to relax, and celebrate a decidedly non-wimpy male narcissism. In Britain this was associated with the phenomenon of the New Lad, tirelessly promoted in the pages of magazines such as *Maxim* and *Loaded* ('for men who should know better'). Men were told they could relax and unashamedly be what they always had been. A sample: *Maxim*'s idea of the main issue for new fathers seemed to be 'how horny "she" was during and after pregnancy', as Harry Browne observed in a cutting article in the *Irish Times* (3 June 1995). With breath-taking hypocrisy an Australian New Lad editor told *Advertising Age* (26 June 1995), 'men are tired of being labelled' and want to be treated as they really are, then proceeded to label today's man as the 'post-SNAG'. The New Man was a fallacy, and 'lads have never been away', the editor of *Loaded*, James Brown, told the *Daily Mail* (14 April 1995). Since gender change was complete ('most women I know burp and talk about shagging'), there was no further need to tie new images of men to the vehicle of gender change.

Even New Laddism can be assimilated by the rhetoric of optimistic gradualism. Jonathan Margolis (*Sunday Times*, 23 April 1995) implausibly told his readers that 'just as we are all socialists now, we are all New Men now, New Lads included ... inside the majority of New Lads, I promise you, you will find a future nappy-changer'. However, he rather confused the picture by remarking that 'few of us, least of all the New Lads, would ever want to be a New Man, with all the yukky wimpish connotations that label has'. His point seemed to be that men had changed a great deal but didn't want it to be thought of in terms of sexual politics: 'It's all a bit like political correctness. Nobody in their right mind wants to be overtly PC, going around renaming everything in sight with bland new definitions ... And yet PC has its heart in the right place.'

We will not pursue here the New Lad, or similar triumphant American images such as *Esquire*'s retro-macho 'post-sensitive man' (May 1994). However, *Esquire*'s editor, Ed Kosner, is worth quoting, as he looked back over shifts in the construction of American masculinity (words in parentheses indicate interjections from the PBS talk-show host, Charlie Rose):

> Well, now we have the post-sensitive man (Right. But this was) Alan Alda, the new man, the guy who's doing the dishes a lot of the time (Phil Donahue), the person who wants to cry at every opportunity, afr- [sic] willing to show your sensitiveness at every moment. And the truth of the matter is, as all the editors who participated in creating the new man know, is that that was a little wishful thinking on the part of some people who hoped that there would be more evolution of men towards those goals than I think ever actually happened. And part of ... the renewed confidence of men in their own manness is a willingness to say 'Well you know I do like to watch football (*Yeah*) and I don't really like to take the garbage out. I will (*Yeah*) but – and I am going to look at a pretty girl' (*Yeah*) (PBS network, 11 May 1994).

Like the man said, yeah.

Meanwhile, 'serious' mass-media treatments of issues concerning men and social change have largely moved on to other issues, especially the psychological issues promoted by the developing men's movement, discussed in chapter 7. Robert Bly's (1990) *Iron John*, with its mythopoeic concern for wounded male psychology and the need for men to heal the relationship with their fathers, provided commentators with a whole new set of issues which had little to do with gender convergence (see Connell 1992 for a critique of Bly's work and the associated proliferation of 'warrior therapy', and Schwalbe 1996 for a superb critical ethnographic study of a group of mythopoeic men). Some idea of the sexual politics of this agenda can be gleaned from this interchange at one of Bly's retreats:

> [participant] Robert, when we tell women our desires, they tell us we're wrong.
> [Bly] So, then you bust them in the mouth because no one has the right to tell another person what their true desires are (in Kimmel & Kaufman 1997).

Journalists looking for the latest trends need look no further than Promise Keepers, an American Christian revival movement for men. At large rallies men promise, for example, to pursue ethical and sexual purity, to forge strong marriages and protect their family, and in general to be both 'humble servant' and 'spiritual leader' of the family (Van Leeuwen 1997). The movement criticises men who have abandoned family leadership, or abandoned their family altogether. Abusive husbands and fathers should stop being bad masters and become good masters. In other words, benevolent domination is the norm (Minkowitz 1995). As I mentioned in the Introduction, one of the leaders, pastor Tony Evans, exhorted stumbling husbands and fathers to 'take back' their role:

> I'm not suggesting that you ask for your role back, I'm urging you to take it back. If you simply ask for it back, your wife is likely to say 'Look, for the past 10 years I've had to raise these kids, look after the house and pay the bills . . . You think I'm going to turn everything back over to you?' Your wife's concern is justified. Unfortunately however there can be no compromise here. If you're going to lead, you must lead. Be sensitive. Listen. Treat the lady gently and lovingly. But lead! (Promise Keepers 1994: 79–80).

By the mid 1990s, the image of the domestic New Man was just another stock image in the cultural agenda. He had his niches still, and in some he was not a joke. But in the wider world the domesticated New Man had to compete for attention with a host of other images, more robust images with built-in wimp protection. To many, the domestic New Man has become boring, as psychologist Robin Skynner, co-author with actor John Cleese of the best-seller *Families and How to Survive Them* (1983) explained to Maggie Tressider (*Sunday Telegraph*, 14 February 1993):

> [Skynner] He is trying to avoid upsetting the woman. He is tying himself to the home in order to be fair. It's like standing on either side of the tennis net and being careful not to hit the ball in a way that the other person can't hit it. And I think that is terribly boring.
> [Tressider] Not for the woman, it's not. Not if that means he is helping at home.
> [Skynner, speaking firmly] It is boring.

CHAPTER 5

The New Father:
The 'Masculine' New Man

While the New Man uneasily combined nurturer and narcissist, I argue in this chapter that the tension was resolved in new representations of men as fathers. The figure of the New Father combines the narcissistic consumer and the male nurturer in a way which flirts with the feminisation of men, but manages to neatly restate gender difference and male right. Superficially the appearance is one of sharing and gender convergence, but the underlying story is rather different.

Although we should be sceptical about the extent to which the domesticated New Man has featured on the public agenda, there is no denying that there have been significant shifts in the imagery of fatherhood. Even Mother's Day is an occasion for newspaper stories about fathers who care for their children, since 'many men are proving that they, too, can mother' (Melbourne *Age*, 9 May 1993). Absurd over-statement about social change is common: 'A baby these days is no longer handed back to the mother when something is wrong' (Roeber 1987: 181). Fatherhood newspaper columns became fashionable, for example, 'Dad at Large', a fortnightly column by Pete Barron, deputy editor of the English paper *Northern Echo*. The *Independent* (14 April 1996) described the way Barron wrote 'without blushing' about haircuts, crazes and crushes in 'every doting detail'. Barron could not be home to help put his children to bed, but the family had a ritual: 'They ring me at the office to say goodnight. You have a strange conversation with your son about how he's learned to use his potty, right in the middle of the newsroom.' He admitted, however, that full-time childcare would 'drive me mad'.

In fact it seems to have become easier for men to publish idealised, personal accounts of parenthood than it is for women. When a letter written by Fergal Keane, the Hong Kong correspondent of the BBC, to

116

his one-week-old son was broadcast on radio during 1997, countless requests for copies were received and the letter was reprinted in the *Radio Times*. What caused this rush of public interest? The letter is a sentimental, loving account of the new father's feeling for his son and the events which led up to it: 'Daniel, these memories explain some of the fierce protectiveness I feel for you, the tenderness and the occasional moments of blind terror when I imagine anything happening to you', and so on. Apparently it is remarkable to find a man with strong feelings, ready and able to express them.

Representations of the new, participant and nurturing father are more common and are spread over a much greater range of sites, than is the case with representations of the generally domestic New Man. Representations of the new involved fatherhood are often addressed directly to men, something which the generally domesticated New Man only rarely achieved. Overall, the main legacy of domesticated New Man imagery was the New Father: this term is commonly used in popular accounts to label fathers who are intimately involved in day-to-day activities with their children. I will use it as a shorthand term for the figure constructed in discourses which speak about men's greater involvement in fatherhood and childcare. The basic term 'New Father' can appear in numerous guises. For example, describing himself as a 'Sensitive New Age Father', the leader of the conservative rural-based National Party in Australia, Tim Fischer, explained 'I've already changed seven nappies. The people at the hospital believe it's important for bonding to take place between the father and the baby. I've got it down to two minutes a nappy' (Melbourne *Sunday Age*, 21 November 1993).

As with the term New Man, 'New Father' rhetoric implies a major break with imagined tradition: 'The new fatherhood surprises us because we didn't know it was even possible' (Astrachan 1988: 234). Those who wish to report that everything has changed are particularly fond of examples of men caring competently for children. A newspaper account of fathers who share childcare explains how such men dispel the notion that there are things a man can't do for children, 'things like wiping tears and brushing the fine tangled hair of a little girl'. One of the fathers is quoted: 'I cuddle and comfort my Alexandra, get up to her in the middle of the night. It's a myth that fathers can't nurture as well' (Melbourne *Age*, 9 May 1993). A great deal of effort has gone into shattering this supposed myth, by demonstrating that fathers have all the practical competencies required for the care of infants – as one text puts it, 'daddies make good mommies too' (Robinson & Barret 1986: 31).

Research by Parke and his colleagues in the 1970s has been widely cited. Parke et al. (1972) observed the behaviour of parents with their newborn offspring and found that fathers behaved very similarly to mothers in a variety of tasks such as touching, talking, looking, kissing and moving their babies. Parke and Sawin (1975, 1980) also measured parents' ability to bottle-feed their babies, concluding that although men spent less time in feeding, the amount of milk delivered was comparable to that delivered by mothers, and that fathers exhibited just as much sensitivity to infant cues. The Parke studies were frequently cited in textbooks of child psychology as evidence of father competence (e.g. Campos et al. 1983), often accompanied by an illustration of a man caring for a baby (e.g. Hall 1982: 355). Less often mentioned was the methodology of the Parke studies. They had not involved observations of spontaneous fatherly behaviour, but were conducted in a laboratory setting. The behaviour had been requested by the researchers. Given the frame of thought about breaking myths of male incompetence, this makes sense: the researchers simply wanted to watch men to see if they could do it. Another finding of these studies was particularly telling: the fathers tended to 'yield responsibility for caretaking to their wives', as the authors politely put it, when not specifically asked to demonstrate their competence for the investigators (Parke & Sawin 1975, 1980).

Naturally, most of the general discussions of men and domestic work focus on the issue of men caring for children, and earlier chapters in this book have made many references to fatherhood. The treatments which focus on fatherhood exhibit the familiar rhetorical tendencies, including this summation by *Esquire*: 'The feminist movement changed forever our view of raising children ... by putting women in the work-force and putting us by the bassinet' (November 1989). Most New Father texts do seem to advocate a more equal sharing of childcare tasks. Certainly the rhetoric of sharing is widespread, for example in titles such as *Shared Parenthood: A Handbook for Fathers* (Roeber 1987). However, as we have seen in other contexts, sharing does not require equal work. This is particularly clear when the issue is the amount of time the New Father should devote to baby care. An interview with well-known Australian journalist George Negus, who was said to be 'totally committed to the idea of sharing the parenting', revealed that he spent a week at home with his new son and partner: 'It was a good week, which he would have liked to have lasted a little longer. "It would have been nice to have an open-ended situation", he said' (*Sydney Morning Herald*, 16 October 1987).

In fact, although New Father texts use the rhetoric of shared parenting, the sharing can be detached from sharing the work of childcare. The term 'shared parenting' is applied, in some texts, to *all* cases where the mother is employed (e.g. Roeber 1987). The presumed logic is that a mother who is employed must be sharing the work of childcare with someone, and that someone will be the father. Sharing is very often constructed in terms of male help. This understanding of sharing has been extensively discussed already and will not be laboured here, though there are some intriguing aspects specific to fatherhood, a topic which provides great scope for flexibility in the discursive construction of sharing.

For example, sharing may be spoken of in terms of joint responsibility for decision-making about such matters as child discipline (Melbourne *Age*, 14 June 1989). Or men can be said to 'share' such experiences as pregnancy and lactation; thus we read of the 'breastfeeding father' who helps his wife with advice on 'the mechanics and positioning of nursing' (Rich-Shea 1987: 29). We are told that 'fathers get pregnant too' (Dodson 1973: 6), and many texts refer to the 'pregnant father' (e.g. Russell 1983b). It is usually the positive aspects of pregnancy which are shared, however. As Harry Brod (1987a: 16) observed, while it has become possible for couples to say that 'we are pregnant', it is still 'she' who has the miscarriage. A particularly strong theme is the sharing of competence in childcare. Since fathers have been 'proven' to have all the nurturant attributes traditionally associated with mothers, we are meant to assume that competence translates into performance.

Fatherhood also has rich possibilities for performing tasks which are highly symbolic and appear to break taboos, but which don't require a great amount of time or effort. *Esquire* summed it up this way: 'We've learned to diaper. We've learned to say, "Breathe, honey, breathe"' (*Esquire*, November 1989). In this one sentence are the two principal markers of new fatherhood, changing diapers ('nappies' in Britain and Australia) and attending the birth. Men's involvement in these two messy (and hence feminine) bodily functions is constantly remarked upon as indicating a complete break with the past. If, as the *Chicago Tribune* (10 July 1988) put it, the 'essential difference' between the sexes is that women 'come in contact with the business end of a baby' and men do not, then men changing diapers does amount to a minor cultural revolution. Journalists looking for ways to begin their articles on men and change have found diapers indispensable. A general discussion on National Public Radio (20 January 1995) began: 'Over the past few years traditional male and female roles have changed radically. Today, more men change diapers, more women work outside the home.' Similarly, *Psychology Today* in 1994 (3 January) took readers on a rapid journey forward to now: 'Fast-forward to a time of fax machines and heart transplants, when real men change diapers and women carry guns'. *Redbook* (June 1993) began its analysis with the triumphant metaphor 'Yes, all across the nation armies of fathers are waving the white flag of enlightenment: a clean diaper' before going on

to somewhat disingenuously remark that for some reason people invariably seem to equate a man's willingness to change diapers with a
commitment to childcare. The question 'does he or doesn't he?' has
been asked about every celebrity new father. Mostly they pass the test.
Rachel Hunter, wife of singer Rod Stewart, told reporters, 'Rod is
doing very well as a father, he is changing nappies and things' (Press
Association, 4 January 1993).

Male attendance at birth has become almost obligatory in many
sectors of society. Even in 1980, 80 per cent of Australian fathers were
attending the births of their children, a huge increase on the 1962 rate
of only 1 per cent (Russell 1983a). Such a rapid change suggests that
birth attendance may have little connection with wider issues. The bulk
of the change was achieved almost before the culture of the New Father
began, and there is evidence that men who attend childbirth exhibit
no greater support for egalitarian attitudes than do other men, and no
greater subsequent involvement in childcare (Richman 1982; C. Lewis
1986). All the same, much was made of growth in fathers' attendance at
birth. The 'delivery room barrier has been broken', the *Chicago Times*
announced in 1985 (25 January). Later that year, an article on fathers
and change in the same newspaper (14 June 1985) explained that the
changing role of women forced a shift in division of labour: 'In the last
few years we have witnessed the emergence of the new father. In some
areas the changes are indeed substantial. Participation by fathers in the
birthing experience has increased noticeably ... The changes are far less
significant in other areas, however.' Five years later the *Los Angeles Times*
(30 October 1990) heralded the change with 'They've come a long way,
baby. Everyone knows that it's simply *de rigueur* for a modern father to
cut the umbilical cord.'

A fascinating aspect of the rhetoric of the New Father is that performance of these iconic tasks – diaper changing and birth attendance
– is often constructed in terms of the emotional significance for fathers.
As we will see, the New Father emotions are central to this new way of
imagining men. In the next section we meet the emotionally sensitive
New Father at his most triumphant.

The Sentimental Patriarch

In 1985 the *Los Angeles Times* (25 December) carried a book review
with the headline 'Fathers Becoming Full Partners in Parenting', about
The Birth of a Father (1985) by psychiatrist Dr Martin Greenberg. The
book's cover stated that it was an 'invaluable guide to fatherhood', and
carried this endorsement by Benjamin Spock: 'An extraordinarily
sensitive book on what it feels like to become – by gradual steps – a

father. I recommend it highly to parents of both sexes'. The introduction to the review is worth quoting at length:

> A quiet revolution is happening. Fathers all over are coaching the labour and
> delivery of their children and then sharing childcare equally with the
> mothers. Stories of famous fathers involved with their infant children – Gary
> Trudeau and his twins, Kurt Vonnegut as househusband, David Stockman
> breaking off a congratulatory call over his $2 million book advance to feed
> his daughter, Canadian Prime Minister Brian Mulroney at the delivery of his
> fourth child – betoken a new era. The inveterate assumption that mothers
> are the primary caretakers of children is being eroded.
>
> In this context, Dr Martin Greenberg's book is most welcome. It
> encourages fathers to be full partners in parenting, from prenatal decisions
> through labour and delivery to feeding, changing, comforting and enter-
> taining their infants. It offers convincing evidence of the benefits of being
> more than good providers and stoic patriarchs. And it brims with practical
> advice on how to become a fully participating father.

This passage beautifully exemplifies some of the optimistic pop-
sociology themes which this chapter will discuss – the fascination with
the role of fathers during labour, the slide from participation at birth to
full partnership in parenting, the reliance on celebrity anecdotes, the
excited tone of myth-breaking. First, however, let us look at the book
itself, especially at its 'practical advice'.

In the introduction to *The Birth of a Father*, Greenberg told how the
birth of his first child was an emotional turning-point. 'Preoccupied and
absorbed' in the infant Jonathan, Greenberg found himself initially
'buffeted by emotions and forces' over which he had no control; he
found, however, that working through that stage led to a 'bountiful
harvest'. The process of 'getting in touch' with the 'multi-faceted and
often tumultuous emotions' of the new father was one of 'reawakening'
which increased the 'breadth and depth with which we view the world'.
This awakening is available to all fathers who break free from the narrow
cultural definition that expression of feeling is a weakness.

Greenberg's surprise at the strength of his reactions is a little
puzzling, since three years before the birth of his son he had jointly
conducted some of the first psychological research into the interaction
between fathers and their newborn babies. The research appeared in a
short paper in the *American Journal of Orthopsychiatry*, titled 'Engrossment: The Newborn's Impact Upon the Father' (Greenberg & Morris
1974). As the title indicated, the research focused on how men felt
about their babies. Based on interviews with fathers of newborn
children, the findings were that new fathers perceived their offspring as
'attractive, pretty and beautiful' and as 'perfect', 'desired to touch and

hold the baby', experienced increased self-esteem and 'extreme elation ... often described as a "high"'. The authors labelled this complex of responses 'engrossment', and concluded: 'It is hypothesised that engrossment is a basic, innate potential among all fathers' (1974: 527).

This simple study, in which science revealed that men love their babies, has been surprisingly influential. Within a few years child psychology texts (e.g. Helms & Turner 1978) were citing it as evidence of father competence and, by implication, involvement, thus making two unstated assumptions: first, that strong positive feelings are proof of competence, and second, that competence is sufficient proof of performance. That the rhetoric was plausible enough to appear in a textbook suggests that conventional assumptions about maternal childcare were taken for granted. In the ideology of motherhood, maternal love, maternal competence and maternal practices are all part of the same package. So, if fathers love their babies, they just have to be involved in childcare.

The concept of paternal engrossment entered the literature on fatherhood. Greenberg continued to promote it, both in *The Birth of a Father* and through activities such as editing *Nurturant News*, in which he described engrossment: 'The father feels swept off his feet, carried away by his feelings. He feels fascinated by the sight, sound and touch of his baby, sees his baby as perfect and feels drawn to the baby as if it were a magnet' (quoted in Melbourne *Age*, 18 May 1988). Much of the 'practical advice' in *The Birth of a Father* is in terms of the possibilities for engrossment: 'Be alert, as you wipe your baby's behind, for he [sic] may look you in the eye. And you will feel the unique touch of his skin and the pleasure of gazing on his little naked body. The diaper-changing was just an excuse, a reason for setting up this whole experience for you' (1985: 218).

Men were reassured that there was nothing feminine about such intimacies. The touching moment is part of 'diaper patrol', during which fathers perform all diaper-changing during agreed periods (1985: 212). Indeed, diaper-changing can lead to a new kind of male-bonding ritual: 'Fathers experience a kind of camaraderie in being able to talk about their struggles ... The anecdotes about dirty diapers are frequently shared in the kind of aura that exists in a tightly closed secret society' (1985: 216). Similarly, walking the baby is an opportunity to combine male-bonding fantasies with a book-writing project:

> I began taking my tape recorder on our walks. And as Jonathan drifted off to sleep, I would talk into the microphone while walking through the forest. I imagined myself seated on the floor of a wooden cabin somewhere in the wilderness, speaking with a small and friendly group of fathers, as the embers in the fireplace brightly flickered, casting its [sic] intimate glow upon us (1985: 8).

How much time do these engrossing intimacies require? Take the recommendation for 'spelling' tired mothers: 'You can take over with the baby and let your wife lie down, get out of the house, or just get on with other work she needs to do, *momentarily* freed from childcare. I call this relief "spelling"' (1985: 194, emphasis added). Consider also the following recommendation to mothers about that trying time of day when 'Daddy Comes Home':

> After 15 or 20 minutes of rest, reading or conversing, your husband *may* have shifted gears enough to feel like spending *some* time with his infant ... Resist any temptation to demand rather than request that your husband care for the baby ... It is this atmosphere of sharing with and caring for each other that enhances the vibrant energy of the marital relationship (1985: 190, emphasis added).

That was from a 'A Chapter for Mothers: Helping Fathers'. In this construction of sharing the joys of baby, even limited and occasional help appears not to be the mother's right, but is a gift from the father. Engrossment itself appears to require encouragement from the mother. In a remarkably contradictory section, Greenberg admitted that unfortunately there was no way of knowing in advance how engrossed a father would be, so special efforts were needed for fathers who failed to become engrossed: 'A woman must take an especially active role in getting this father involved' (1985: 177); and even engrossed fathers could be easily distracted, so mothers were advised to 'provide a protective space for the family' by hiding the newspaper and the mail before fathers came home (1985: 183). Rather as if they were themselves the infants, fathers needed a great deal of patient encouragement. However awkwardly he held the baby, the mother should remark upon 'how well he's doing it' (1985: 184). Sample scripts were provided:

> Simply say something encouraging such as, 'Isn't she beautiful? She's so much fun to hold. Why don't you try?' ... Above all don't criticise ... When she smiles at him, say, 'Look, she's smiling at you honey' ... You could say something like 'She's pursing her lips the way you do. Isn't that fascinating?' etc. etc. (1985: 181).

Similarly, 'to enhance your husband's relationship with the baby', the mother should organise family walks, and ask if the father would like to try carrying the baby. Once this routine was established: 'Encourage him to try it without you ... [If] the baby is tired, hungry, wet, or soiled you can suggest that he simply bring her home to be taken care of ... This kind of leisurely, prolonged contact will both stimulate and recharge your husband's parenting battery' (1985: 185).

While the self-important sentimental patriarchy of Greenberg's book is striking, Greenberg himself may not be quite so self-important. In an interview in the *Los Angeles Times* he partially problematised the engrossed father:

> It is possible to get very fascinated with the image and idea of being a father that is captured by 'my son is asleep and I'll talk to you about my feeling about being a father'. [But] there is also a down-to-earth aspect about being a father and that is my son wakes up and is on my back and I need to respond to him. There were times when I was up in the air and Jonathan would wake up and I would feel like saying, 'Would you stop bothering me for a second, I want to finish talking about how wonderful it is to be a father' (4 December 1985).

Such accounts, which at least hint at the reality of routine childcare, were not in the book. There it was a father's psychological journey which mattered.

The Birth of a Father usefully introduced, though sometimes in an extreme form, many of the key themes in the new agenda about men and family life. It was not necessarily typical, though neither was it particularly unusual. In a *Family Circle* piece 'Mother Stress: How to Get Dad to Share the Parenting' (18 July 1995), popular pediatrician T. Berry Brazleton recommended, among other manipulative strategies, that when the father was away from home the mother should ask him to phone his children periodically, and to allocate some time with each when he returned. Greenberg's influence has persisted: a 1996 *Psychology Today* (May) feature on the encouragement of father–child bonds offered Greenberg's father and baby bonding walk as one of its key techniques. Another was, 'Persuade mom to go out of the house so you can have the experience of being the parent.' The review of Greenberg's book described it as a manual for the 'fully participating father'. The term 'participant' was apt, given the recommended practice; 'participation' carries no sense of quantitative equality and so expresses involvement without any requirement for comparison of effort. In an advice text by Dr William Sears (1988, the participant father was advised to 'be a back-up caretaker' who relieved his wife when she was exhausted; such 'emergency relief' was shared parenting: 'The benefits are manifold. Mother will love you for it, and will run out of physical and emotional energy *far less frequently*' (my emphasis). Sears called such relief 'solo fathering'.

More importantly, the New Father participates fully in the emotional joys of parenthood: 'You know about those special looks that have meaning to just the two of you, the sense of innocence and wonder that defies description. You know a kind of love that you've never known before, and a kind of satisfaction that you've never had.' This appeared in 'A Message to Dads' (*Parents* magazine, July 1992). Read out of context, it was reminiscent of romantic fiction for adolescent girls. Similarly, an ad for Omega watches showed a man seated at a piano, cradling a naked baby. Perhaps he was singing a love song. The caption was, 'For a moment, there were just the two of you and the whole world to discover' (*Time Australia*, 6 February 1989).

It is quite an achievement to incorporate men into such sentimental-ised romanticism. This can happen in the most unexpected places, even in such havens of unrepentant old-style masculinity as *Esquire* magazine: 'Fatherhood is neither a science nor an art. It is a state of being, a triumph of instinct, and above all, an opportunity for joy' (*Esquire*, November 1989). In this way men can justify their 'newness' as fathers purely on the grounds of their love and need for their children. When the father of the girl who won the British Post Office's competition for the design of a stamp for Father's Day was asked if he was a New Father he replied: 'No question about it. I couldn't be without the children. It might sound like a cliché, but it seems to have made life complete' (*Sunday Telegraph*, 19 June 1994). The next question was 'did he change the nappies?'

Consuming the Joys of Fatherhood

The real shift in the imagery of fatherhood is not so much to do with men undertaking childcare, as with men falling in love with their infants. I must stress again that the shift being discussed is one of imagery – no doubt many fathers were in love before it was prescribed by the rhetoric of the New Father.

Before the 1970s, remarks addressed to fathers in the childcare literature were few and far between. In *Child Care and the Growth of Love*, Bowlby's famous analysis of the child's need for consistent nurturance by one person to whom it becomes attached, fathers were summarily dealt with: 'while continual reference will be made to the mother–child relation, little will be said of the father–child relation: his value as the economic and emotional support of the mother will be assumed' (Bowlby [1953] 1965: 15–16). Similarly, Ribble's *The Rights of Infants* (1943: 101–2), in a very short chapter for fathers, recommended avoiding direct involvement in the child's routine until after the third month: 'irregularity is such a disturbing matter to a young baby'. Spock's *Baby and Child Care*, which first appeared in 1945, made few references to fathers. One passage explained how boys needed 'friendly accepting' fathers, which could be expressed in brief periods of play requiring a 'reasonable effort' since it is 'better to play for 15 minutes enjoyably and then say, "Now I'm going to read the paper", than to spend all day at the zoo, crossly' (Spock [1945] 1968: 320).

In *Parents Ask* (Ilg & Ames 1962), a compilation of answers to parents' questions by experts from the influential Gessell Institute of Child Development, there were occasional questions from fathers. One man wrote about his desire to spend less time playing with his two-year-old son without appearing to reject him. The experts reassured him, and transferred the problem to the mother and to paid help:

> His mother needs to think through his total day and set up a good schedule of his being with people, and being away from them. This is the kind of boy who needs, if possible, a house with many wings (or at least rooms) so that you, the father, can get away from him ... It isn't too exciting to play with a child this age – he will be more fun later on ... A good relationship with a responsible babysitter can do much to relieve pressure on other members of the family (1962: 106).

Today this expert advice must appear laughably out-of-date. Little or no interaction was then expected between fathers and their young children, though in comparison to Greenberg's advice the greatest difference is in the tone. Greenberg's expectations of fathers were not highly time-consuming either, but the time which was spent on father–child interaction was rich in emotional and symbolic significance.

By the 1970s, childcare experts began to speak of fatherhood in distinctly different ways. Salk's *What Every Child Would Like His Parents to Know* deplored earlier professional attitudes which tended to 'deprive father of the pleasures of fatherhood', and argued that fathers 'have been pressured into accepting a somewhat limited role as a parent' (Salk 1972: 20, 33). Intimate and pleasurable association with infants on a daily basis was enjoined, but Salk nevertheless remarked that 'the infrequency of an event shared by a child with his father does not detract from its importance' (Salk 1972: 33). The popular advice book *Becoming a Father: How to Nurture and Enjoy your Baby*, by William Sears, began with this invitation: 'Babies are fun, kids are a joy, and fatherhood is the only profession where you're guaranteed that the more effort you put into it the more enjoyment you will get out of it. And guess what? You get to experience these joys 24 hours a day.'

Sears meant what he said. Fathers could experience the joys full-time, not the work. Fathers could experience 'quality time'; 'quantity time' was for mothers. To ensure that quality time would be enjoyable when a father returned from a trip, he should, 'Suggest that your wife tell the children stories about you and your childhood while you're away.' If the children were too young for stories, a photograph of the absent father could be displayed, so that 'Baby can awaken and see Dad's face.' An illustration showed a photo of Dr Sears watching over a baby in a cot (1988: 155, 164).

Men are often reassured that not too much will be asked of them. The concept of quality time first served to allay the concerns of employed mothers, by reassuring them that fewer hours spent with their children need not be harmful. But, as with Sears, the advice literature for fathers uses the rhetoric of quality time to reassure men who spend less time with their children than do their wives: 'It is the quality of the time spent together which is important and not the number of hours' (Roeber 1987: 12). In *The Essential Father* (1985), Tony Bradman stated: 'I have written many features in *Parents* about the problem of reconciling involved fatherhood with the demands of a full-time job. I've often said in those features that it's not so much the quantity of the time that you spend with your child that matters, as the quality of the time.'

Similar views about quality time and fatherhood are espoused by psychological researchers. For example, Weinraub (1978), in a review article titled 'Fatherhood: The Myth of the Second-Class Parent', argued, against the psychological orthodoxy as she saw it, that there was no evidence that fathers were second-class parents. By this she did not mean to claim that fathers do, or should do, as much childcare as mothers; her point was that, just as much as the mother, the father 'plays an important role in influencing the child's development'. Indeed, Weinraub made it clear that this role need not take up a great deal of the father's time:

> However, differences in the quantity of time fathers and mothers spend with their children do not necessarily imply that mothers and fathers will have differential impact on their children. It is increasingly recognised that the amount of time parents interact with or are available to their children (beyond a minimal amount) has very little effect on the quality of the relationship (Weinraub 1978: 114).

Stevens and Mathews (1978: 85) made the same point even more clearly: 'Infants establish enduring relationships with fathers who exhibit responsive, sensitive behaviour even though they may not devote much time to caregiving activities.'

Thus fathers who fear that their children may one day reproach them for not having spent enough time with them have a remedy at hand: a few key meaningful interactions will create sufficient happy memories of daddy, as Brazleton explained in *Family Circle* (18 July 1995). When his children were young he used to read the story 'Goodnight Moon' as a bedtime ritual. When, as adults, they chided him for not having spent enough time with them, he recited the story by heart: 'In a great green room/there was a telephone and a red balloon/and a picture of a cow jumping over the moon/a comb and a brush/a bowl full of mush/and an old lady whispering "Hush".' This was surprisingly effective. 'That always gets them, and it lets me off the hook ... Everything you share with them today is treasured always.' This kind of sentimentalisation of the father–child relation is very common. As one father interviewed by a reporter said: 'Just coming home at night and the kids running to the door and saying "G'day Dad" and they tell you what they did at kinder, and I just think of the joys of having them around, seeing them grow up' (Melbourne *Sunday Age*, 1 September 1991). Here is Greenberg on the same topic:

> Homecoming has been a very special time for me as a father. When I came in the door Claudia would say to Jonathan, 'Look, Daddy's here!' And by two months Jonathan, perhaps in response to her enthusiasm, began greeting me with a grin that seemed large enough to swallow the room. When that happened, Claudia would often comment, 'Marty, see how much he loves you?' Coming home from work was a moment I looked forward to with eager anticipation (Greenberg 1985: 183–4).

A key emotional reward for the New Father is his engrossment at the first sight of his offspring, a strong theme in accounts of men attending childbirth (Melbourne *Age*, 30 March 1983). Views reminiscent of paternal engrossment are found in many of the texts, which speak, for example, of the way fathers find babies 'enthralling' (Roeber 1987: 170). References to Greenberg and Morris's original paper are frequent, as in Sears' description of engrossment as a form of fathers' addiction to their offspring. The wording is very revealing: 'Engrossment doesn't so much describe what the father does for the baby as what the baby does for the father. A father who is "engrossed" in his baby is totally absorbed in the baby's unique features ... He can't wait to hold him [sic], to talk to him, and interact with him' (Sears 1988: 10, 29).

In these and other ways, New Father texts stress the opportunity fatherhood offers men to fulfil themselves by 'getting in touch with [their] true emotions' and improving their 'expressive abilities' (Foreword by Gardner in Dodson 1973: x; Greenberg 1985: 3; Balswick 1988: 199). The editors of the social science anthology *Dimensions of Fatherhood* claimed that change is 'self-actualising' for men: 'Men recognise the value of male parenthood not only for their children and their families but for their own personal growth and fulfilment. Indeed, men are discovering that parenting is self-actualising' (Hanson & Bozett 1986: 15). Another text stated that baby care is a 'unique opportunity for personal growth', whereby the New Father can discover and enjoy the 'nurturing, caring side of his personality' through this 'ideal opportunity to evolve a complete and whole personality of his own' (Roeber 1987: 2, 9). Manifestly, the idea that baby care is a 'unique opportunity' to express male nurturance takes it for granted that men do not nurture other family members, for example their wives.

Media accounts show a similar understanding of the wonders which fatherhood can work. In an article on Hollywood's 'hottest and most exclusive fraternity', namely older male stars who have found the joys of 'late-life diaper duty' (*Dallas Morning News*, 7 June 1994), Shirley MacLaine spoke about her brother Warren Beatty. Explaining how the famously philandering actor had found contentment, she added that 'he's happier than I've ever seen him'. Beatty himself put it this way: 'Fatherhood's beyond description, it's the zenith of existence.'

The New Father's psychological gains are often contrasted with the traditional father's losses. Men's movement activists often suggest that pointing out the emotional loss of traditional fatherhood is the best way to motivate men to change (e.g. Brannon in Franks 1984). Bernard's (1972, 1982) work is sometimes cited, though without its feminist understanding of the way marriage works in men's interests, to show that men's psychological health suffers outside the family setting. Anecdotes of the losses experienced by traditional fathers are common: 'One grandfather spoke wistfully to me of his gradual realisation of lost chances after his son died at an early age. "Looking back I think our relationship had the ecstasy of a few close encounters, but the sadness of many lost opportunities"' (Roeber 1987: 14). Similarly, Spock's remark, near the end of his life, that he mourned the fact that he had not hugged his sons, was widely quoted (*Time Australia*, 22 August 1988). In fact, wistful paternal realisations of this kind predate contemporary New Father rhetoric by many centuries. Writing in the 1570s, Montaigne reported that an acquaintance whose son had died had spoken of 'the heartbroken grief that he felt at never having opened his heart to the boy. He had always put on the stern face of paternal gravity, and had thus lost the opportunity of really knowing and appreciating his son, also of revealing the deep love he bore him.' In contrast, Montaigne offered himself as a model for emotional 16th-century New Fatherhood: 'I am open with my family, to the extent of my powers. I quite freely reveal to them the state of my feelings for them, also my opinion of them, and of everyone else' (Montaigne 1958: 149–50).

The flexibility of the concept of sharing is particularly clear when it comes to the New Father's emotional rewards. I do not intend to denigrate the pleasures and emotional rewards of intimate association with children. The important issue is whether the New Father is offered such rewards while remaining free of the obligation to perform the work of childcare. Full participation in the emotional joys of parenthood does not seem to require equity in time spent with children. Contradictions between optimistic accounts of the convergence of sex roles and the acknowledgement, implicit or explicit, that women still do the bulk of childcare can appear to be resolved through stressing the emotional rewards. Despite the rhetoric about male nurturance, what is shared between men and women in these texts is largely a common personality orientation. Sharing the pleasures of involvement with children, and the emotional and therapeutic rewards thereof, means sharing consumption rather than production.

A noteworthy instance occurs in historian Thomas Laquer's (1990) account in 'The Facts of Fatherhood'. In a very interesting move, Laquer invoked the labour theory of value to argue that ownership of the child belongs to those who perform the 'emotional labour of the heart'. The logic was not materialist, belonging rather to a narcissistic and consumerist understanding in which *desire* authorises possession. Laquer's description of the father's emotional work concerned the father's state of feeling, rather than work done on and for the child: 'If a labour theory of value gives parents rights to a child, that labour is of the heart, not the hand. (The heart of course, does its work through the hand; we feel through the body).' This confusion between feeling and doing, and between desire and agency, in a theoretical text purporting to extend the materialist paradigm, is very revealing. Narcissistic and consumerist understandings have overwhelmed the distinction between caring for and caring about (see Ruddick 1990 for a critique of Laquer's discussion).

Fathers are not Wimps

In a discourse which speaks about men becoming more like women, largely framed in psychological terms, it is no surprise to find the rhetoric of the 'masculine' and the 'feminine'. For example, the psychological feminisation of men through association with children is often discussed. The lesson some writers drew from the film *Three Men and a Baby* was that popular culture was beginning to 'tap into the more feminine side of the masculine psyche' (*Australian*, 20 January 1990). In an interview with a musician father, which stressed the value of intimacy with children and the unexpected benefits of psychological change, the same rhetoric of masculinity and femininity was at work:

The experience of caring for Matthew has affected his music and changed his outlook on life. 'I'm more mellow, I have a more feminine view of the world. For example, the song "For the Children", which I wrote for my son and for all the children of the world . . . I wouldn't have thought about a song like that had I not spent a year at home watching him grow' (*Australian Women's Weekly*, May 1988).

As we have already seen, a psychological version of the revolving door is often invoked: changes in women's personality lead to changes in men's personality. Well-worn dichotomies of the rhetoric of gender are trotted out, women becoming more assertive and men becoming more receptive. On the face of it, the discourse of the New Father constructs men's psychological capacities for the nurturance of children, and the receipt of pleasure from children, along lines markedly similar to the discursive construction of motherhood. But it turns out that incorporating men into a rhetoric previously reserved for motherhood does not seem to undermine its ability to legitimate the sexual division of childcare.

As has often been said, the discursive construction of nurturant women and non-nurturant men is a key ideological element of patriarchy: the ideology of motherhood attributes to women – and only to women – the qualities of nurturance necessary for the physical and emotional care of children, and so legitimates women's responsibility for domestic labour (Wearing 1984). Game and Pringle (1983: 127) noted how the emotionalisation of women's domestic labour over the course of this century has reinforced the division of labour by offering emotional rewards, especially for middle-class women now stuck with the housework as a result of the disappearance of servants. In contrast, fatherhood can be constructed so that men share with women the emotional rewards of parenthood without being stuck with the job. This is apparent in the way New Father texts speak in terms of male choice. As Diane Ehrensaft observed in her early critique, personal accounts of fatherhood tended to describe the rewards men can experience, if they choose to take that option. In a memorable passage, she noted the ability of the father to 'slip off his fathering cape and do a psychological disappearing act. He simply makes himself less accessible to the child' (Ehrensaft 1980: 63). Many New Father texts show this clearly:

> It seems to me that, unlike mothers, fathers exercise the luxury of choice. It's all very confusing. There are no rules, no defined tasks or delineated roles any more . . . 'Fatherhood' generally begins in blissful ignorance, and it may proceed to a state of supreme indifference or one of positive rewards from maximum involvement (Melbourne *Sunday Age*, 1 September 1991).

The notion that delineated roles no longer exist applies only to men. Male 'confusion' can only be read in terms of a choice predicated on women's continuing responsibility for childcare.

Thus Bettina Arndt, in a piece titled 'The Joys of Fatherhood Should Come Naturally' (Melbourne *Age*, 18 August 1988), criticised the excesses of New Fatherhood, arguing that the compulsory 'joyous welcome of the pregnancy, nine months of cheerful curiosity and support, a spiritual, peak birth experience, following [sic] by full-on engrossment' was reminiscent of earlier, oppressive, constructions of joyous motherhood: 'It is wonderful that more males are discovering and talking about the special relationship between a man and his children, but let's not prescribe just how and when that should happen. Paternal feelings are far more likely to flourish if we try not to make them compulsory.' The article assumed that routine childcare is performed by women, driven by maternal feelings. Women are given permission to 'react in many and varied ways', but it is fathers (at least, those with an office to go to) who are given permission to be uninvolved: 'Who can blame them for sometimes being grateful to escape into the office?' (Arndt's career progress from youthful editor of the raunchy sex-chat magazine *Forum* to middle-aged voice of conservative middle-class commonsense has been a continuing source of comment in Australia.)

Other texts, if not directly referring to choice, nevertheless assume it in their accounts of fatherhood. The common journalistic practice of basing articles on interviews with a few differing stereotypical figures means that involved fatherhood can be constructed as just one of many lifestyle options. One Father's Day article titled 'Daddy Dearest' concerned four fathers, 'all, in their own ways, examples of concerned, caring fatherhood'. One of the fathers spoke of himself as highly involved in routine childcare, but otherwise the issue did not arise. Instead fathers spoke of their love and concern for their children: 'It's been a pleasant cheerful world, with these extra humans around' (Melbourne *Age*, 31 August 1988).

In connection with choice, the concept of paternal engrossment is particularly interesting. On the face of it, the discourse of engrossment constructs fatherhood on the model of motherhood: fathers and mothers both have a natural capacity to become absorbed in their babies, thus fitting them for involved parenting. However, male engrossment can be constructed as a matter of choice and desire, as shown in Greenberg (1985). One text for fathers spoke of mother's engrossment in quasi-natural terms: 'It is almost as if the umbilical cord was still intact with mother and baby still attached to each other's inner world.' Father's engrossment was seen differently: 'I have observed that some fathers become equally engrossed with their infants – if the environment is encouraging and the desire is there' (Roeber 1987: 170–1). Similarly, Green (1976: 182) observed that since fathering is *'increasingly a matter of feeling rather than feeding*, the father can direct his paternal interest where he wishes' (emphasis added). This is a wonderfully revealing summation, coming not from a critic but from a wholehearted advocate of New Fatherhood.

It seems, then, that fathers are simply different. Rhetoric which seems to construct men as similar to women appears to have little difficulty in maintaining gender difference when fatherhood is the issue. An obvious and important point is that the masculinity of fathers, whether 'new' or 'old', is confirmed simply by the fact of being a father, with all this implies about successful heterosexual performance, both in terms of the act of reproduction and the continuing relationship with the mother. This is why, for example, intimate images of men and babies need not feminise men. Commercial poster and card images of men and babies, in which both father and baby are naked, have been remarkably successful. The best-selling poster image *L'Enfant* will be familiar to many readers. The marked eroticism of the image was explained by the photographer, Spencer Rowell: 'I was told women go ape-shit when they see a man cradling a child' (in Chapman 1988: 236). Actually, the 'father' in this famous photo was the very successful and very single model, Adam Perry. Perry later became notorious for his claim to have had sex with 3000 women since the age of 15 (quoted in *Cleo*, September 1997).

'As the father of a baby daughter, it allows me to be caring and emotional without being judged wimpish or gay', wrote Jack Sullivan, associate editor of the *Independent* (Melbourne *Age*, 7 June 1997). The New Man may be problematically masculine, but the New Father is not. An article on 'Fathers' Lib' cited Sam, father of a 12-week-old daughter:

> He wasn't, he said with a flashing grin ... a New Man. He wasn't good with the nappies, he hadn't got the hang of bathtime, and he often slept through her night-time feeds. But he could recite chunks of Penelope Leach's *Baby and Child* as he had once been able to sing the lyrics of every song that Rod Stewart had recorded ... it occurred to me that evening, as I was made privy to the endless minutiae of his daughter's life, that while most men would vehemently deny being a New Man, they would happily concede to being a New Father (*Daily Mail*, 14 July 1994).

In other words, the New Father is fascinated by his child, talks about that child at length and knows the expert advice literature by heart, but he is no wimpy feminised New Man. Overall, New Father representations show little tension between the poles of macho and wimp, and little of the humour which often accompanies other representations of men who stray 'too far' towards the feminine. A newspaper article which caricatured the generally domesticated New Man as a sandal-wearing soy-milk drinker described a New Father with a degree of self-mocking awe: 'There was a large, damp patch on Ted's khaki. "Excuse me," he said, retreating to the house, "his nappy needs changing." In deep shock, we dropped our list of questions. That, we told ourselves, is the Real Sensitive Man' (Melbourne *Age*, 20 May 1988). A reporter assigned to interview stay-at-home fathers remarked 'I am finding it hard not to gush' (*Los Angeles Times*, 1 September 1991).

New Father texts are more likely to be humorous about the defects of the traditional father:

> For years, men did not see fatherhood as a very demanding role. Their function was quite simple; they were supposed to bring home the wage packet, get drunk on Fridays, hit the children when requested to by their wives, and pay for their daughter's wedding. They spent the rest of the time in the garden shed making corner cupboards (*Australian Women's Weekly*, August 1991).

While the New Man's domestic presence is humorous, when fatherhood is concerned it is male absence which is problematic and therefore a subject for humour. Certainly, it is common enough to poke fun at men who, like Tom Selleck's character in *Three Men and a Baby*, can design tall buildings but fumble over the diapers. But such humour is very gentle: the men do learn, and are all the more masculine for it: 'Tom Selleck is muscled, mustachioed, hairy-chested and permanently tanned, thus in the eyes of all Americans a decliner of quiche. Get this fellow to grasp a baby in his huge paws and fatherhood is suddenly glamorous' (Melbourne *Age*, 3 February 1988). Indeed, diapering becomes work fit for heroes: 'I have changed a baby's diaper in the shadow of a condom machine; I can mix infant formula in an airport bathroom' (San Diego *Union-Tribune*, 16 June 1996). In California the Irvine Medical Center instituted a 'Booty Camp for New Dads' which relied on sporting and military metaphors, with a 'head coach' using 'veterans' to teach 'rookies' basic skills such as 'diaper drill'. A news report on Booty Camp was gloriously headed 'Fathers Told to Pin One for the Gipper' (*Los Angeles Times*, 14 April 1996).

Tensions about the New Father's masculinity do arise. In a report on stay-at-home dads one of the men requested the writer to stress 'how macho we are'. The reporter obliged, finishing the piece with 'They are the most macho of men. They are the daddies' (Dallas *Morning News*, 28 August 1994). Advice texts address the same concerns: 'Some men fear that they will simply become surrogate mothers, losing their male identity. This is just not the case, as any baby or toddler knows. When a man takes over the "mothering" role it has a distinctly different flavour' (Roeber 1987: 12). 'The father is not a substitute mother; he has his own unique contribution to make to his child's development' (Sears 1988: 149).

The ease with which concerns about the masculinity of New Fathers is brushed aside is in stark contrast to the situation of the domesticated New Man. The difference occurs in many ways. Sometimes it (and male superiority) is stated with startling directness, as in this account which was concerned that the job of raising children was losing status: 'The fastest and most cunning device for restoring parenting as a central task of adult life, and one that must be tackled seriously, is to recall father once more to the job. Father alone can confer prestige on the domestic setting'(Green 1976: 211–12). Quality time with the father can be constructed as a precious gift, surpassing similar experiences with the mother: 'The time that a mother, or even more so a father, gives to his children ... the walks he takes with them, the explanations he gives on nature, on his own life, his confidences – these are priceless gifts whose memory forever remains engrained as the most beautiful of all childhood' (Tournier quoted in Grant 1983: 18). That passage occurred in an advice text addressed to Christian fathers, who were encouraged to view themselves as 'the mirrors through which our children first visualise the Heavenly Father' (Grant 1983).

Gender difference is sometimes understood in terms of grand social theoretical schema, using, for example, the well-worn functionalist distinction between the public (masculine, instrumental, rational) and the private (feminine, expressive, emotional) spheres. The related notion, common in psychoanalytic writings, that the father 'helps extricate a child from the maternal orbit, facilitating a sense of reality' (Ross 1979: 325) is widely found in New Father texts. The father's connection with the public/social world is contrasted with the restricted maternal sphere where women love their children unconditionally but are unable to represent the 'reality principle ... Mother, ideally, teaches the children that they matter enormously, because they matter to her; father is ideally placed to teach them that there are other people and other things that matter as well' (Green 1976: 176). However, even this aspect of child-rearing can be absorbed by the rhetoric of sharing. In one advice text the mother is said to share the experience of having her child drawn away from her by her husband: 'A father will play, stimulate and draw the child gradually away from the mother, towards maturity. Shared parenting means a willingness to share all these activities' (Roeber 1987: 209). On occasions the father's role outweighs that of the mother to a remarkable degree: 'Weaning means to cause a child to give up mother's milk and substitute other nourishment. Father is the source of the other emotional nourishment' (Sears 1988: 61).

The Playful Expert Father

On the issue of the New Father's difference, two themes deserve particular attention. The first concerns the father's special skills in play.

This can be linked to the grand gender scheme noted above – playing with daddy helps children to expand their horizon and draws them into the wider world represented by men:

> Mothers tend to play quieter, less active games with babies. They focus their play activities in a small area, and babies learn to accommodate these limits. Fathers widen baby's playtime interests with more vigorous climbing and tumbling play. Many dads have trouble sitting still in one place and concentrating on a narrow play activity. They need space and so they naturally use more space when they play. Babies profit from exposure to these bigger play areas (Sears 1988: 151).

As we know, father–child interactions focus on playful and leisure-like activities. New Father texts construct this not in terms of male privilege, but as an obligation. The benefits for children are stressed so much that, in effect, it becomes the duty of fathers to have fun.

The theme is common in social scientific research into fatherhood. For example, Parke and his colleagues (MacDonald & Parke 1984; Parke et al. 1988) reported that fathers' play, compared with that of mothers, is more physical and elicits strong affects, both positive and negative, in children. The authors concluded that playing with the father facilitates a child's ability to decode emotional cues and to regulate affective bonds. Writing in *Psychology Today* (May 1996), Roberts and Moseley summed up the evidence about the 'daddy dynamic', concluding that fathers' rougher style of play pushes children to cope with the wider world away from mother, and to develop a more complex set of interactive skills. Thus rough play helps children to learn to read emotions – 'Is Daddy really going to chase me down and gobble me up, or is he joking?' – and children learn to communicate emotions to others, for example 'the child who by crying lets her [sic] daddy know that he's playing too roughly or is scaring her'. Finally, boisterous fathers help children learn to listen to their own emotional state: 'a child soon learns that if he becomes too "worked up" and begins to cry, he may in effect drive his play partner away'. In such ways children learn they can 'indeed effect change both on internal matters, their feelings, and in the outside world, their father's actions'. Beneath the rhetoric is the assumption that interaction with the mother is a matter of undifferentiated nurturance and acceptance: 'a mother's more comforting manner is just as crucial to her children, helping them foster ... a critical sense of security and confidence'. There is no recognition that the mother–child interaction is very complex, with plenty of opportunity for exercising a wide range of interpersonal skills on both sides (Everingham 1994).

Research into the 'daddy dynamic' was often discussed in media accounts of fatherhood. A study by Russell and Russell (1987) was cited as evidence that the traditional playful role of the father had been 'downgraded in favor of nurturing and caring' and that 'the kind of intimate, romping, physical sort of play between some fathers and their children will help those children relate to people around them' (Melbourne *Sunday Age*, 1 September 1991). Recently, research results of this kind have been summarised and popularised by sociologist David Popenoe in *Life without Father* (1996), which bears the subtitle: 'compelling new evidence that fatherhood and marriage are indispensable for the good of children and society'.

In this spirit, the father advice literature abounds with examples of time spent with children in play and recreation, doing things with children rather than for them: 'Whether playing a game of basketball, building a birdhouse, or taking a walk, quality time means we are fully tuned in' (Grant 1983: 38). Interestingly, that text placed particular stress on the need for fathers to spend large amounts of time with their children. Explaining that children spell the word love 'T-I-M-E', Grant said: 'Material things, I have learned, can't take the place of time spent with our children' (1983: 18). However, the examples of time with children did not include routine childcare.

Often advice about play is much more specific than advice about routine childcare. Consider the following: 'The two of you can chase each other around the couch singing "Where's daddy?" Bob up and down periodically to reveal yourself and say "Here I am." Look for the surprised expression on baby's face and approving chuckles' (Sears 1988: 151). Even discussions of the performance of routine childcare tasks can emphasise play. Fathers are said to approach such events 'with an open mind, often transforming them into exciting "happenings"' (Roeber 1987: 12). The same playful approach to childcare was evident in the account of an exemplary New Father by his widow, in which she urged women to accept that equality means allowing men to perform childcare in their own fashion: 'Brian thought baths were for playing, and if any washing incidentally got done that was a bonus (Melbourne *Age*, 14 September 1984).

Fathers are valued not only for their play but also for their unique expertise, and this is the second theme I want to discuss in this section. The growth in the influence of experts (often male) over mothers, both with respect to childbirth and child-rearing, has been widely studied (e.g. Ehrenreich & English 1979; Reiger 1985). Some writers, for example Donzelot (1980), have argued that this has undermined paternal authority. However, recent New Father texts often give the strong impression that expertise in matters of childcare and child-rearing is embodied in the father. This can apply even in the case of childbirth. One advice text encouraged fathers to write an account of the birth: 'Usually fathers have a keener sense of the exact sequence of the labour which can help the woman fill in any gaps in her memory' (Roeber 1987: 170). The following account of fathers and birth speaks of sharing fathers as those who exhibited a technical interest in the processes of birth:

> The third type was the sharer ... They were often tinkering with the car to make sure it was ready for the hospital run; they picked up baby books and asked questions ... often they were like sports coaches, telling her to move her breathing to 'level C' and timing her with a stopwatch. At the hospital they regretted not having been shown how to read the monitor, and were delighted when they were allowed to play an active part. 'I really liked it when they let me help a bit with things – the tubes, the traces and so on.' They were an immense support to mother all through their often unanxious, logical and above all doing approach. They were determined to be equal parents from the beginning (Jackson 1983: 75).

Even occasional male help can be constructed as a kind of expertise. For example, the expert husband can diagnose the point at which his wife's exhaustion endangers the family: 'Father can have a vital part to play in diagnosing the point at which the mother's *nervous or mental disabilities* have reached a stage at which the children are noticeably suffering, and some outside intervention is needed' (Green 1976, emphasis added). The reference to outside intervention speaks tellingly of the abnormality of father help. The privileging of the children's welfare is also clear, the reference to the mother's 'nervous or mental disabilities' being particularly patronising. Consider too the patronising expert husband in Greenberg's discussion of the protocols of 'spelling' (relieving) the mother: 'Work out your signalling system in advance. A nonverbal cue such as the raising of the pinkie finger could indicate, "It's time for me to take over." It is a reminder that says, "Remember what we talked about before? You're getting into trouble. I think you need help" (Greenberg 1985: 195). The possibility that the mother might simply ask her husband for help is not considered. Similarly, a section of Sears' book (1988: 42, 48) headed 'Be in Charge' states that the 'overwhelming desire to be a good mother sometimes overrules a woman's ability to know her limitations' and so the situation can sometimes 'get out of hand ... fathers are the ones who oversee this balance'. Sears' main message is that the father should 'help his wife be a good mother' by reminding her she is doing the 'most important job in the world'. Above all, the 'breastfeeding father' has the duty to encourage breastfeeding: 'Point out to your wife that the traditional cultural model for a human mother and baby has never been a mother alone in a room with a baby. It has always been mothers and babies sharing their burdens and joys. Encourage your wife to join a support group' (Sears 1988: 46). If the mother replies that she cannot spare the time, the father is encouraged to send out for pizza and to drive his wife to the support group meeting.

The Essential Father

What is most often stressed in current discussions of fatherhood (whether new or otherwise) is that children need their fathers. Plentiful expert opinion and research evidence is on hand to back up any commentator wishing to make this point. One Australian newspaper story quoted an (unnamed) visiting American pediatrician: 'The more Dad stays home, the better a newborn baby's chances of a good sense of humour and a high IQ' (*Sydney Morning Herald*, 16 October 1987). Another cited unidentified research which showed that 'active fathering can be closely linked to high-achieving children' (Melbourne *Herald*, 21 November 1988).

The issues have been extensively researched by social scientists. The much-heralded 'discovery of the father' by social science usually refers to the 'discovery' that fathers, like mothers, influence their children (e.g. Zigler et al. 1982). Most psychological studies of fatherhood concern the effects on children, with gender and cognitive development given particular attention (for reviews of the psychological literature on fatherhood see Fein 1978; McKee & O'Brien 1982; Hanson & Bozett 1986; Lamb 1986; James 1988; Vallender 1988). Stevens and Mathews (1978: 85) typically observed that fathers have a 'significant impact on the development of children's cognitive skills, their achievement orientation and their sex-role development', and concluded that 'researchers can no longer ignore the father'. This new approach rapidly became a staple of child psychology texts (e.g. Hall 1982; Campos et al. 1983) and was taken up in popular New Father texts. In some of those, the absence of a father is depicted as so disabling that any father, no matter how defective, is better than none: 'Those who have had the good fortune to experience a father – however unsatisfactory – have some roots from which their own ability as a parent can grow' (Roeber 1987: 13).

Much of the research compares children with and without father contact, often concluding that children without fathers are disadvantaged in various ways. However, a major weakness of many such studies is that they neglect to control for such variables as class and income. But children living with and without father contact constitute very different groups: for example, children living apart from fathers experience greater poverty. Studies which do properly control for such factors find little difference in outcomes between children with and without father contact (see Marsiglio 1995: Introduction for a comprehensive literature review). One large study of divorced families found what the authors described as a surprising result – that children's educational and psychological outcomes were not correlated with fathers' level of child contact, though they were correlated with the level of fathers' economic support (Furstenburg et al. 1987). Another large study, for the American National Institute of Child Health and Human Development, concluded that the presence or absence of a father mattered less to cognitive development than 'the quality of the child's environment – the presence of caring individuals' (Mott 1993). Another study tellingly concluded that research into the effects on children of father involvement was unlikely to show much difference between father-absent and father-present children simply because 'too few fathers show the high level of involvement needed for a reliable difference to emerge' (Crockett et al. 1993).

However, no amount of contrary evidence can deter those determined to stress the unique importance of fathers. *Parents* magazine (July 1992) was certain that with the New Father 'our children will grow up more content and secure and better able to manage the many roles that they will no doubt juggle one day'. The question of children's interests can lead mainstream commentators to make harsh judgements about men's practices in a way rarely seen in connection with women's interests. The widely respected Australian family expert Don Edgar abandoned his customary rhetoric of optimistic gradualism when, in alarmist tones, he chastised men for their lack of commitment to fatherhood: 'The fact that almost half the adult potential for child development is being denied to children is not just a shame, it is a national disgrace. Men can no longer pretend they don't have time for children when women manage to find it as well as work outside the home' (*Time Australia*, 22 August 1988). After all, men's obligations were not great – a little effort could go a long way. As Edgar explained to a reporter: 'They just have to take an interest in what their kids are doing. They should talk to them, go for a walk with them or look over their homework without interfering' (Melbourne *Herald*, 21 November 1988).

As in that case, when expert views on fatherhood are quoted in the mass media, it is most often in connection with the idea that children (often 'families') need fathers. This need not be expressed in terms of the unique contributions of fathers; rather, fathers may be deemed necessary on the grounds that two parents are better than one. In another article Edgar argued that child-rearing needs two intimately involved parents, both of whose 'talents can be brought to bear on the development of competence', thus providing a 'double engine' for the train of child development (Melbourne *Age*, 5 September 1986).

New Father rhetoric is almost entirely framed within the context of marriage, and individualised solutions to problems of child-rearing. The supposed truism that families need fathers is ceaselessly restated. As one advice text confidently stated: 'The two-parent family still seems the best bet as a framework that allows the whole intricate network of sexual, intellectual and maternal and paternal needs to be worked out together' (Green 1976). In such ways fathers can be drawn into panics about the future for children and into the expanding system of expert influence over private life, associated with fantasies of the perfectibility of society (Harris 1997). Another effect is that single mothers are again attacked: as the headline of Arndt's article on single motherhood (Melbourne *Age*, 30 July 1996) proclaimed, children raised without fathers are consigned to 'a lesser future, something women contemplating motherhood need to know'.

Calls for increased father involvement often ride on whichever moral panic is currently uppermost in the public mind. In *Fear of Falling*, Barbara Ehrenreich (1989) suggested that a general intensification of concern about child-rearing is associated, among the middle class at least, with an increasingly competitive labour market and the resulting intensification of the struggle to maintain class position. This helps explain research titles such as 'Fear of Failure in Families without Fathers' (Greenfield & Teevan 1986). This is not the first era in which concern about inadequate fathering has been attached to general social anxieties. In the 1950s, fears about absent fathers and maternal overinvolvement were strong in both social science and popular culture. The underlying fear was that women would emasculate their sons (Breines 1986). This fear is still evident, along with many others. Father advice books can be marketed with covers proclaiming that involved fatherhood will help 'deal with the drug threat' (Dodson 1973); concerns about family breakdown and declining discipline are easily linked to 'the declining influence of the father in the home' (Grant 1983: 22). The association of fatherhood and discipline is strong, as the following passage shows – the subtext about maternal chaos is remarkable: 'Fathers play a vital role in discipline by providing balance and structure in the otherwise disorganised world of the child' (Sears 1988).

The father's discipline may be required, for example, to prevent women from spoiling their children:

> Some women wait on their children for years, and prevent them from ever learning to look after themselves. Father may need to step in firmly and insist that the children are forced to be more independent. In adolescence he may have to start the long process of untying mother's apron strings (Green 1976).

Note, though, that this text does not problematise the way women wait on their husbands.

Advice texts give considerable importance to the performance of domestic work by children, and the disciplinary role fathers should play in this connection. Relief of stressed mothers is often portrayed as a matter of the father organising the children. Often, a father's responsibility to encourage his children to do housework is greater than his responsibility to do some work himself. One author, concerned about possible sexism in the allocation of chores to his children, wrote that 'both of our children were making their own beds by themselves at age four and were doing a fairly good job of it – not as good as their mother would have done, but passable' (Grant 1983). However, the only reference to domestic work by fathers concerned building a store of happy memories: 'In some homes the father and children can take over the responsibility for preparing the family breakfast or dinner occasionally. This can provide the mother a welcome relief. But more importantly, such shared times spent in common work are often remembered with deep gratitude in later years.'

It is surprisingly common for advice texts to promote non-sexist child-rearing, while at the same time failing to problematise the parents' division of labour. In *The Secret of Happy Children* (Biddulph 1988), the father 'brings on the cavalry' to help child and mother deal with their joint 'problem':

> Peter, aged 13, is hassling with Marjorie, his Mum, about putting out dirty clothes to be washed. He gets louder and begins to swear, and is talking too aggressively. His father overhears this, and walks in. He tells Peter 'Hey! You need to use a normal voice and sort this out with your mother now.' He catches Peter's eye. 'Right?' 'Mmm.' Dad then walks off, but stays within earshot. Peter then has to continue and solve the problem about the clothes.

Nowhere was the sexual division of adult domestic labour (childcare or housework) problematised. Washing was the mother's affair, while the father's role was to oversee the mother–child interaction. A father can apparently do this even while taking his leisure. Biddulph told an audience at one of his lectures that 'when we're sitting behind the newspaper in the living room and you think we're opting out, we're not, you know. Our radar is on; we're monitoring the family' (Melbourne *Herald-Sun*, 7 August 1996). In the literature on parenting, a remarkable example of the failure to problematise the adult division of labour occurred in the popular Australian manual *Becoming Better Parents* (Balson 1987). Speaking of the widowed father, Balson observed that 'it is particularly difficult for children when the mother dies suddenly, leaving the father who has not developed particular skills with, or interest in, the children ... The father should use the death as an opportunity for teaching independence at an earlier age, to teach that children have an opportunity of contributing to the family rather than simply being waited on.'

There is considerable concern about the appropriate gender development of children, particularly that of boys. It is well-established that fathers are more concerned about the appropriate gender development than are mothers (e.g. Henshall & McGuire 1986). Advice texts for fathers certainly play on this concern: 'It often takes a man really to understand the adventurous, aggressive nature of little guys' (Dodson 1973). The same text said that daughters also need their fathers, but in a different way: 'A father is equally important to a preschool girl, not as a model to imitate, but as the first man in the little girl's life. You are the model for your daughter's future husband.' Likewise, Sears considered that fathers played a part in producing the next generation of good (i.e. full-time) mothers: 'Daughters who report a satisfactory relationship with their fathers are less likely to seek careers outside the home' (Sears 1988: 209).

There is little or no evidence that it makes a difference which parent is the principal carer (Russell 1987). All the same, New Father texts often insist that boys are disadvantaged in the acquisition of gender identity: 'Female domination of infant care has long been recognised as a potential hazard, leaving boys at a distinct disadvantage where emotional and psychological development is concerned' (Roeber 1987). In his best-seller, *Manhood*, Biddulph (1994) stated that 'boys who do not get very active fathering ... will never get their lives as men to work. It's as simple and as absolute as that.' Having been raised myself by women, I am inclined to disagree. Authoritative expert pronouncements are only a little less extreme. According to the director of a centre for adolescent health: 'The bulk of boys are completely and utterly devoid of a mentor figure who will enable them to go through adolescence and come out as a psychologically mature man' (Melbourne *Age*, 23 July 1996).

Rhetoric of this kind is often associated with general fears about social breakdown. According to Biddulph, the 'astonishing disappearance' of men from family may be the 'key to most of our social problems'. One of the most significant recent achievements of the American right has been repackaging its support for marriage and traditional family values by restating the necessity for a strong institution of fatherhood (Kraemer 1995). In *Fatherless America* (1995: 30), David Blankenhorn, director of the Institute for American Values stated boldly: 'There are exceptions, of course, but here is the rule. Boys raised by traditionally masculine fathers generally do not commit crimes. Fatherless boys commit crimes.'

For Blankenhorn the highly involved feminised father is problematic. He may be available as a role model, but what kind of model does he provide? The New Father is an aspect of a 'culturally impoverished conception of fatherhood ... the new father closely resembles the unnecessary father' (in *Chicago Tribune*, 30 January 1992). Similarly, psychologist and fatherhood expert Jerrold Shapiro told *Time* (28 June 1993), 'If you become Mr Mom, the family has a mother and an assistant mother. This is not what good fathers are doing today.' This tends towards paranoia – equity in parenting is seen as an attack on fatherhood. Perhaps the fear is not only that without clear gender differences fathers will be unnecessary and women will raise children alone, but that without clear gender differences women will no longer be subordinate.

Lynne Segal's (1990) qualified optimism about New Father imagery was noted earlier. Writing a few years later (1993) she was more cautious, arguing that recent emphases on fatherhood might involve reasserting men's significance in families given that women are no longer completely dependent upon marriage. Sometimes she said so quite baldly. Another advice text advocated shared parenting for fathers in order to establish a good relationship with the children in case of divorce (or perhaps in order to prevent divorce): 'These increasingly common situations suggest that the father needs to establish powerful and direct relationships with their children as early as possible' (Colman & Colman 1988: xvii). Fatherhood is the last role a man can hang on to in a world where relationships (marriage) are no longer secure: 'For the average man living in a world where male/female relationships are confused and often unsatisfactory, fatherhood has come to be a more important role than ever' (*Daily Mail*, 14 July 1994).

But more usually the rhetoric of father difference is employed to justify the necessity of marriage as the site of child-rearing. According to Blankenhorn (*Chicago Tribune*, 30 January 1992), children need both the tough love of the father and the soft love of the mother. The National Fatherhood Initiative, led by Wade Horn, formerly commissioner for children, youth and families in the Bush administration sponsors mass rallies which culminate in men signing the Fatherhood Pledge:

> Many people believe that fathers are unnecessary. I believe the opposite. I pledge to live my life according to the principle that every child deserves a father; that marriage is the ideal pathway to effective fatherhood; that part of being a good man means being a good father; and that America needs more good men (*Kansas City Star*, 18 June 1995).

According to Horn, the NFI aims to counter 'this sense that mother and father do the same thing' and foster a return to the 'ancient fatherly virtues' of breadwinning, teaching and discipline (*Guardian*, 20 June 1994). As Agger commented, about a similar proposition in a standard sociology text which criticised female-headed families on the grounds that a father 'is more effective at commanding obedience than a mother' (Light & Keller 1985: 348):

> To conclude that the family needs men because men are the most appropriate leaders and role models would simply be zany if it were not so perverse. Women do not command obedience because they do not enjoy the status and charisma accompanying power; let a woman run the family, and she quickly becomes as prepotent and as likely to 'command obedience' as the absent father (Agger 1989: 259).

Domesticating Men through Fatherhood

This chapter has described dominant trends in the literature about New Fathers, including the research and advice literature, personal accounts of fatherhood, expert commentary and the mass media. There are exceptions to the trends. For example, although most personal accounts of New Fatherhood focus almost exclusively on the joys of involvement, more realistic accounts do appear:

> As I became familiar with diaper rash and fits of colic and finger food and water play, I would learn to get out of bed like a robot ... In caring for a child, I would see, there is no woman's work and no man's work. There is just work, and responsibility, and bad hours, and small rewards that appear like sudden snowflakes and then quickly go glimmering by (Clary 1982; quoted in Astrachan 1988: 214).

After reams of positive hype about fatherhood this comes like a breath of fresh air, echoing my own experiences caring for children. So too does the following unromantic account of an afternoon in the park with a two-year-old daughter:

> We go for a walk, to do something different. I have a plan that stretches out the different amusements of the park to last the afternoon. Play on the grass. Read. The swings. Look at the animals. I am out of key with myself this afternoon. I am lonely. I am just trying to get through. I feel bad about this. I wish I was more 'there' for Corey. I don't want her to feel I'm pulling away. But I do feel underutilised. I want someone to talk to (Morrison 1991: 105).

Such passages show complex and ambiguous responses, very much like those reported by mothers (e.g. Fallows 1985), but they are all too rare.

In general New Father texts are curiously deficient in providing the kind of detailed information necessary for anyone who expects to be, at least some of the time, fully responsible for childcare – even though hands-on involvement is ceaselessly stressed. In this they resemble the texts constructing the domestic New Man, which are similarly short of practical information. Again, there are exceptions. One was the Australian *A Practical Guide for Fathers* (Russell 1983b), which discussed matters such as feeding babies and toddlers, and techniques for minimising the resulting mess, revealing hard-won personal knowledge of the nitty-gritty of childcare. A minority of New Father texts do argue for straightfoward equity in the work of childcare (e.g. Russell 1983b; Colman & Colman 1988), sometimes linked to issues of social justice for women. Bradman's (1985) advice text described how the author came to connect his political views and his domestic practices: 'To say I was a supporter of equal rights for women, and at the same time never to do any ironing, was a contradiction, and a hypocritical one at that ... I began to realise the vague guilt I was feeling was a lot to do with that contradiction, and began to take steps to do something about it.' However, he still felt free to say that 'a little willingness, a little volunteering goes a long, long way in a relationship'.

While women's interests are not prominent in New Father discourse, those of men and children are. The following passage unproblematically put men's interests ahead of those of women: 'Father must be encouraged to spend some of his time working and playing within the family setting. Not primarily to ease mother's burdens, but to construct a place for himself, to ensure that he is seen to be needed' (Green 1976: 201). Even more explicitly, one psychological study encouraged men to participate in childcare not 'for the sake of social justice' but in order to take 'an important step in one's personal growth' (Hawkins et al. 1993). In most New Father texts, the interests of women are considered met if their husbands are sufficiently helpful, though in some texts even this limited notion of women's interests is absent; stress is placed instead on the interests of the children or the family as a whole.

In an analysis based on empirical studies of Italian family life, sociologist Chiara Saraceno argued that men seem to be re-enacting the birth of the modern family. Social historians of the family such as Ariès (1973) and Shorter (1976) documented the increasing significance of emotional life, mediated especially through the increased interest in children. Wealthy women experienced this most fully, as they had the necessary leisure to enjoy their children's company, while servants performed the domestic work and routine childcare. Saraceno concluded, from her observations of men's right to enjoy pleasurable times with children while remaining free from the obligations of routine childcare, that contemporary men were being incorporated into a similarly emotionalised relationship with their children, materially supported by the modern equivalent of the domestic servant: 'Today's men do not have servants to enable them to do this: they only have their wives. That is, men make this important discovery and carry out this appropriation of a previously prohibited dimension ... at the expense of their companions' (Saraceno 1987: 202).

Similarly, Segal (1990: xi) suggested that changes in fatherhood may allow men to have 'the best of both worlds', retaining power in the public sphere 'while having greater access to the satisfactions (often without the frustrations) of family life'. Both the empirical and the textual evidence suggest that this is a major tendency: sentimentality is the privilege of those who have a choice about involvement. A revealing instance occurred in a Father's Day article titled 'The New-Era Father is Becoming More Like His Mum': 'The new-era father is poised at that moment in history when he can taste the best of both worlds: a work life mostly uncompromised and uncomplicated by his status as father and a family life unshackled by the old, confining social roles' (*Sydney Morning Herald*, 28 August 1990). This makes sense only if we assume that the basic division of labour is intact. The point being made was not that men's lives increasingly resemble the lives of women, in having to juggle responsibility for childcare with the demands of employment. Rather, fathers are 'freer to be more like mothers' in that the New Father can, 'thanks mainly to the women's movement ... enjoy an intimacy with his children his own father never knew'. In fact, the text stated that men are 'freer to be more like mothers are meant to be', implying that men can be the true mothers, untroubled by the demands of juggling time.

However, another reading is possible. It is hardly likely that anyone can experience all the benefits and none of the frustrations of family life, especially someone who does little of the family work. New Father texts may be as much about desire as practice, as Judith Williamson (1988) suggested in her discussion of the imaginary resolutions of the tensions of fatherhood in New Father films. In 'Having Your Baby and Eating It', she suggested that films like *Three Men and a Baby* touched on deep tensions men felt about parenthood; a desire for perfection was evident, a desire to 'avoid conflict and choice through imaginary resolutions – indeed to "have it all"'. Such imaginary resolutions, she argued, typify the culture of consumerism, in which social contradictions such as those between employment and family life reduce to issues of 'what you can *have*' (emphasis in original). Suzanne Moore offered a similar argument about the resolution of tensions through fantasy in films about fatherhood in which 'designer dads cuddle babies at their convenience': 'Every father/child interaction is painted in glowing colours as though a few minutes with junior is enough to make up for all those nights spent working late. These fantasies, propelled by male guilt and female dissatisfaction, obscure the everyday hassle of childcare that so many of these designer dads are not around to see' (Moore 1990: 42).

So, while the diagnosis by writers such as Saraceno and Segal of the male appropriation of affectivity bears a clear relation to fathers' practices, it may be even more applicable in the textual representations of desire, with New Father texts constructing and encoding a narcissistic male desire to have it all – pleasure without guilt. Perhaps the most significant way in which the issue of equity in the division of labour has come onto the public agenda is that male guilt has become a little evident.

However, it would be naive to analyse New Father texts only in connection with men's desires. It is very likely that the principal readers are women: these and other texts on personal life purportedly addressed to men may have a largely female readership (Clarke-Stewart 1978). Father advice texts often include sections specifically addressed to women. If the generally domestic and sensitive New Man can appeal to women's fantasies, so too should the the nurturant sensitive New Father figure. Since the New Father is evidently an emotional being who loves his children, the deduction that he loves his wife equally and that he will remain a good father and husband, can be appealing. A magazine article which detailed one woman's experiences of her husband's resistance to sharing the domestic load concluded that, after all, love is enough:

> Even when in my own humble estimation my husband has fallen flat on his face our children never notice that Daddy has so much as stumbled. They do not care who folds the laundry, as long as it's in their drawers when they want it. They do not care who takes them to the doctor, as long as they get the medicine they need. And they are not angry with Daddy for being late; they are excited when they see him. Maybe my children are smarter than their mother. They love Daddy for what he does, not despite what he does not do (*Redbook*, June 1990).

A figure notably absent from the optimistic New Father texts is the bad father. The abusive, incestuous, violent father has been the subject of very different discourses. Accounts of participant fatherhood sometimes refer to the likelihood that increased contact with infant children will strengthen the incest taboo and so reduce the incidence of child sexual abuse, for example 'the male who is remote from his children has fantasies about them' (Kraemer 1995). In one way, at least, the bad father is a strong subtext in New Father accounts, in connection with the anxiety that a husband might have been (or might become) a bad husband and a bad father: 'Men, first of all, need to find their children satisfying, to be stabilised themselves by the demands of the generation who look to them for guidance ... Fatherhood supports the uncertain masculine ego and gives him a source of pride; it provokes him to use his energies by giving him a motive and harnesses them to socially useful goals' (Green 1976: 201–2).

A very broad cultural current is apparent. The idea that men are naturally wild and dangerous and that they must be tamed is deeply rooted. So too is the notion that women's role is to civilise men. The New Father is, at least partly, another stage in a long history of making men fit for civilisation, with women as the civilisers.

PART III

The Blocked Door

CHAPTER 6

Blocked-Door Theory: Misrecognising Resistance

The Puzzle

While many of those impressed by the logic of the revolving door emphasise the extent of change, others express surprise at the persistence of the sexual division of domestic work. In a society thought to be changing rapidly, the stability of household organisation can be seen as a 'major puzzle' (England & Farkas 1986). In this chapter I examine various ways in which the puzzle is said to be solved, through analyses of supposed obstacles to change. To search for obstacles is to abandon a sexual-political analysis at the outset. At best, obstacle analyses are 'empirically true, but theoretically false', as Saraceno described the supposed contradiction between motherhood and paid employment, and quite often they are empirically false as well.

Investigating obstacles to change does not mean adopting the kind of naively optimistic view of change seen in earlier chapters, but those puzzled by the lack of change mostly remain within the general framework of optimistic gradualism. To be profoundly puzzled about the matter is to assume that change is inevitable and is blocked only temporarily, though some writers have a foot in both camps – interpreting optimistically the evidence of small changes and at the same time arguing that obstacles are impeding the more rapid change which had been expected.

The position of puzzlement often involves a naive assumption about widespread social change, compared with which domestic work can be seen as a 'puzzling backwater' (Brines 1994: 652). Certainly the gendered social order has not been static, but general change is often exaggerated. According to the rhetoric of post-feminism, women have already made great advances. This makes it possible, for example, to portray men as confused, searching for a new identity in a world where all women 'speak proudly' with the new voice offered by feminism (Melbourne *Age*, 15 May 1993). More soberly, a father advice text spoke of men as lagging behind: 'Women have achieved a lot so far, and it's now time for men to start catching up with them' (Bradman 1985: 262). The rhetoric about male lag can rapidly become alarmist. Writing in *New Statesman and Society* (8 March 1996) Paul Lashmar claimed: 'In the 30-year war, men are in retreat. By the year 2000 there will be more women in employment than men. Women are performing better academically.'

To be fair, that article did note that some issues of equity for women, such as pay inequalities, remained – an understatement. The labour market remains strongly gender segmented, and women's success in education is hardly translating into dominance in the professions, politics or business. Having a job is not the same as having equality. All the same, although general change can be exaggerated, the idea that change in the division of domestic work is particularly slow is not unfounded. The best evidence is perhaps that women whose public lives resemble those of highly successful men are still usually responsible for domestic management and child-rearing. The predictions of revolving-door theory have not come true. To discuss the various attempts to rescue revolving-door theory by uncovering obstacles to change, I will extend Young and Willmott's metaphor and use the term 'blocked-door theory' as a convenient shorthand.

The failure of the door to fully revolve is not news to conservatives, who never endorsed the project of change. If women found it 'impossible to feel carnal desire' for SNAGs, 'weak, soft, limp [and] totally devoid of sex appeal' (Melbourne *Age*, 29 August 1992), no red-blooded man in his right mind would risk even putting his foot in the door. That organ of economic rationality, the *Economist* (18 May 1996), stated that the whole idea of the New Man was flawed. Men should stick to roles for which they were well equipped, 'killing mastodons, say'. The metaphor was a joke but the point was serious: the division of labour is part of the natural order. However, the article's conclusion was not just a triumphant 'we told you so'. It complained that the effect of the misguided New Man rhetoric had been to 'devalue men's traditional value to the family' as breadwinner, leading to a crisis of masculinity. A similar view was expressed by Ann Leslie in the *Daily Mail* (14 January 1995). Biological rhetoric again came in handy: 'They are not going to turn into nappy-washing New Men. Instead, their veins bursting with redundant testosterone, they're going to roam the estates, looting, pillaging and burning: they will become the 21st century's warriors without a cause.' 'They' are young males, disenfranchised from their traditional roles by unemployment and the rise of single mothers (hence the redundant testosterone), with no possibility for bread-winning and no one to win bread for. I will return to the notion of crisis masculinity later, but will not dwell further on the obvious fact that opponents of gender equity find no difficulty in citing obstacles to change in the division of domestic labour. My interest is in more progressive understandings, ways of re-imagining men in the context of a belief in (or at least the rhetoric of) gender equity.

Blaming Women

In a letter to the *New York Times* (25 November 1982), Bernice Okun of New Jersey expressed exasperation with women who were unhappy about the 'Jobs vs Baby' dilemma, which had been the subject of a feature article a week earlier:

> It is a paradox that women who achieve so much in their careers are fearful of asserting themselves in personal relationships (a throwback to the unliberated generation). There is concern about asking their men to share the domestic burden. In the same situation men are rarely reluctant to ask their wives to do chores for them or hire others. Many men are pleased and more than willing to participate in childcare and look forward to parenting. Most men in their 30s are not reluctant to be involved (it is the woman who is reluctant to ask) ... Women should realise that a relationship must be a two-way street.

One of the most surprising aspects of blocked-door theory is the relatively common tendency to suggest women are the key obstacles to change. While women are the stated object of these critiques, much is also revealed about the way men are understood. For example, men may be constructed as beyond criticism, so that any tendency to criticise them proves women's obstructiveness. Thus women who criticise their husbands for, say, 'playing too rough, for dressing the kids funny' (*Parents* magazine, June 1991) are part of the problem. Evidently, the father's way is beyond reproach. As we saw in Chapter 1, most helpful husbands receive considerable praise from wives and other women. Such praise is not fulsome enough for commentators such as Arndt: 'The helpful husband often finds himself surrounded by critical women ready to jump on his every mistake ... greater effort is needed to make them more welcome – lest that comfy chair continue to beckon' (*Australian*, 27 September 1989). That 'comfy chair' itself acknow-ledges men's interest in leisure, but in a naturalised 'boys will be boys' fashion.

Some arguments are breathtaking in their obfuscation of the issues. Responding to the release of yet another survey which pointed out the persistence of women's double burden and men's greater leisure, a leading article in the *Independent* (21 December 1993) suggested that women need to understand what men, being more 'culturally attuned to the distinction of work and leisure', already 'wisely' know – that the household should be viewed as a place of leisure as well as work. Some commentators are simply exasperated with women for failing to produce a revolution. In *Our Treacherous Hearts* (1992) Rosalind Coward concluded from her interviews that women are 'scared of a fundamental confrontation with men'. Many women have given up challenging their partners since 'they seem to be afraid that asking men to change will involve losing men's love and support'. However, her interviewees may have been right. A letter-writer to the *Guardian* (18 April 1996) made the inevitable reply:

> Emboldened by Ros Coward's book ... I sought to persuade my partner to do more. His eventual response was that the stress of juggling work and home was what 'we feminists' wanted: it was my problem not his. Reader, I left and became a single parent ... I want men to join women in juggling work and home ... Can Ros Coward please focus on why so few men feel able or willing to do so?

Searching Coward's book for an answer to that question, we find that it is taken for granted that men will not change unless confronted. Radical critics of male exploitation of women would agree – but this does not make everyone who expects men to resist change a radical critic of male exploitation. Coward constructed men's resistance as natural, rather than an active maintenance of a privileged position, while at the same time stressing women's agency. In effect, it is women who are said to maintain the status quo:

> It goes without saying that men, if women do let them get away with it, will ... provide too little childcare, working ridiculous hours, taking too little responsibility for their homes ... Women have let men get away with it. When it came to the crunch, most made it clear they didn't want conflict with men. Rather than have conflict, which they saw as a symptom of disturbed and angry people, they would prefer to keep the traditional structures of masculinity and femininity intact, even if it meant not coming to terms with themselves, even if it meant burying aspects of themselves in men and in children, even if it meant harder work and more pressures for women (Coward 1992: 147).

This amounts to blaming the person in the weaker position. A similar view was adopted by sociologist Pepper Schwartz when she also took for granted men's resistance, and placed much of the responsibility for the lack of change on women 'wimping out':

> Women often don't ask, they don't expect, and I think that's part of the blame we have to take on. Men are selfish. They're looking for a way to get out of yukky stuff, so men have been, I think, appropriately criticised for their lack of contribution, but I also think women have to stop wimping out and say 'Hey', you know, 'this is a marriage and here's your part of the deal' (CNN TV News, 31 July 1994).

Apparently, men just need to be told the new rules.

Probably the most common argument I am told by men trying to explain the sexual division of labour is that women have an excess of domestic power and refuse to cede it to men. The rhetoric of female territoriality and male exclusion is common: Richard Seel, author of *The Uncertain Father*, told the *San Francisco Examiner* (28 January 1992) that 'new mothers can be very territorial and working mothers are probably worse. They offer crumbs from a table of riches'. Shirley Fader (*Working Woman*, December 1985) claimed that 15 years of interviews with women had forced her to give up the idea that men were standing in the way of change: instead, 'to ease her Superwoman overload, she must give up total control and permit him to be an equal partner'. In a particularly misogynist article Anne Smith (*Sunday Times*, 25 October 1992) argued that some women want their husbands to be mere domestic servants once the children arrive: 'If women were honest, they would admit their territorial attitude to their children, and the effect this has on their men, whom they sometimes seem to wish to transform from lover to butler as soon as the doors of the maternity ward close behind them.'

The argument that women exclude men from full and equal participation in the work of the household sits very badly with the evidence of women's widespread desire for greater male participation and of men's resistance, outlined in Chapter 1. Male exclusion undoubtedly occurs but it is hardly the dominant trend, especially in marriages where wives are employed outside the home. If some women do appear to be territorial about some aspects of their domestic work, this needs to be understood more broadly. In an interview in *Ladies Home Journal* (July 1984), sociologist Sarah Fenstermaker Berk explained that some women were reluctant to give up the authority that came from being in charge of the house: 'there's a measure of control in determining what the family will eat or in ordering them "Stay off my clean floor" ... some men claim that when they try to pitch in, women will stand over them and criticise. So they stop doing it.' However, to someone responsible for cleaning the floor, a dirty floor means more work. To try to keep control is really just to be efficient. This applies in all divisions of labour:

consider a secretary becoming annoyed when the boss muddles up the files. Like all jobs, the job of housework requires a degree of territorial behaviour.

Another important point is that what seems like territoriality may be resistance to the extension of male privilege. Fatherhood provides a clear example. Fatherhood involves a greater proportion of play and leisure-like interaction than does motherhood, though this does not stop women being chastised for monopolising 'all the good stuff of parenthood while delegating the dirty work to their husbands' (*Parents* magazine, June 1991). As Saraceno (1987: 202) has argued, it would not be surprising if some women felt themselves 'once again the losers' if the playful and joyous dimensions of maternity – severely limited by other domestic duties – are appropriated by their husbands, 'freely chosen, freely given, free from domestic schedules'. Thus women may resist losing their monopoly on affectivity, not wanting to be left with only 'the monopoly of domestic toil, material problems, boring and non-gratifying routine work, including the work of using services external to the family'.

Territoriality about children is one area where women appear to resist change. Another area concerns the issue of domestic standards, a constant source of humorous puzzlement: 'I tell my husband "This room needs dusting" and he says "What dust?" He doesn't have a clue' (*San Francisco Examiner*, 10 March 1994). For men, the belief that women's standards are excessive provides a very common self-justification. Wrapping up a relatively hard-hitting report on Hochschild's study on the American TV show *20/20* (ABC TV, 1 November 1991), reporter John Stossel and anchor Barbara Walters staged a short humorous battle of the sexes. It is worth quoting at length:

> Stossel: But I think part of the problem is that some of you women expect too much … why make the beds every day, why vacuum once a week?
> Walters: Why not eat right out of the can, right?
> Stossel: Why not? You can eat canned peaches and stuff right out of the can.
> Walters: So, so, okay. So, then you don't make the bed, you don't set the table, you don't make dinner. The husband comes home and says 'You lazy slob, I'm divorcing you.'
> Stossel: The husband, in most cases, he doesn't mind. He doesn't want all these fancy things.
> Walters: Like a clean bed? That's fancy?
> Stossel: Clean bed, but why have a made bed?
> Walters: I'm going to call – Hello, Mrs Stossel?
> Stossel: Well, she thinks I'm a cretin for feeling this way. But when you're pressed for time why do all these things?

Walters: I – You floor me. [To co-host Hugh Downs] Hugh?
Downs: Ruth [his wife], if you left the dishes I'll do them when I get home.
We'll be right back.
[Commercial break]

Even qualitative sociological studies rarely achieve such richness. Among other things, Stossel's rhetoric constructs men's supposedly lower standards as an instance of male rationality. Male tolerance can also be constructed as evidence of tough masculinity. A *Psychology Today* (December 1988) article explained that women are 'weak when it comes to resist the urge to order, straighten and polish. Men are stronger than dirt. It is women's weakness, not men's, that gives rise to the imbalance in the household chores account'. The article was headlined 'humour', but unlike the average humorous piece it relied on the academic literature for its key point, using a quantitative study by Benin and Agostinelli (1988) which found that although men said they were in favour of an equitable division of domestic labour, they did not want to spend much time actually doing any work. Taking at face value men's stated opinion about equity, the authors hypothesised that the apparent contradiction could be the result of a difference in standards: 'Husbands want equality, but they don't want to spend a lot of hours on family work. This suggests that they may desire lower standards of house-keeping than their wives.' *Psychology Today* took its cue from there.

Interestingly, despite the ubiquitous rhetoric of sex differences in domestic standards, little research data is available. A recent valuable study by Bittman and Pixley (1997) aimed to test the view that men have lower expectations of housework, with a series of survey questions about the preferred standard, timing and frequency of performance of a range of tasks. Their data did show small sex differences in some cases, but overall they concluded that both sexes had very high expectations. For example, over 75 per cent of both men and women believed beds should be made daily, that at least one meal should be fresh and home-cooked each day, and that the laundry, the vacuuming and the cleaning of bathrooms should be done at least weekly. Less than 3 per cent thought washing-up should be left undone overnight and, despite men's particular reluctance to iron, men shared women's high ironing standards. Finally, the ranking of the urgency of domestic tasks was very similar between the sexes. The most significant difference was that women were more concerned than men about the cleaning of bath-rooms and refrigerators.

Further highly suggestive evidence was presented by Luxton, who found that the standards of some men appeared to vary according to the presence or absence of a wife: disorder could be tolerated in her absence but not in her presence. As one of the female respondents put it: 'When my husband is on his own, he is happy to live in a pigsty. Mess doesn't bother him. But the minute I get back he insists he can't live in the house unless it's spotless' (Luxton 1983: 34). This calls into question an assumption which underlies much of the debate about standards, namely that individuals assess domestic work using a set standard, and thus have a fixed tolerance for a particular level of domestic disorder. However, it is not just the satisfactory completion of a given task which determines the meaning, the significance and the degree of satisfaction. The context is also important. Perhaps it is the most important aspect, especially the context of who performs the task and under what conditions. To extend Delphy and Leonard's example, discussed in Chapter 2: a fresh home-cooked meal is not just a fresh home-cooked meal – a meal prepared by and for yourself is not like one which is prepared and served by someone else for you, with love, attention to your preferences, anticipation of your unexpressed desires and some ceremony which confirms the loving interpersonal relations of cook/waiter and diner.

This brings us back to the the task/job distinction: a household is not just a place where certain tasks are done. The tasks are done in certain relations of production, and confirm those relations through their performance. In particular, task performance by a wife confirms that the tasks are her job. A clean house is not just a clean house; it is a house cleaned by a particular person in a particular social situation, a particular relation of production. A man who tolerates a pigsty in his wife's absence would not necessarily tolerate the pigsty that would occur if his wife were present but refusing to clean the house. The former requires him to tolerate his own slovenliness; the latter to tolerate a political strike. His masculine privilege is not called into question by his own mess, but it is called into question if the mess can be construed as his wife's responsibility.

Society Resists

Writers baffled by the lack of change can make remarkably vague observations. We hear that men are simply 'not aware' of the 'revolution in gender roles' which has been going on for two decades (*Ladies Home Journal*, August 1990), or that they just have 'not adapted' to change, using rhetoric which simultaneously affirms belief in change and concedes the lack of it (Melbourne *Age*, 8 January 1998). This language is not used only by journalists. The family expert Edgar explained that blocked change is caused by men's failure to 'adjust to reality' (ABC radio [Australia], 8 May 1992).

One way of making this plausible is to argue that change is always slow. To many it is self-evident that traditions are hard to break, and studies which show the failure of revolving-door models often have titles such as 'A Residue of Tradition' (Berardo et al. 1987). Hochschild's explanation of the stalled revolution was that men have not 'adjusted themselves to this new reality' (in *Washington Post*, 4 June 1989), and that 'changes this deep take time' (*Chicago Tribune*, 1 November 1992). Likewise, Levine explained that increased father participation in child-care is a 'not a revolution, but an evolution', since 'the sense of duty dawns slowly' (*St Louis Post-Dispatch*, 27 January 1992). According to Gershuny's lagged-adaptation thesis (1992), each new generation can differ only slightly from its predecessors. The overall effect of such arguments is to naturalise the view that change is inevitably slow. This is wrong: there is no law of slow social change. Change, including gendered change, has often been rapid, sometimes beyond all pre-dictions. The rapid growth in dual-career middle-class marriages is one example, and others were mentioned in Chapter 1. Some traditions collapse almost overnight.

In a related move, blocked-door theory often posits society itself as the obstacle to change. Psychologist Lucia Gilbert, author of a book on men in dual-career marriages, explained in an interview that 'Society doesn't help at all because it's so hard for societal change to occur' (*Dallas Times Herald*, 13 January 1986). Similarly, Edgar pointed the finger at 'a society that is too rigid for the realities of modern family life' so that 'men are dragging behind because social conditions have not altered enough to affect them' (Melbourne *Herald-Sun*, 17 July 1992). A common variation on the theme of society as obstacle is attributing resistance to the population at large. According to James Levine, director of the Fatherhood Project: '[Men] still want to be providers, the economic and physical protector of their families. That's how men feel at a gut level, and it's what women expect. We all buy into it' (*Boston Globe*, 16 June 1991).

Accordingly, it is often said that both partners in a marriage collude to maintain the division of labour. For example, struck by the ways in which men and women justify their household arrangements and their (manifestly incorrect) belief that domestic work is shared, researchers may argue that through such practices couples 'impede progress towards any real change' (Backett 1987: 87), or speak of 'covert contracts' by which the sexual division of labour is maintained (Smith & Reid 1986: 402), with most people simply not being interested in equality, merely paying it 'lip service' (Brannen & Moss 1987: 141). Media accounts of Hochschild's research emphasised aspects of her work which could be read in terms of the joint responsibility of men and women for the division of labour, with each sex following 'gender strategies that pre-vent progress', through, for example, maintenance of the belief that domestic work is fairly shared (*Time Australia*, 7 August 1989).

To speak of joint activities is to obscure relations between husbands and wives. The view that married couples collude to inhibit change towards the symmetrical family is hardly consistent with the evidence in Chapter 1 that the division of labour is a site of conflict between men and women, with many women experiencing considerable dissatisfaction and engaging in various forms of largely unsuccessful struggle, while many men exhibit satisfaction with the division of labour and resist change in a variety of ways. While undoubtedly many men and women do justify their domestic arrangements in various ways, two very different subject positions are involved. Both wives' and husbands' justifications are designed to explain the low levels of participation in domestic work by husbands; women justify their husbands and men justify themselves. In the latter case, men's acts of self-justification often amount to a strategy of resisting more domestic work. In the former case, women's justification of their husbands often involves the rationalisation of inequality. Such rationalisations are only partially successful. Bittman and Lovejoy (1993), whose female respondents had affirmed the fairness of their household organisation, observed that: 'major cracks in the wives' presentation of self were seen in the inability to maintain a plausible impression of harmony and unity ... Powerful feelings of unacknowledged toil, of unequal exchanges, of less than total resignation kept poking holes in the wives' careful presentation of un-rehearsed family harmony'. Indeed, maintaining a plausible impression of family harmony is itself a form of emotional domestic work, and is disproportionately performed by women.

To argue that society, or the population as a whole, acts to obstruct expected change is exceptionally vague, amounting to little more than a description of a static situation. Such arguments overlook questions of human history and human agency, and the operations of power. Who is doing what, and to what end? How did it happen that these actions and motives are possible? What is the source of the power which renders social action effective? After all, some traditions are swept away, not everyone conforms to their conditioning, society isn't just 'like' any one thing, conflict is endemic, stable situations arise only if the status quo is actively and successfully reproduced by people motivated to do so, change is always the result of conflicting actions by various groups. Society is the setting for social life, not the power behind social life. Explanations of social life based on 'society' are tautological, just as much as explanations of biological phenomena in terms of the 'nature of biology' would be.

'Doing Gender'

A new variation on the idea that it is the population at large which resists gender change has gained considerable credibility within the social sciences. Significant studies include Berk (1985); West and Zimmerman (1987); Fenstermaker et al. (1991); Shelton and John (1993, 1996); Brines (1994); South and Spitze (1994); West and Fenstermaker (1995); John and Shelton (1997); and Tichenor (1997). This new gender model provides a good example of the way in which mainstream sociology can reproduce uncritical common sense as theory. Some details are necessary to put the new perspective in context.

In her large quantitative study *The Gender Factory* (1985), Sarah Fenstermaker Berk (later known as Fenstermaker) produced devastating evidence of the failure of revolving-door models, some of which I relied on in Chapter 1. Unlike many other quantitative sociologists, she did not try to extract every least bit of evidence of change from the data in order to support revolving-door models. On the contrary, she remarked upon the 'astounding stability' of the division of labour, and stressed that the clear presumption that women were responsible for domestic work explained the consistent asymmetry in the division of labour. *The Gender Factory* was framed in the language of the economic theory of efficient resource allocation, particularly the ideas of the school of New Home Economics, articulated by Nobel Prize winner Gary Becker in *The Economic Approach to Human Behaviour* (1976). Fenstermaker Berk's principal conclusion was that no plausible assumptions about the efficient allocation of resources within the household could explain how human effort was applied to the production of household goods and services. For example, Fenstermaker Berk challenged any economically inclined theorist who might try to rescue the model with a last-minute proposal that women were simply more efficent producers of domestic goods and services than men; this would be 'rampant ad-hocery'. To try in such a way to show that the division of labour was a rational allocation of effort would require that 'even dead on their feet, wives are more productive in the household than husbands'. Putting it equally forcefully, Bittman observed that rational allocation models could be saved only if it could be shown, for example, that it took a man six minutes to boil an egg that a woman could boil in three minutes (Bittman 1991: 13).

The obvious conclusion might appear to be that economic models simply are not applicable, the household being not an efficient business but a hierarchical political system. However, while Fenstermaker Berk did observe that men benefit directly by appropriating women's labour, she did not abandon the economic model. Rather, she argued that it had not been applied with enough imagination. This move ranks with the collapse of the domestic labour debate as a key moment in the retreat from the possibility of a materialist analysis in terms of men's interests. There are important similarities, which will be discussed later.

Fenstermaker Berk criticised studies by household economists that assumed that what is produced is simply goods and services. They ought to have seen that something else – gender itself – is produced. This is not a material but a symbolic product, with a rich range of meanings including dominance and submission: 'Simultaneously household members "do" gender, as they "do" housework and childcare, and what I have been calling the division of household labour provides for the joint production of household labor and gender; it is the mechanism by which both the material and symbolic products of the household are realised' (1985: 201). 'In households where the appropriation of another's labour is possible ... the expression of work and the expression of gender (dominance and subordination) are inseparable' (1985: 204).

What are we to make of this theorisation of gender as a product? Is it a powerful way of radicalising liberal economic theory by forcing it to acknowledge that people are busy producing not only goods and services but also symbolic goods expressive of domination and subordination? Or is it to mask inequality in the cloak of a symbolic household product?

Fenstermaker Berk relied on the sociological tradition of symbolic interaction, which placed great weight on the relation between social actions and their reception by the wider audience of observers. Through interaction between actor and audience meanings are produced, thus all human interaction is a process of symbolic production. Goffman's (1977) notion of gender as an ongoing accomplishment in which actors continually have their masculine or feminine status reaffirmed was crucial to Fenstermaker Berk's analysis. So was the refinement by West and Zimmerman (1987), who argued that gender display is a 'stance towards the conventions' of gender, through which we render ourselves 'accountably masculine or feminine' by producing 'configurations of behaviour which can be seen by others as normative gender behaviour'.

About the specific content of gender accountability, West and Zimmerman said 'it may be that the primary category-bound activities are, for men and women respectively, dominance and submission'. This is a very coy way of speaking about dominance and submission; they just happen to be the relevant gender categories. The task for everyone who wishes to be gender-accountable is, for West and Zimmerman, to 'devise out of the stuff of mundane interplay situationally responsive means of doing dominance and submission'. Accordingly, what might seem to be irrational in the division of labour is actually rational – gender as well as housework is being produced, and as a whole the arrangements optimise the joint production of the two goods.

The political ramifications are clear. The analysis does mask in-equality. Consider the scenario I used in Chapter 1, of the husband watching TV and drinking beer while his wife cooks and manages the children, both tired after their day in the labour market. According to the 'doing gender' model, two people are devising out of mundane materials situationally appropriate performances which express the norms of gender behaviour. In other words, we see a man acting dominant as a man should and a woman acting submissive as a woman should. Dominance and submission happen to be the primary category-bound activities with which to express gender, but they could easily have been something else, according to the analysis. Power does not exist in the model. If dominance and submission are to be understood as per-formances to achieve gender accountability, we have no way of thinking that one performer in the duet may be in a position to exercise power over the other. A change of scene may help. The person watching TV and drinking is a white female; the person cooking is a black female in a maid's uniform. Is this also to be thought of as the 'doing' of dominance and submission, which happen to be the primary category-bound activities with which to express race?

In such a framework we can conduct quite rich empirical investi-gations, and I relied on evidence from such studies earlier. Every aspect of gendered practices could be brought into this framework, though it would have some difficulty with dealing with evidence of conflict or variation. Moreover – and significantly – the analysis may well corres-pond with the justifications and explanations people often use for their practices, along lines such as 'well, that's what men do' or 'doing it makes me feel like a woman'. But as social theory it has given up right at the start, given up any attempt to grasp the wider significance of gendered practices. Why, for example, are dominance and submission the primary signifiers of gender? Might this not result from the male power to enforce such definitions? Questions like this are outside the frame of the model. Where power is recognised it is considered only a side effect of doing gender, as one exponent of the model recently put it in a paper titled 'Marital Power Dynamics as a By-Product of Doing Gender' (Tichenor 1997).

The ability of the gender display model to explain away inequity is quite remarkable. In Chapter 1 I relied partly on the data of South and Spitze (1994) to illustrate the net drain effect. On separation from her husband, a woman's domestic workload (including childcare) decreases, thus husbands are net consumers of domestic production, their domestic work not even matching the work created by their presence. South and Spitze did not, however, conclude that marriage is a site of labour exploitation or hierarchical gender relations. Rather, they saw marriage as the site of a 'symbolic enactment of gender relations'. This amounted to the claim that what we see is not material domination and subordination but their symbolic enactment. In other words, the tired bodies of women are not really being exploited, they are just bearers of coded messages of subordination. Accordingly, South and Spitze's explanation of the lower workload of a husbandless woman is not the straightforward and political point that there is less work to do because the husband's needs no longer need to be considered. They held that when no man is present there is no one available to display love for or subordination to; the necessary audience is missing.

Similarly, Shelton and John (1993) concluded from their carefully controlled quantitative comparison of different household types that the situation of married women is unique. It is the presence of a husband (not just a cohabiting male partner) which is the key determinant of married women's high domestic workloads. This is consistent with the feminist materialist analysis of marriage, but the authors saw it otherwise, as supporting West and Zimmerman's view that gender is produced in social situations. Thus, they held, the status of 'wife' is produced through household labour. The assumption was that that is just what marriage is like.

Most revealing of all is the treatment of the kind of quantitative evidence which I have discussed in terms of male resistance. As Chapters 1 and 3 showed, the most glaring failure of revolving-door models is that husbands do not perform significantly more domestic work when their wives are employed or when they are unemployed themselves. The gender display model is well aware of this, indeed it developed largely in response to the failure of revolving-door models, as we have seen in the case of *The Gender Factory* (see Shelton & John 1996; South & Spitze 1994). But men's failure to behave equitably is not seen as resistance by those with the power to resist. Rather, it is another case of doing gender. The term 'resistance' may be used, but only in a formal sense. For example, Brines (1994) presented quantitative evidence that unemployed husbands do no more housework than do employed husbands, perhaps even a little less. Although she described this in terms of resistance to housework, the resistance was not viewed politically. The striking failure of unemployed husbands to spend even a portion of their available time on increased housework was viewed as a heightened performance of gender in circumstances where the usual breadwinner avenue for the performance of masculinity was blocked.

The gender display model relies on shared values, on norms and expectations about what counts as an appropriate gendered performance. It has nothing to say about the ways in which norms are produced. By treating norms as a given, a kind of external input to the model, all it can do is point to ways in which behaviour is said to reflect norms. This can become circular – we discover what norms are by watching behaviour, and then discover that behaviour reflects norms. In this and other ways the model has strong affinities with models of gender which dominated earlier in the history of mainstream sociology, models which manage to renew themselves despite having been subjected to devastating theoretical critiques. The following critique relies on the extended analysis of Connell (e.g. 1997).

The most significant case is the sociology of sex-roles. The 'male sex-role' was indispensable to most analyses of men from the 1950s to the 1970s, and appeared capable of explaining almost anything – and thus nothing – about men. The male role was a collage of supposed norms, attitudes, practices, values and ideals connected with men. *Relations* between the sexes were anaesthetised as *differences* between roles, as if it so happens that his role is to be assertive and hers to be submissive. That thinking power is impossible in this framework is clear if we try to employ the language of role in a situation where power is impossible to ignore. Do we understand imperialism as the result of colonised and coloniser following a 'black role' and a 'white role'?

The gender display model is a revived form of role theory combined with a contemporary emphasis on the realm of the symbolic, in broad alignment with writers in a much more radical tradition. As shown in Chapter 2, the domestic labour debate was discussed along Marxist lines. When it proved impossible to show that capitalism benefited from the domestic division of labour, the materialist analysis could have turned its attention to men. Instead, attention turned to the realm of the symbolic, refashioning the Marxist analyses of the ideological reproduction of capitalism to fit the world of gender, which was primarily seen as a symbolic world. Thinking economically about the family was abandoned in favour of seeing it as the site of 'ideological processes and the familial construction of gendered subjects', to repeat a key passage from Barrett (1980: 173). In other words, theorising about a household economy was replaced by theorising about a symbolic order.

Fenstermaker Berk and her colleagues followed a very different tradition, the theoretical economic analysis of efficient resource allocation, grounded in analyses of the operations of individual capitalist enterprises. They held that the data simply could not be explained by the orthodox assumptions of the school of New Home Economics. The move replicated, at the level of mainstream social theory, the move advocated by Barrett and others within the radical tradition. Where Barrett and others had argued for the abandonment of economic theorising in favour of theorising the symbolic domain, Fenstermaker

Berk and others argued that economic theory had to incorporate the symbolic. The overall effect was not all that different. Where Barrett had proposed that the family was the site of the production of gendered subjects, Fenstermaker Berk argued that it was the site of the production of gender. The difference was that Barrett abandoned economic theory, whereas Fenstermaker Berk remained within it.

Both approaches ignored the possibility of analysing men's interests. The Marxist economic theory which Barrett rejected was grounded in the analysis of exploitation, and so to retain it would be to risk discovering men were exploiters. The liberal economic theory Fenstermaker Berk continued to embrace was framed so as to deny the possibility of exploitation, and so could be harmlessly applied to the practices of men.

No Choice: The Male Model of Work

Holding that the revolving door is blocked by vague entities such as society or gender means remaining at the level of general description. Such approaches cannot ask why society or gender takes the form that it does. Where specifically should advocates of change focus their activities? Another kind of sociological approach promises to be much less vague. Analyses of social structures, which examine specific social-structural obstacles and their interrelation, should make it possible to identify the key obstacles to change and thus identify the most effective sites for action for change. To be fair, this is what some of the discourse about 'society' means, the term being used to indicate large-scale social phenomena, such as this jumble of structures, policies and attitudes: 'Society is equally responsible for the lack of male participation at home. The stringent demands of the workplace, the government's refusal to back pro-family legislation, and the pervasive attitude that domestic work is not "real work" help keep family roles rigid' (*Mothering*, 22 September 1993).

The structural obstacle to men's performance of domestic work which is most often cited is the structure of the labour market – 'work', to use the common (misleading) term. The rhetorical progress of the male model of work is very revealing. The model was first developed by feminists concerned with women's labour market disadvantages, who argued that male holders of privileged labour market positions relied on full-time wives to take care of them and of other family responsibilities. However, slowly the model has come to be thought of as also, or even mainly, a constraint on men. Men are said to be frustrated by the limited roles available to them, compared with women's 'multiple options' (*Time*, 1 October 1990). The plaintive lines in the 1989 film

Parenthood were widely quoted as summing up the plight of fathers: 'This is the difference between men and women. Women have choices. Men have jobs.' Until work structures change, 'no matter how much men want to assume a bigger role in childcare and homemaking' they will be unable to do so (Edgar & Glezer 1992: 39). The time demands of men's jobs are 'the big issue ... women take the burden of caring because their men are working long hours' (Melbourne *Age*, 14 January 1983). This is an article of faith for many commentators. The *Guardian* (10 November 1996) summed up a recent study on parenting in Britain with the claim that the main cause of the 'blight on family life' was men's increased working hours, even though the report had noted that fathers' time with children was not sensitive to their hours worked. Not only men in top jobs suffer: 'The majority of men (be they senior executives who do not leave the office until after 7 pm, or men on shift work) are excluded from the caring work of home and family life' (Weeks & Batten 1991: 43). Similar rhetoric about men's exclusion appeared in the *Scotsman* (23 April 1996): 'Fathers generally come home too late even to put the children to bed. At the weekend the knackered breadwinners stagger back into the bosom of the family ... But fathers are realising that they have rights too, that they have been excluded from fulfilling the emotional contract with their children.'

The problems of men who attempt to overcome their exclusion are discussed in terms very similar to the problems of women. Fatherhood expert James Levine used the term 'daddy stress' to describe the experiences of men who have significant conflict between work and family (*Arizona Republic*, 30 March 1993). As well as Superwoman we now have Superman, Lucia Gilbert told a reporter: 'They're putting up a good front and trying to do it all, just like Superwoman' (*Dallas Times Herald*, 13 January 1986). The involved New Father has his own version of the double burden, engaging in 'a complicated balancing act between the demands of family and work' (Roeber 1987: 179). An article on the heavy psychological toll suffered by men in a time of change cited the opinions of a psychologist specialising in stress issues: men are 'still expected to go out and make a living, but they're also supposed to change the diapers, be more sensitive and more flexible'. The result is that men are frustrated because they cannot properly carry out all the roles expected of them (*Record*, 24 January 1994). The stresses of modern life can be constructed as more difficult for men than for women. One of David Cohen's interviewees observed: 'I just think that for men like myself who have opened the gates, balancing work and family life is bloody difficult ... I don't think society offers men alternatives. I'm not resentful, but I do think the pressures on men attempting to be a breadwinner and an involved father are greater than those on Gilda' (*Guardian*, 4 May 1996). Some New Father texts completely ignore women's double burden. The author of one father advice text who, as shown in Chapter 5, had offered men 24 hours a day of fatherly joy later explained that 'I can't allow myself the luxury of developing a 24 hour a day, seven day a week, commitment to Matt ... Martha, however, can.' The point was illustrated with a cartoon showing the harassed father, dressed for the office, being pulled in two directions by a baby and a pregnant wife in night attire, while wondering to himself 'Is there enough of me to go around?' (Sears 1988: 12, 157).

Earlier chapters discussed how men and the sexual division of domestic work most commonly featured on the public agenda in connection with fatherhood issues. As the examples above show, the discussion of structural obstacles to change follows this trend. This also generally holds true in public policy. The general sexual division of domestic labour has been the subject of some publicly funded campaigns, such as the 'halb-halb' (50-50) campaign in Austria in 1996, encouraging sharing domestic chores. Another recent Austrian initiative has become notorious. Under the old Austrian marriage law, one of the grounds for divorce was the wife's neglect of domestic duties. The relevant section was reworded to be gender-neutral, though commentators doubted that courts would grant a divorce to wives on the grounds of husbands' domestic inadequacies. The change resulted in a wave of jokes about 'housework police' peering through windows and children acting as paid informers (*Sunday Times*, 14 April 1996). Men around the world must have hoped the Austrian disease would not spread, given the way the issue was reported internationally as a new law under which 'Austrian men slow in performing their household chores' could be taken to court (*Chicago Tribune*, 7 February 1993).

However, the majority of significant policy initiatives have focused not on housework but on greater male involvement in childcare. For example, the concluding recommendations in *Fatherhood and Family Policy* (Lamb & Sagi 1983) proposed more flexible working hours, provision for paternity leave and changed attitudes to male employees with family responsibilities (see Pleck 1987 for a cross-national survey of policy debates). Often such initiatives are supported by arguments about the advantages for child development and the psychological benefits for men, along the lines noted in Chapter 5 (e.g. Edgar & Glezer 1992). The most widely implemented initiatives have been in the area of paternity leave. A common initiative is extending maternity leave provisions by adopting a gender-neutral regime of 'parental' leave. It is worth noting that much, though certainly not all, of the political pressure for change has come from women. Male unionists have been slow to support greater flexibility of male employment conditions to allow men to undertake family responsibilities (Deem 1987; Lake 1989; Wolcott 1990).

This is not the place to give a detailed account of policy implementation, which varies considerably, but I will note that Britain and America have some of the least liberal paternity leave provisions among Western industrialised countries. For example, although some company policies are more generous, all that American workers were guaranteed under 1993 law was 12 weeks of unpaid job-protected leave for the birth of a child, to be shared by the parents as they decide. Two years after the introduction of that right, a study by the National Institute of Mental Health found that most fathers missed work for five days or less, and only 1 per cent took three or more weeks leave (*Chicago Tribune*, 7 May 1995). From its interviews with new fathers, the study concluded that most families could not afford the loss in income and that the workplace culture socially stigmatised men who could be considered less than fully committed to their jobs. Colin Harrison, writing in the *New York Times* (31 August 1993), perpetuated the stigma even while regretting it: 'Men may not like this state of affairs, but it's so built into our understanding of things that we don't protest. Although I'm now a father twice over, I'm afraid I would secretly look upon a male co-worker who took a long paternal leave as someone who was less serious about his work. I'm not proud of this feeling, but there it is.' This was in an article broadly sympathetic to the value of paternity leave, in which Harrison described how he had been forced to take annual leave to be at home for two weeks after the birth of his first child, who was hospitalised twice in that time.

Even when income is less of an issue and major efforts have been made to remove the social stigma against paternity leave-takers, the take-up rate is low. Sweden legislated in 1974 to guarantee both parents a total of seven months shareable parental leave. Parents would receive 90 per cent of their regular salary and would return to work without loss of entitlement. Each parent was also entitled to 10 days sick leave on full pay at the time of birth (Lamb & Levine 1983). The provisions have been progressively increased; by 1994 fathers and mothers could share up to 13 months leave, after a maternity leave of four weeks (Hojgaard 1997). Despite nationwide advertising campaigns picturing macho sports heroes 'holding, feeding, and strolling with babies and exhorting other men to share the joys of parenthood' (Hwang 1987; Eveline 1994), few men have taken parental leave and the rate appears to have stabilised. Only about 14 per cent of parental leave days are taken by fathers, and those are concentrated in the recently implemented 'daddy days' on full pay which are taken by fathers straight after birth; 50 per cent of fathers take only these days (Haas 1993; *European*, 6 October 1994).

It is worth contrasting the modest effects of paternity leave policies with other policies. Differences between the domestic work and child-care of Australian and Finnish men are slight; if anything, Finnish men perform less domestic work than do Australian men (Bittman et al. 1992). Nevertheless, Finnish women's double burden is markedly less than that of Australian women. This does not result from greater help from Finnish husbands, nor is it attributable to liberal Finnish paternity leave, since the participation rate is low. The crucial difference is Finland's implementation of fully state-funded childcare, the provision of parental leave to mothers with full entitlement to return to employ-ment, and women's high level of participation in the full-time primary labour market. Policies directed at women appear to have a much greater effect on reducing the quantitative division of domestic labour than do policies directed at men, by reducing women's responsibilities for the sole care of their children.

In her general analysis of parental leave in Scandinavia, Lis Hojgaard (1997) argued that the policy rhetoric of gender-neutrality appears to include men but in fact represents the transformation of woman/mother to parent; the gender-neutral term covers the power relation-ship between the sexes. Since there was no compelling incentive for men to take parental leave, the partnership between men, labour market and state remained in effect, with fatherhood a 'fairly unaccept-able interruption' to working life. This meant that men who wished to spend more time on childcare had to find their own solution to the contradiction that official policy supports parental leave for men and most men complain about their lack of time with their families, but the male workplace culture encourages views such as the one expressed by one of Hojgaard's interviewees: 'Have you heard of a career man who took parental leave? That says something about the ones who do, doesn't it?'

What, then, of the argument that the nature of work is a major obstacle blocking the revolving door? Men's low take-up rate of parental leave could be seen as undermining the argument, since it seems that even when obstacles are removed men do not walk through the door. In reply it could be pointed out that changes, such as the right to parental leave, have had little effect on workplace culture. Perhaps the general culture of work, then, could be said to constitute the real obstacle, but it is misleading to speak of a culture of work without acknowledging that the culture is gendered. It is not the fact of being employed, even in a highly demanding job, which is the obstacle, but the fact of being an employed *male*. Many women manage to undertake demanding family and domestic responsibilities despite being highly placed in the labour market. There is some reason to believe that employment represents a greater practical obstacle to women's domestic work than it does to men's. Game and Pringle (1983) found that since women felt they might be criticised as being more concerned with family than with employment, in many cases they kept their work and home lives more separate than men did. The phenomenon of women having to outperform men to be judged as of comparable worth is well known. A survey by Bielby and Bielby (1988) found that women tend to put more effort into their paid employment than do men in comparable jobs, while also putting more effort into domestic responsibilities. With scientific detachment, perhaps intended ironically, the authors concluded: 'For women to work just as hard as men, if not harder, despite their greater household responsibilities, they must be able to draw on a reserve of energy that is either not available to the typical male or, more realistically, that men choose not to draw on.'

As I argued in Chapter 2, the public and private divisions of labour are mutually dependent and mutually reinforcing aspects of the overall sexual division of labour whereby women's labour is exploited for men's benefit, in both the labour market and the domestic sphere. To argue that the organisation of the public sphere blocks change in the domestic sphere, or vice versa, is to explain one part of a whole in terms of another. Men's dominance in the labour market requires the exploitation of women's domestic labour, and reinforces that exploitation through creating economic dependence in women. An aspect of that dominance is men's higher incomes, which can then be constructed as an obstacle to change: 'Whatever views the family members may hold about the naturalness of childcarers being women ... it will still be logical in the average working-class family for the man to be the primary breadwinner and the woman to be the childcarer on either a full-time or a part-time basis' (Curthoys 1988: 58).

It *is* logical, from the point of view of the particular household, but that does not mean that we should conclude that the structure of work is the key obstacle to change. Doing so assumes, first, that the interests of married women can be identified with the interests of the couple as a unit. Delphy and Leonard (1992: 97) remarked that those who speak of the rationality of such decisions, feminists included, 'avoid facing unpalatable facts' by attributing the family division of labour to external factors: 'They want to see marriage (or at least contemporary Western middle-class marriage) and cohabitation, and especially their own marriages (or living situations or heterosexual relations), as voluntary agreements arrived at between equal and complementary partners.' Second, it isolates the structure of employment from the organisation of the household. In effect, the rhetoric about labour market obstacles to men's greater domestic work claims that men's privileged position in the public sphere, based on the exploitation of women in both spheres, prevents them from reducing that exploitation in the private sphere.

Undoubtedly, from the perspective of a man wishing to devote more time to domestic activities of any kind, paid work is a constraining factor. But if what constrains him is simply having a job, women should be equally constrained from participation in household and family work. Moreover, if he occupies a privileged position in the labour market, with high demands on time and energy, the supposed constraint could instead be viewed as enabling both for him and for men collectively. The possibilities for bad faith are considerable. Speaking about his lack of time at home, a New York lawyer interviewed for an article about juggling career and fatherhood complained about his 12-hour working day and two-hour commute: 'It stinks. It's a constant pain. It's terrible for them. It's terrible for the family, terrible for me.' When asked why he continued in such a demanding job, he explained: 'Greed. I want to live in a certain kind of a neighbourhood and take my wife out to dinner ... a certain lack of imagination. This is the one way I know to make a living ... work is very satisfying. I must find it more pleasurable, less painful, to spend my time with my associates than my kids. Kids can wear you out' (*New York Times*, 13 April 1986).

According to the same article, millions of fathers are experiencing stress as they 'try to fulfil long-term career goals and satisfy new family demands'. I do not in the least intend to minimise the stresses and strains, indeed the suffering, which some men experience due to conflict between paid work and the demands of family life. The crucial point is, though, that men do not have a monopoly on suffering: men's stresses cannot explain the blocked door. Certainly men cannot have it all, as one investment banker who wanted to be a 'world-class player' in business and have a 'world-class home life' described his goal, now abandoned, in another interview in the same *New York Times* article. But to conclude that since men cannot have it all the demands of employment have priority, is to take for granted the very division of labour we are trying to explain – it amounts to taking for granted that men will not change unless no sacrifice is involved. A radical critic of gender relations would make the same assumption, but couch it in terms of the active pursuit of interest rather than in the obfuscatory terminology of 'obstacles'.

Any discussion of social factors which considers them only as constraints on social action is unsociological (Crook 1989). The widespread stress on structures and constraints in sociological accounts of the organisation of family life loses sight of power, male supremacy and agency (Delphy & Leonard 1992: 190). The organisation of the labour market is one structural obstacle which is proposed to explain the resilience of the division of domestic labour and other aspects of gender relations, but the critique can be generalised. Since almost any social phenomenon can be conceptualised in terms of social structures, the scope is immense. As David Morgan (1992: 40) observed, all the institutions of patriarchy can be the site of over-structural and over-socialised analyses of men's practices. He argued that accounts of the power and pervasiveness of the various institutions can reduce the question of men's agency in perpetuating the institutions to 'near zero', so that 'patriarchy is everywhere and nowhere'.

This does not mean that accounts of social structures are apolitical. The concept of social structure is indispensable in this study; structural analysis does not inevitably work against a political understanding in terms of interested practice. For example, Iris Young's (1984: 143) definition of (feminist) structural analysis recommended 'a structural analysis of relations of authority and dependence, and a description of the transfer and appropriation of benefits of labour', guided by the questions: 'which gender has access to what social resources as a result of performing its gender-differentiated activity, and what do the resources give members of the gender the capacity to do?' Not enough structural analyses are of this kind, though. All too often 'structure' is a code for social phenomena said to be external to the matter at hand. But as soon as a phenomenon is considered external, it moves beyond critical attention. Much of the talk about obstacles to change in men's domestic lives does just that.

Too Much Choice: Male Confusion

In apparent complete contrast with the argument that men lack choices, it is also claimed that men are deeply confused about the choices they face. Men are confused, subject to conflicting demands, role models and expectations and this supposedly explains men's inability or unwillingness to change, or at least the difficulties of doing so: 'Fathers' roles today are not so clear-cut. What sort of dad should I be to my children? What roles do I take in my family?' (Melbourne *Age*, 4 August 1996). 'In Britain in the 1950s, roles were clear-cut. The father went out, earned the salary, and came back, had a token play with the baby, and that was the end of it. Now it's not exactly clear what is expected' (*Sunday Times*, 31 December 1995).

Male confusion is spoken of both by those who are broadly sympathetic to change and by those who are more ambivalent. In a piece titled 'What Do Men Really Want?' (*Time*, 1 October 1990), Sam Allis explained men's anger and exhaustion:

> There is profound confusion over what it means to be a man today. Men have faced warping changes in role models since the women's movement drove the strong, stoic John Wayne type into the sunset. Replacing him was a new hero: the hollow-chested, sensitive New Age man who bawls at Kodak commercials and handles a diaper the way Magic Johnson does a basketball. Enter Alan Alda. But he, too, is becoming quickly outdated. As we begin the '90s, the zeitgeist has changed again. Now the sensitive male is a wimp and the object of derision.

Arnold Schwarzenegger was also mentioned. The article's language was overheated but its thrust was common. Three assumptions are generally made. One is that men really are unusually confused now. The second is that men in earlier times were not subject to similar conflicts – they were simply 'traditional'. Historical studies tell a different story. In earlier chapters I traced the evidence of historical variation in men's domestic practices and in ideals of fatherhood; images of general manhood have varied as well. For example, in early 20th-century Australia, two major models competed for men's allegiance: the 'family man' who was a good provider and handy round the house, and the 'real man' who engaged in 'drinking, gambling and whoring' (Gilding 1994: 107; see also Lake 1986a). The third assumption is usually unstated, but is necessary if the rhetoric is to be effective in justifying male defensiveness. This is that women are not subject to the same conflicts. I will not dwell on the perversity of this. The different views about the effects on children of 'stay-at-home' and 'working' mothers are one example of the intense contradictory pressures faced by women; another is the constant injunctions to be simultaneously sexily feminine and assertive.

A defensive joky rhetoric of male confusion is often resorted to by men to express exasperation with pressures to change. 'Eat the quiche. Don't eat the quiche. What is the 90s guy going to do?' moaned Sean Piccoli in the *Washington Times* (8 June 1993), in an article which hoped that the current sex wars could be resolved through compromises such as 'an acceptable balance' between 'sensitivity and the urge to whistle at women in their lunch hour'. The fact that competing images exist is enough for some to argue that men are in an impossible situation. In the *Guardian* (21 December 1997), novelist Fay Weldon spoke for young confused men. Her point appeared to be that no sensible response can be expected from men until society speaks with one voice:

> It is left to me to speak for men, it seems, while they get their act together. Young 90s men complain that they are in a hopeless double bind. They care desperately for the good opinion of women. They want nothing more than to live a domestic life. If they show sensitivity, strive to be New Men, they are despised as wimps. If they keep a stiff upper lip they are derided for their insensitivity.

Do the same women who despise wimps also deride stiff upper lips? Or is it just that young men are aware that anything they do could be criticised from some perspective? Weldon laid at the door of all young women the competing images of masculinity. More honest are accounts of New Men which make it clear that other men are the main problem. An article on men's difficulties with sharing childcare cited one father's 'most embarrassing moment': 'He was playing softball and his wife stopped by after work to find out whether he had fed the baby. "Hey mommy on second base", yelled the umpire, "did you feed your baby yet?" The otherwise easygoing Parisi told his wife never to ask that question in public again – "just feed the baby"' (*Forbes* magazine, 23 May 1983).

Not all commentators are alarmed by male confusion. Analyst Andrew Samuels told David Cohen (*Guardian*, 4 May 1996) that men should welcome choice, not in a 'panic-stricken way, but in a reflective way': 'We can admit that we don't know much about being a man. We have a chance to ask: is it simply power, orgasm and career success that we want? Or do we tear up the list and start again. It's a free-for-all. Everything's up in the air. Post-modern man is here.' In certain sectors there is a positive interest in promoting confusion, or 'choice', a term which sheds a positive light on having options. As Mort (1996) observed, confusion about the definition of the New Man was very welcome to industries such as fashion, which thrive on diversity. Rosie Boycott, editor of British *Esquire*, saw the commercial possibilities: 'I sense a lot of men out there are angry in the confusion of what to do. And this is where magazines come in' (Melbourne *Age*, 17 June 1992). An article titled 'The Brave New World of Men', which appeared in the marketing journal *American Demographics* (Crispell 1992), helped readers target various segments of the male consumer market. Citing market research for *GQ* magazine, the article explained that men know they have choices. Some welcome the choices and others fight them, but overall the situation of choice is healthy for men and the women in their lives – and for marketers, of course, as long as they remain aware that 'these two groups of men shop for different items, and they shop in different ways' (men who welcome choice are more likely to shop for their own clothes, for example). The simultaneous promotion of confusion and offer of resolution through consumption can reach ridiculous heights. A lift-out style guide for men declared: 'You may be confused about who you are, or who you ought to be. But be in no doubt about what you should be wearing and who you should be watching in the long hot months ahead. *Good Weekend* tells you, the modern male, how to come out of the shade and into the sun' (Melbourne *Age*, 29 August 1992). This appeared in a newspaper colour supplement titled 'Men in a Time

of Change: Who Are They Supposed to Be?' The leading article discussed social change in terms of masculine identity and imagery: 'The
issue many academics, social workers, counsellors and writers studying
contemporary masculinity are looking at is this: for centuries there has
been a clear image in society of what constitutes a Masculine man. What
is the image today?'

Once again we are face to face with difference. Gender convergence
is toyed with, but difference must be maintained. Richard Seals, author
of *The Uncertain Father*, complained that 'there is nothing distinctive any
more for fathers to do or be' (*Chicago Tribune*, 2 October 1994). So how
do we define 'manhood' when 'Today more men change diapers, and
more women work outside the home. American men are left
trying to redefine manhood' (*Morning Edition*, National Public Radio,
20 January 1995)? Masculinity may need redefinition but nevertheless
men are men and women are women. An article on 'Floundering
Fathers' began with a wonderfully dense passage: 'John Lawrence is a
typical 90s father. He is at the sharp end of a battle that men increasingly
feel they are losing, a battle to reconcile a chronic shortage of time,
their freedom and their own sense of masculinity' (*Independent*, 20 April
1996). The fantasy is one of having it all – freedom (leisure rights?)
combined with the satisfactory performance of paid and unpaid work,
while remaining thoroughly masculine. The plea is for tolerance while
men take time to adjust to the new realities of life, grappling with
unprecedented stress levels: 'Besides sharing in child-rearing and
housework chores, men still feel obliged to be wage-earners. Juggling all
that while keeping his identity as a male has made being a 90s guy a
study in angst and tension' (*Record*, 24 January 1994).

Thus the problem of change for men is cast in psychological terms.
The next chapter shows that psychological understandings are at the
heart of blocked-door theory. The psychological account of damaged
men portrays the blocked door as male tragedy.

CHAPTER 7

The Separated, Defensive Male: Psychologising Sexual Politics

Dear Mr President, now that you've won the budget battle, you are relieved of the immediate pressure to defend your presidency. Perhaps, then, you have the time to consider some suggestions about how to be more effective in combating the conservatives' assaults.

So began Michael Lerner's plea to Bill Clinton (*Tikkun*, September 1993) to take up the 'politics of meaning' articulated by his wife Hillary. Lerner's starting point was Clinton's capitulation to conservatives on the issue of homosexuality in the military. Clinton had failed to understand the psychology of conservatism, Lerner argued. Since it flows from deep psychic trauma, rational argument is pointless. Instead, liberals had to develop empathy with the 'basically decent people' who support moral conservatism, learn to 'speak to their pain' and to talk about their 'deepest desires for caring and mutual recognition': 'We must continue to resist the content of the homophobia, racism or sexism, or anti-semitism that these people exhibit. But if we want to effect change, we'd better understand the underlying trauma and begin to develop strategies aimed at addressing that trauma and dislodging it.'

How should this underlying trauma be understood? To become individuals boys must psychically separate from their mothers, their primary sources of nurture. This requires them to identify with the world of the masculine and to repudiate the feminine. To demonstrate masculinity, bonds are formed with other boys and men and the caring, nurturant, feminine side of boys is repressed. Men grow up fearing their repressed feminine potential and fearing their dependence upon women. One result is that gay men arouse deep anxieties in straight

179

men by reminding them of the part that caused them so much pain to repress, hence the ban on gays in the military – men fear even being in the same room as a homosexual man. The only way to overcome the conservative social agenda, Lerner argued, was to understand its psychic roots then articulate a sympathetic healing vision. Conservatives had to be brought to the realisation that they hold a 'mistaken model' of manhood, based on continuing pain based in childhood, and helped to learn that to be a 'real man, a powerful man', they could be strong yet soft, masculine yet nurturing.

In taking up this position Lerner had tapped into an important tendency in thinking about men. The idea that the trauma of separation from the mother is the key to masculine identity, and thus to a host of regrettable attitudes and behaviours, has become very influential. In particular, since the resulting model of the male psyche is said to explain men's resistance to such feminine traits as nurturance, it forms a major aspect of blocked-door theory. This quote from the developing field of men's studies shows how the model can explain any male refusal to enter the world of the feminine:

> The establishment of a boy's identity and his individuality is a psychic process in which the boy struggles to renounce identification with mother and the nurturing she represents ... manhood is defined as a flight from femininity and its attendant emotional elements, particularly compassion, nurturance, affection and dependence ... as a result most men are afraid of behaviour or attitudes that even hint at the feminine (Kimmel & Kaufman 1997).

This line of argument applies also to the division of domestic labour and to much else besides. In this chapter I will concentrate on the way the issue of domestic labour is represented in the model, but the rhetoric of the wounded male is very wide-ranging and on occasions the discussion will be more general. The model is certainly not confined to academic men's studies. It has, for example, received the imprimatur of very distinguished social theorists. When Anthony Giddens discussed the issue of gender relations in *The Transformation of Intimacy*, his explanation of male resistance to change concerned men's 'defensive repudiation of nurturance'. He held that male identity involves a deep sense of in-security and loss because basic trust has been 'intrinsically compromised, since the boy is abandoned to the world of men by the very person who was the main loved adult'. Men's need to control women originates in a 'repressed emotional dependence upon women', and the need to 'neutralise such repressed desires, or to destroy the object of them' results, among other things, in violence (1992: 53–4, 115).

The origins of this model of male identity formation lie in the work of certain feminist psychological theorists who reworked the ideas of the object-relations school of psychoanalysis developed by theorists such as Balint, Fairbairn, Guntrip and Winnicott (see Chodorow 1978: 226, note 26 for a bibliography of these writers). That school had stressed a primary drive for human contact and relationship, and the related processes of identity formation through the internalisation of object worlds. Nancy Chodorow's *The Reproduction of Mothering* (1978) is the best-known work of the feminist revision of object relations theory, and was the main source for the ideas of Lerner et al. just noted. Other writers including Dorothy Dinnerstein (1976) and Jane Flax (1981, 1983) were also very significant, along with writers such as Jessica Benjamin (1988), whose work was similar. Though the various writers are often considered together, they made considerable differences of emphasis. For example, Dinnerstein's work was less concerned with the construction of gendered personality than was Chodorow's. Dinnerstein's main aim was to explain how both male and female personalities tend towards misogyny, leading to an acceptance of male domination. The misogyny is rooted in the fact that both sexes have experienced, through mothering, a woman as the first source of frustration (for a critique of Dinnerstein see Bart 1977).

Feminist object relations theory has been very influential within feminist theory, but it has also been widely acclaimed outside feminist academia. In 1996 the review journal of the American Sociological Association listed the 10 most influential sociology books of the preceding 25 years (*Contemporary Sociology*, May 1996). Chodorow's book ranked alongside works by Foucault, Said, Wallerstein, Geertz, Bourdieu and others. In fact, it is fair to say that object relations theory is the feminist theory most favoured by male writers. Often it is the only feminist theory cited by a male author, or the only one cited with approval. For example, a model curriculum for teaching anti-patriarchal men's studies, which largely relied on male-authored texts, included the work of the feminist object-relations school in its course outline. The absence of other kinds of feminist theory was explained under the heading 'materialist theories', in an orthodox Marxist way: 'Materialist theories privilege the workplace and relations within the state as major sites structuring masculinities and men's power' (Pease 1992: 7).

I mentioned earlier Agger's scathing critique of the bland optimistic gradualism and blinkered positivism of mainstream sociology. It is interesting, then, that in *Gender, Culture and Power: Towards a Feminist Postmodern Critical Theory* (1993: 142–3) Agger singled out Chodorow as the author of a 'sensible' kind of feminism which stresses that men, like women, fall 'blindly' into male supremacy, and offers both sexes liberation from the sufferings induced by the division of labour. I will give more examples of the male endorsement of Chodorow's model, and its allies, but first we should look at the original work.

Feminist Object-Relations Theory

I will begin with Chodorow's feminist interpretation of object-relations theory, since it is most often relied upon in the literature on men and masculinity. Chodorow's main purpose was to explain the division of labour of child-rearing – in her own words 'how do women today come to mother?' (Chodorow 1978: 4). It might seem surprising that a text whose declared concern was the psychology of women should have become so influential in the literature on men. However, the text also discussed why men do not undertake much of the care of children, building a comprehensive account of male psychology in the process. It is this account which has been taken up by writers on men. In later work Chodorow (e.g. 1989) revised her position substantially. However, that more subtle and complex position has not had the same impact on the literature on men, which is why the following discussion is based upon her early work.

We have already seen hints of Chodorow's account of male psychology. The starting-point is the fact that children's first love object and point of identification is their mother. To develop a masculine identity, the boy struggles to break free from his dependence on and identification with his mother, assisted by his mother's treatment of him as different from herself. As a result men are overly concerned with maintaining interpersonal boundaries, do not define themselves in relational terms and have diminished relationship capacities. The same processes also explain the contempt men express towards women. Thus, it is 'demonstrated unequivocally that the very fact of being mothered by a woman generates in men conflicts over masculinity, a psychology of male dominance, and a need to be superior to women' (1978: 214).

The conflicts over masculinity are heightened because of the usual absence of the boy's father from primary childcare. Since boys have to learn masculine gender identity and male roles in the absence of their father, the process of identity formation is fraught with anxiety. Because of the father's absence, masculinity remains abstract for the boy. In this sense a true masculine identity is unattainable, and so is fantasised and idealised. Chodorow relied on accounts such as those of Horkheimer (1972b) and Mitscherlich (1969) to develop her argument about the production of an abstract and insecure masculine identity. Those writers explained the production of personalities suitable for alienated roles as consumers and workers under capitalism, and focused on father–son relationships. Chodorow extended such analyses to cover gender relations, focusing on the mother–son relationship. Given the remoteness of the model of masculinity provided by the father, the boy's masculine identity is largely defined negatively, in terms of what the mother is not. Consequently masculine identity remains doubly uncertain, based upon rejection of the concrete feminine identity represented by the mother and the uncertain adoption of an abstract masculine identity represented by the idealised father.

It is interesting to compare this with Chodorow's account of female development. Girls do not have to suppress their identification with their mother, and so their relationship capacities are unimpaired. The acquisition of feminine roles is less fraught with anxiety, since femininity is concrete, embodied in the constantly present mother. Another advantage is that the girl's psychic world is more complex, in that her father is added to her world of primary objects. Thus her relational sense is triangular and requires, in adulthood, completion by both husband and baby. The contradiction – between the boy's experience of a remote father and the girl's experience of a father sufficiently concrete to be added to her world of primary objects – is noteworthy, as is the heterosexual subtext.

Overall, Chodorow concluded that normal psychological development produces women with, and men without, the 'particular psychological capacities and stance which go into primary parenting' (1978: 206). Men do not desire to engage in the intimate care of others and neither do they have the relevant capacities; the opposite applies to women: 'feminine identification processes are relational, whereas masculine identification processes tend to deny relationship ... the basic feminine sense of self is connected to the world, the basic masculine sense of self is separate' (1978: 169). This is Chodorow's central proposition about the reproduction of mothering in particular, and the sexual division of labour in general. Women's work outside the family extends their concern with personal and affective ties (for example as secretaries, service workers, private household workers, nurses, teachers), whereas men's public life is less likely to involve the affective domain.

Clearly this work offers a wide-ranging explanation of men and gender relations. Interestingly, it has sometimes been hailed as the kind of materialist analysis feminism needs. Sarah Harding (1981: 154) claimed that the work of Chodorow et al. provided what was conspicuously lacking from the feminist materialism of writers such as Hartmann, Delphy and Leonard, namely a plausible explanation of the male desire for domination. The missing material base of patriarchy is revealed, she argued, when we understand the way in which the boy's experience of being mothered 'emerges in adults to make men want to dominate others'. Similarly, Bonnie Fox (1988: 168–73) argued that Delphy and colleagues supplied no plausible motive for men's desire to exploit women's labour, there being no 'reasonable motive force' equivalent to the capitalist profit motive to explain why men would want to dominate women. Since the source of men's need or desire to control women's labour power was not specified, the analysis relied on implicit assumptions of an 'innate desire for power' among men, and so 'falls flat'. Materialist feminists, she argued, should be problematising domination, not putting it at the centre of their theories: object-relations theory is a promising extension of the materialist paradigm since it gives patriarchy a referent, a goal-directed activity in the production of gendered subjectivity. This, Fox argued, puts the theorisation of patriarchy on an equal footing with Marxist analyses of capitalism, which rely on the goal-directed activity of production for profit. The failure of both Fox and Harding to recognise the material benefits of patriarchal exploitation is striking.

Why does the feminist object-relations model have a particular appeal for many men? One clue is that it permits analyses which are critical but at the same time quite sympathetic to men. A few examples of the employment of feminist object-relations theory by male writers will suffice (see Richards 1982; Lewis 1983; Osherson 1986; Craib 1987; Kaufman 1987; Astrachan 1988). Victor Seidler in 'Fear and Intimacy' (1985: 159) partly relied on Chodorow's account to explain men's resistance to feminist demands for equity in personal relationships, describing male psychology in terms of self-estrangement, denial of need, fear of personal and intimate life, emotional undevelopment and a 'terrible isolation and loneliness'. Jack Balswick in *The Inexpressive Male* (1988: 191–7) asked why men did not engage in more intimate and nurturing relations with their wives and children, given that such behaviour was now, he believed, part of the 'cultural definition of masculinity'. He relied on Lilian Rubin's (1985) popular account of male–female relations, itself based upon feminist object-relations theory, to argue that the pain of having to reject mother and identify with an absent father led to men with 'ego boundaries that are fixed and firm', unable to express emotions or to meet the intimacy needs of women. Tom Ryan, in 'The Roots of Masculinity' (1985), explained his clinical observations of men's 'fragile gender identity and related problems of fear of commitment and intimacy' and 'emotional shallowness' in similar terms: 'Masculinity, then, can be viewed as a defensive construction developed over the early years out of a need to emphasise a difference, a separateness from the mother ... To ensure a separateness many men deny their feelings of need or dependency, finding them a threat to an already fragile identity.' Ryan relied particularly on the work of Stoller (1975), based on studies of male transsexuals.

It is remarkable how far analyses of this kind can be taken. Male violence against women is a good example: 'I think of the man who feels powerless who beats his wife in an uncontrollable rage' (Kaufman 1994: 149). David Lisak surveyed rapists and concluded that they fear 're-engulfment' by women, and relied on Chodorow to explain this in terms of 'the male's need to reject parts of himself identified with the mother' (Lisak 1991: 256–7). Tony Eardley (1985: 105) cited a study of convicted rapists (Groth & Birnbaum 1979) which characterised the typical offender as possessing 'unfulfilled emotional need resulting from a feeling of powerlessness', an impoverished emotional life (except for anger) and 'deep-seated doubts about his adequacy and competence as a person'. Eardley argued that this was a reasonable description of 'normal masculinity', and relied on Chodorow for an understanding of the production of such a masculinity, stressing the processes whereby a boy must reject his mother and so suppress 'his own potential qualities of nurturing'. Thus, he said, men seem 'to exorcise, in the only way they know how – by force – the fear of accepting what they are and what they may have lost in the process of becoming what they are'.

I have often heard that my analysis of men is far too critical. However, my point that men try to maintain their advantaged position in the division of labour is really quite bland when compared with some of the depictions of fearful, defensive, violent wounded men. Some writers go further still, and attempt to explain all forms of male domination in object-relational terms. In *Fathering the Unthinkable: Masculinity, Scientists and the Nuclear Arms Race* Brian Easlea (1983) presented a devastating discussion of men's practices in terms of the material domination over women, nature and each other. He argued that Chodorow's account best explained all forms of unwelcome male behaviour, including the preparations for nuclear destruction.

Empirical Difficulties

The following sections contain a broad theoretical and political critique of feminist theory's object-relations account of men. First, however, it is worth exploring the empirical basis of the theory. As far as the theory concerns the division of labour, it seems to be on sound empirical grounds – women do perform the bulk of routine nurturing work. How valid, though, is the specific account of gendered personality? As Pauline Bart (1984) observed, Chodorow's account is quite abstract, tending to disregard evidence in favour of a selective reading of psychoanalytic theory. For example, in Chapter 1 I showed that men's childcare practices tend to favour the more pleasant and playful activities with a high relational content, over practices of routine or mundane care. Men also receive care from women, and value and depend upon it. Ideas about men's rigid ego boundaries sit awkwardly with the evidence that men are able to receive nurturance and to engage in pleasurable interactions with children.

Another important point is that women generally take on the bulk of domestic labour and childcare, no matter what their personality orientation. A study by Russell (1978) tested the relationship between individuals' scores on a masculinity/femininity scale and their performance of childcare. The result was that whatever their score women performed most of the childcare, whereas men who scored higher on 'femininity' tended to perform more childcare than other men. This recalls the findings, noted in Chapter 3, that women perform the bulk of routine domestic work whether or not they support shared roles and whether or not they report satisfaction with their role as housewives and mothers. Men's attitudes, however, do show some correlation with their domestic task performance. I do not intend, in citing Russell, to give validity to psychological measures of 'masculinity' and 'femininity', which are usually based on answers to questions based upon stereotypes. The point is simply that psychologists have been unable to demonstrate a relationship between 'femininity' and the propensity to care for children. Evidence about male psychological development also calls Chodorow's account into question. There is much more variety than the model can allow. For example, cross-sex identification, where some men identify strongly with femininity (at least at the psychological level) is not rare, but it is impossible to theorise in the standard object-relations model (Elshtain 1984). Connell's empirical work on adolescents demonstrated how several distinct male and female personality types can be produced within the one milieu (Connell 1987). William Goode made a similar point, arguing against the literature's description of a tough, competitive, unemotional masculinity: 'The macho boy is admired, but so is the one who edits the school newspaper, who draws cartoons, or who is simply a warm friend' (Goode 1982: 135).

As Segal (1994: 153) observed, despite their supposed stress on the 'fragile, unstable, layered, precarious, fragmentary' nature of the psyche, psychoanalytic accounts find 'bedrock' in sexual difference – sexual difference never changes. This too is empirically implausible: the evidence about psychological sex differences is very damaging to the object-relational account. The search for sex differences has been exceptionally diligent, yielding largely negative results (Duncombe & Marsden 1993). As Connell said, if it were not for the persistence of cultural biases, research into sex differences would be known as 'sex similarity' research (Connell 1987: 170; see also Segal 1993). In those few traits where sex differences have been consistently demonstrated, the differences are small compared to the widespread variation within each sex, and even small sex differences in such crucial traits as domination, nurturance and fear of intimacy, as measured by psychologists, cannot be reliably established (Tavris 1992). Psychological tests are not, of course, based on practices in ordinary social settings, but measure attitudes and orientations using questionnaires and laboratory studies. All the same, it is significant that attempts by psychologists to operationalise sex differences yield consistently negative results.

In evidence about behaviour in ordinary social settings, further empirical and political difficulties for object-relations theory appear. Fathers tend to be more concerned about appropriate gender development than are mothers, and so more concerned to avoid producing a 'mummy's boy', but the object-relations texts stress the determining role of the mother in separation from the son, because of his perceived difference from her (Chodorow 1978: 207). Accordingly, Seidler (1985: 167) spoke of male superiority as a 'way of dealing with the primal betrayal of our feelings by our mothers', lending credence to Brittan's (1989: 195) suggestion that object-relations accounts can be read as offering support for the proposition that it is women who reproduce the gender system: 'if mothering [is] to blame for male domination then, in the final analysis, men are blameless' (see also Bart 1984).

Without accepting the hype characteristic of the literature about New Men and New Fathers, it is true that some apparently quite unexceptional men, products of conventional mothering, routinely perform primary care of others. This involves care of frail elderly spouses and parents, care of sick spouses, and care of their young children (Russell 1986; Grbich 1987; Arber & Gilbert 1989). A common factor in this kind of role-reversal is the unavailability of a suitable woman to do the caring work, a point stressed in Chapter 1 – men do the job when there is no alternative. Reviewing his experiences of patients and colleagues in group therapy sessions, sociologist and psychotherapist Ian Craib explained why he had revised his original support for Chodorow:

> The men who could be stereotypically masculine could also talk with sensitivity and insight about their own feelings, engage in comforting and supporting others and take part in all the routine emotional interchanges of the group's life; and women who could be stereotypically feminine could also be hurtful, emotionally obtuse, defensive and blind and unable to engage in nurturing (Craib 1995: 155).

Similarly, Dinnerstein acknowledged that none of the five people best known to her fitted the composite portraits of masculinity and femininity she presented (Dinnerstein 1976: x). In her Afterword, Chodorow (1978: 215) also retreated from the universalistic positions taken up in the body of the work:

> *All* women *do not* mother or want to mother, and *all* women are not 'maternal' or nurturant. *Some* women are far more nurturant than others, and want children far more. Some *men* are more nurturant than some women. I agree that all claims about gender differences gloss over important differences within genders and similarities between genders. I hope that this book leads people to raise questions about such variations, and to engage in the research that will begin to answer them (emphasis in original).

However, this was not heeded by most writers who adopted feminist object relations theory as the definitive theory of men.

Theoretical Critique

Feminist object-relations theory makes a critique of male domination, and suggests that equal parenting would break the vicious cycle of reproducing gendered personality and the gender order in general: 'My expectation is that equal parenting would leave people of both genders with the positive capacities each has, but without the destructive extremes these currently tend toward' (Chodorow 1978: 218). The clear path to reform through equal parenting explains part of the theory's popularity among those who desire change. Chodorow did acknowledge that the shift to equal parenting would be difficult, since women's mothering was fundamental to gender ideology and the sex-gender system. Her proposal for equal parenting was seriously undercut by the theory itself: the optimistic vision of change based on the equal sharing of parenting begged the question of how that way of breaking the cycle of reproduction of mothering could be achieved. Since the theory showed how men's inadequacy for the task is reproduced, it is hard to see how or why adult men would initiate change (Bart 1984). Some writers have actually relied on object-relations theory to oppose shared parenting, on the grounds of men's unsuitability for the intimate care of the young (e.g. Peterson 1984).

We must also ask why change is supposed to come through caring for the *next* generation – apparently caring for a wife is less important. This is another instance of the emphasis on the care of children which has been noted throughout this study. But if men can change enough to become equal parents, why can they not change enough to become equal carers for their spouses? Moreover, the challenge to men is framed entirely within the context of heterosexuality and the possibilities for the perfectibility of marriage. Bart (1984) suggested that this is one reason why feminist object-relations theory received widespread mainstream acceptance, unlike feminist critiques of the very institutions of marriage and the family.

Another likely factor in the theory's popularity is that it reverses traditional valuations of masculinity. For example, male independence becomes a sign of inner weakness and relational deficiency. Similarly, while orthodox Freudian accounts stress discontinuity and lack in *female* psychological development, object-relations theory constructs *male* development in terms of the discontinuity of identity formation, and the resulting psychology of lack. The appeal to feminists is clear but the appeal to men is less so; nevertheless male writers who adopt such approaches can produce remarkably critical accounts of men. Men come to be viewed as lacking certain 'feminine' qualities and may be conceptualised in terms of 'difference' or 'otherness' with respect to women. Thus, male writers accuse their own sex of fearing intimacy and lacking awareness of their own or others' emotional needs (Seidler 1989). As we will see, this critical account of the wounded man is not as politically helpful as it might seem.

Sociologists who criticise psychological approaches are always accused of a naive or wilful rejection of the whole psychic domain. I am going to be critical of the particular psychological approach outlined above, but not because of a general disregard for the domain of psychology. Like Delphy (1984: 216), I do not accept that objecting to psychoanalytic theory amounts to a 'lack of interest in its object'. The point is that there is more than one way to think about this object. The materialist theoretical position discussed in Chapter 2 also puts psychological practices at the centre of the analysis, but in a very different way. To think of the practices of care and nurturance of concrete human beings as forms of socially necessary labour is to take them very seriously indeed. This is one of the major ways in which feminist materialism has broadened the materialist paradigm, though to orthodox Marxists this is moving too far towards the psychological. Clearly the needs met by the practices of nurturance and care belong to the traditional subject matter of psychology, and the significance of the psychic level is thus recognised within feminist materialism. Undoubtedly a great deal remains to be done: for example, the crucial concept of emotional labour requires much research and theoretical development, but the idea is not foreign to psychology.

What follows is not a critique of psychology as a whole. It is a critique of a particular psychological approach to gender relations, an approach grounded in early childhood development and holding that gendered personalities are fixed in the first few years, resulting in the division of labour between adults. The materialist account suggests, in contrast, that the division of labour involves a continuing construction of gendered personality. For example, women's emotional labour continually sustains the seeming independence of men. However, this anticipates my argument.

A useful beginning is to recall the task/job distinction emphasised by Delphy and Leonard. Under the division of labour men do perform domestic tasks such as childcare, but are not under the same obligation as women to perform it routinely. The empirical basis for the idea that men are not nurturant is not that men *cannot* nurture others, but that men *do not* engage in a great deal of routine nurturing behaviour. Men are themselves the objects of nurture, and gain the freedom to engage in other kinds of practices. What must be explained is why men do not take on the *job* of domestic work, but the theory seeks to explain why men cannot perform the *tasks*. The main point about the division of labour is missed at the start. Writing about the rhetoric of the new nurturant father and the research showing that fathers can be as nurturant as mothers, Ann Oakley (1986: 90) observed that 'men's potential to be active and involved fathers is not in question; what is in question is why so few of them assume this commitment'. Men's potential as fathers is questioned by the object-relations model, and Oakley's general point applies also – the important question is not whether men can do the work, but why they do not assume the commitment. The belief that men lack the capacity for childcare overlooks the possibility that what men really lack is the 'inclination to burden themselves with the demanding labours of love and personal maintenance' (Segal 1990: 41).

As Hilary Graham (1986) noted, Chodorow's account of motherhood stressed psychological aspects of nurturance and gave little emphasis to the routine meeting of physical needs. To Chodorow mothering was a role which, unlike others, requires particular 'psychological capacities and a particular object-relational stance' (Chodorow 1978: 205–6). Valerie Walkerdine and Helen Lucey (1989: 152) argued that Chodorow and similar theorists of female nurturance participated in a discourse of the 'sensitive mother', offering a patriarchal account of femininity which stressed 'passivity, receptivity and nurturance' (see also Rose 1987). Object-relations theory holds that women look after children because they are nurturant – suited to the job – and that men do not do it because they are not suited. This explains a division of labour in terms of the supposed nature of the people occupying different positions in that division, and has great popular appeal. The common-sense view is that all observable differences between men and women result from their different personalities and identities. The feminist object-relations model of gendered personality is, in effect, a theorised version of the popular ideology about the natures of men and women. The model differs from conventional wisdom in that gender is seen to be socially produced and not simply given by nature. However, it is in accord with popular wisdom's basic notion that differences between men and women explain their differing positions in the social world.

However, might it not be the case that gendered social positions are produced and maintained in other ways, and gendered attributes are the result? For example, women's emotional competence could well 'derive *from* their social location as carers and dependants' (Jackson & Scott 1997: 568, emphasis in original). The attributes are those of the job. As Katha Pollitt (1992) observed in her critique of feminist difference theory in general, if mothers are patient, peace-loving and attentive to emotional context it is for the same reasons that 'accountants are precise, lawyers are argumentative, and writers are self-centred' – in each case these are the qualities needed to get the job done (see also Okin 1989). This point will be further developed below. For the moment, though, it reminds us that a much more fruitful analysis might start from the nature of the jobs, rather than the job-holders, in the division of labour. This leads to the most important point about the object-relations model.

Like other forms of blocked-door theory the model seems to find the sexual division of labour puzzling. The versions discussed in Chapter 6 speak of various sociological obstacles to change, with the net effect of glossing over men's agency. The social location of men and women in the division of labour is seen not as primary but as an epi-phenomenon, the effect of some other process, requiring an explanation beyond itself. The psychological version discussed in this chapter does something similar. It finds the explanation in the reproduction of a new generation of males and females – within the division of domestic labour itself – but its approach is still indirect. All versions of blocked-door theory avoid the point emphasised by feminist materialists, that the division of labour is a political/economic division which serves men's interests more than women's interests. Contrary to Harding, theory does not need to uncover the 'missing material base' of patriarchy in the psychic domain: the material base is plain in the countless instances of men being served by women. This is clear if the analysis begins with a critique of the jobs themselves rather than the attributes of the job-holders.

I have argued that male resistance to change is not hard to explain. Men's continued ability to resist change is another matter, always contingent and contested, constituting an empirical, historical question.

Delphy, writing about psychological accounts of men's supposed need for superiority expressed through female deference, argued that the important unanswered question is how men manage to get their needs met: 'It may be that men want and need respect. (And are they alone in this?) But what gives them the *means* to obtain it? ... We are given reasons for men's domination *which presuppose it*' (Delphy 1984: 192, emphasis in original). Similarly, in her critique of feminist object-relations theory, 'Is Male Gender Identity the Cause of Male Domination?', Iris Young argued that it is all very well to explain the production of a male desire for power, but unless we assume that a psychological propensity to wield power itself makes men powerful, this gives no insight into how men obtain and maintain power. If men are able to dominate women and to receive benefits from exploiting their labour, it is hard to see why we need to theorise specific psychological mechanisms which produce a desire for domination. Young concluded that the accounts of domination offered in feminist object-relations theory are abstract: men simply want to be superior to women. They are also, she argued, idealist, failing to grasp that the 'bases, structure and operation of power and domination are necessarily concrete' (1984: 139). Even if we grant validity to object-relational accounts at the psychological level, the question of the source of male power is left untouched: 'Phenomena related to gender differentiation cannot by themselves explain structures of male domination, because the former category refers to ideas, symbols and forms of consciousness, and the latter refers to the appropriation of benefit from women by men in a concrete material way' (1984: 140).

Even texts which are clear about women's service to men are inclined to rely on psychic explanations. For example, Rubin (1985) spoke of men's benefits from marriage, whereby men rely on women's support 'in all the ways we know so well', but constructed gender relations in terms of men's primal trauma upon the loss of their mother and their resultant inability to acknowledge dependency. Similarly, Formaini (1990: 33, 85) discussed the way women are 'asked by men to belong to a servant class and, as such, to take care of men in the name of love', but went on to argue that male domination flows from a need to control others caused by men's unacknowledged sense of their own powerlessness, originating in pre-Oedipal traumas. Throughout Chodorow's account there was a reluctance to place male advantage at the centre of the analysis, even where it was clearly required. For example, the relatively common jealousy experienced by husbands upon the birth of a child was explained by Chodorow in terms of working out unresolved Oedipal traumas. A somewhat more direct explanation would be that the husband has to compete with the baby for his wife's attention and care. Similarly, Chodorow explained men's generally harder adjustment to marriage breakdown in terms of the male psyche's simple fantasy structure based upon the narcissistic recreation of their relations with their mother, compared with women's more complex triangular object world which gave them 'other resources and a certain distance from their relationships to men' (1978: 198, 207). Again, a simpler explanation would be that men have more to lose in terms of material well-being upon marriage breakdown.

As with 'doing gender' theory (Chapter 6), domination becomes an effect, not the thing itself. Balswick (1988: 192) discussed power and domination largely in terms of fantasy rather than practice, arguing that while men seemed 'to show a contempt for women based upon arrogance', such contempt was really born of fear of the power of the rejected mother. Quoting Rubin, he said: 'It's a fear so great he can only live with it by disempowering her – by convincing himself that she's a weak and puny creature.' Similarly, Chodorow constructed male advantage as a *consequence* of the division of labour. The subject positions which result from the mothering of children involve men who are inclined to dominate women. She wrote: 'The structure of parenting creates ideological and psychological modes which reproduce orientations to and structures of male dominance in individual men, and builds an assertion of male superiority into the definition of masculinity itself' (1978: 185).

Like some of the sociological accounts in Chapter 6, the object-relations account allows us to speak in terms of male power, domination and advantage while proposing an explanation in terms of the agentless reproduction of a social structure, in this case the organisation of child-rearing. Rather than understanding men's position in the division of labour or any other aspect of male domination in terms of interested practice, the division of labour is seen as determined by the hypothesised male psyche, itself produced by the division of labour. While much of the literature is undoubtedly critical, the sexual-political effects are conservative, since attention is directed away from interested male practices and towards a fetishised personality. This is not a great advance on conventional wisdom about the different natures of men and women. Psychoanalytic theory is claimed to promise a materialist account of gender relations, but 'under the cover of introducing materialism into subjectivity, one in fact introduces the enemy in its place: one introduces idealism into history' (Delphy 1984: 215–16).

The Self-sufficient Male

Two aspects of feminist object-relations theory and similar models are worth examining, as they bring us closer to popular ideologies about men. Object-relations theory is known only to experts but everyone has some acquaintance with the first aspect I want to discuss, men's supposed need for autonomy, and there is increasing public debate about the second aspect, men's emotional wounding. The next two sections discuss the issues at the level of theory, but many of the points would serve just as well in a critique of the related popular ideologies.

First, men's supposed desire for autonomy and their consequent fear and hence denial of their own dependence and need. To Chodorow (1978: 181), the mother represented regression and lack of autonomy for both sexes but for a boy 'dependence on his mother, attachment to her, and identification with her represent that which is not masculine; a boy must reject dependency and deny attachment and identification'. This point is particularly important in Benjamin's work, which has much in common with feminist object-relations theory. She argued that the chief manifestation of male hegemony is the dominance of the ideal of the self-sufficient individual, which arises from the processes whereby boys separate from their mothers (Benjamin 1988). Similarly, Seidler, relying on various psychoanalytic perspectives including object-relations theory, argued that although men want to have their needs met they find it difficult to articulate those needs, since 'the very acknowledgment of our needs compromises our image of self-sufficiency' (Seidler 1985: 174).

The idea that men fail to articulate their needs may seem odd, since household life often revolves around the expressed demands of husbands, and men frequently acknowledge their dependence on marriage and family life (Chapters 1 and 3). However, the main claim concerns the supposed failure of men to communicate emotional and psychological needs, particularly to women (Balswick 1988). This too is empirically questionable since, as Jeff Hearn concluded from his studies, men's greatest reluctance to acknowledge emotional dependency concerns other men: 'Any sign of emotional or social dependence of one man on another is ... an invitation to take the mickey. Such dependent relationships are seen as more appropriate to a woman in marriage' (Hearn 1985: 125; see also Sherrod 1987). Self-revelation to other men is particularly difficult because men are often competitive with each other. Thus many male secrets are told only to wives, lovers or female friends (Komarovsky 1976; Phillips 1986), consistent with the materialist analysis of women's obligatory (physical and emotional) care of men.

The most plausible evidence for the claim that men fail to disclose themselves to women is that in heterosexual relationships men tend to articulate their emotional needs less often than do women (Thompson & Walker 1989; Rubin 1985). This may suggest a reluctance to place emotional demands upon women, which would count against the materialist critique of women's emotional labour on behalf of men, but there is no necessary contradiction. In fact, the failure to explicitly acknowledge certain needs can be crucial in maintaining a system of appropriation which meets those needs. The point was made forcefully by Carol Hanisch: 'If men cry less than women, then it's because men have something to gain by withholding their feelings, withholding valuable information so they can control the situation. *He who controls the truth controls*' (Hanisch 1978: 75, emphasis in original). In a related vein, Kathy Ferguson (1984) argued that women's emotional displays enhance male power by providing valuable information. See also Sattel (1989) and Hite on the strategic value of male inexpressiveness (in Acker 1989).

The work of Wendy Hollway (1983, 1984) is very insightful on this issue. Although I am relying on her arguments at this point, I am not claiming that Hollway identifies her position as a feminist materialist one. The same point applies to some other writers discussed below. Hollway's qualitative study of the discourses employed by heterosexual couples discussing emotional matters revealed a strong tendency for men to deny their emotional dependence upon their female partners, and a degree of unwillingness to acknowledge emotional needs in general. Hollway argued that this confers power on men, through suppressing indicators which would undermine power. Thus, men's abstract mode of speech about emotionally fraught matters 'purports to give people information, but the information it denies the other person is what really matters. It conceals value, importance, desire, the person's commitment to an issue or position' (1984: 258). This is why women often do not realise how much their male partners depend on them until it is too late for the information to be of practical value, such as when male distress becomes evident at the termination of a relationship. Hollway concluded that men construct women as the ones needing intimacy; this projection protects men from acknowledging the 'risk associated with their own need, and the consequent power it would give women' (1984: 246). The result is that a man can 'eat his cake and have it', able to experience being loved without any 'strings attached' (1983: 131).

Benjamin's (1988: 187) analysis of men's desire to appear self-sufficient appears to invoke the materialist tradition: 'Feminist theory has exposed the mystification inherent in the ideal of the autonomous individual ... the feminist critique of the autonomous individual closely parallels the Marxian critique of the bourgeois individual.' When the bourgeoisie denies its dependence on the working class and sees its wealth as the result of its own labours, we are inclined to see a self-justifying mystification. We might expect Benjamin to go on to argue something similar to Hollway: that since men are dependent on the appropriated labour of women, the mystification of this dependence is an important masculine strategy. However, in another example of the abandonment of a materialist analysis just when it seemed to be coming to fruition, Benjamin invoked the psycho-sexual realm. The dependence which men deny is not the material dependence of a man upon the labour of his wife and other women, but is the original psychological dependence of the boy upon his mother. The denial is a repudiation of 'the primary experience of nurturance and identity with the mother' (1988: 188).

Another (male) writer who combines materialist rhetoric with contradictory psychological explanations is Seidler, who discussed critically the way men expect their partners to do their emotional work for them. This work is, he said, an aspect of 'invisible female domestic labour', but the analogy with other forms of labour was not pursued. Seidler's explanation of men's failure to acknowledge their dependence on women's emotional work is that men are alienated from themselves. Men have 'little sense of [their] own needs'; this can be traced back to fears of intimacy induced by the Oedipal trauma (Seidler 1989: 162). Thus 'we are fearful that if we ever contact our unmet needs they would be so overwhelming that no one would want to have a relationship with us' (1985: 174). The fact that women do men's emotional work is presented as a kind of male tragedy whereby emotionally undeveloped men are unable to care for themselves, and are so afraid of their own emotions that women's care for men must remain invisible lest men be forced to confront their own needs.

In some analyses of this kind, the sexual-political nature of men's practices is particularly obvious to the reader, if not the writer. Therapists Barry Gordon and Richard Meth (1990: 64) wonderfully mystified what is, judging by their own description, a master–servant relationship:

> Men can generally allow themselves some attentiveness without feeling unmanly. Despite their unwillingness or inability to voice most of their significant needs, men commonly define some needs they consider acceptable. They use this list to measure attentiveness by their female mates. For some husbands this means having dinner on the table, the house clean, or their wives dressed up when they return. Many men will react with strong, even irrational, anger to such 'slights' or 'disrespect' if these expectations are not met. Underlying this anger is a fear of abandonment. Few men make this emotional connection because they are not in touch with their more fundamental needs.

Among other things, this remarkably obfuscatory argument constructs a female other who is not alienated from her own needs. This point will be criticised shortly. Let us accept, for the sake of argument, that men are particularly likely to be unaware of their emotional needs. A more parsimonious explanation is that of the perspective of feminist materialism. Dorothy Smith argued that the abstracted conceptual mode of action characteristic of dominant individuals depends upon the servicing of their concrete and particular needs by others who also 'produce the invisibility' of their own work. Those who so serve are able to see how the whole thing is put together, to know the world 'immediately and directly in the bodily mode', but those who are served do not:

> The organisation of work ... in managerial and professional circles both constitute and depend upon the alienation of members of this class from their bodily and local existence. The structure of work in this mode and the structure of career assumes the individuals can sustain a mode of consciousness in which interest in the routine aspects of bodily maintenance is never focal and can in general be suppressed (Smith 1987: 81. Smith's analysis is an elaboration of Hegel's ([1807] 1977) parable of master and servant).

A lack of conscious awareness of some of one's needs can thus be an aspect of having a dominant position, in which those needs are continually met by others who have (indeed, who are obliged to have) such an awareness. The point was made particularly well in connection with women's emotional labour by therapists Susie Orbach and Luise Eichenbaum. Men's 'dependency needs' (their term for the human need for emotional nurturance and support) can remain hidden precisely because they are more regularly satisfied:

> A boy can feel secure in having his mother look after him, clothe him, prepare his meals, clean up after him, encourage him, nurture him. *More importantly, [a] boy can look forward to this in later life from another woman, his wife, who will replace mother* ... At the same time as men acquire power in the outside world – by being born male in a patriarchal culture – they continue to be looked after (as children are) at home (Orbach & Eichenbaum 1983: 59, 61, emphasis in original).

Thus men come to take nurturance for granted, as part of the fabric of life. 'Men more often than not do not have to crave emotional attention and connection because they receive it' (1983: 75). Orbach and Eichenbaum considered that the widespread view of men as independent was a myth arising from this lack of awareness, and discussed this understanding as a 'camouflaging' of men's dependence upon women, implying that it is not in men's interests to acknowledge how this dependence enables them to 'go out into the world and be "independent" and successful' (1983: 59). The *continuity* between men's experiences of female nurture as children and adults is in marked contrast to object-relations theory's stress on male experiences of *discontinuity*. This leads to the other aspect of the object-relations model of men to be discussed in detail, the wounded man.

Wounded Men

A remarkable feature of male writers' employment of feminist object-relations theory is the discussion of 'normal' male psychology as pathological. This is also the case with many popular accounts of men written by women; a good example is Formaini's *Men: The Darker Continent* (1990; see also Ingham 1984). The male psyche is damaged, wounded, in need of repair: men are said to be 'emotional illiterates with self-deluding ideas of independence' (Eardley 1985: 107) and 'deskilled' in the area of human relations (Edgar in *Time Australia*, 22 August 1988). As Brittan (1989) observed, object-relational accounts lie at the heart of many contemporary diagnoses of a crisis in masculinity. In this genre, which Betsy Wearing (1994) called the 'poor boy' school of writing, men can appear in a distinctly tragic light. In some cases the claim seems to be that men have a monopoly on suffering. At the very least, white middle-class men now have permission to construct themselves as victims, thus writing themselves into one of the dominant discourses of the late 20th century.

The remarks of the British writer Brown (1995) about arguments of this kind are refreshing: 'Oh, poor things. What is missing is any understanding of how aggression is functional within the way masculinity is performed and that it leads to payoffs. Men who aggress are often not short of friends, or even sexual partners, and may indeed be widely approved of or admired. It's wimps like me who are, as I am regularly informed, "inadequate".' I must reiterate that I recognise that men can and do suffer. Experience tells me, though, that no matter how much this point is stressed, views like mine will be dismissed by many as cruelly unsympathetic to men's pain. As William Goode (1982) observed, men, like all members of dominant groups, tend to take their privileges for granted, while (I would add) being painfully aware of their burdens. This kind of bad faith is no basis for theory.

In any case, much of the grief in men's lives results from the actions of other men, something many men seem unwilling to acknowledge, as Schwalbe argued in his criticism of Robert Bly's mytho-poeic movement: 'Sometimes this is a matter of injuries and insults inflicted as men compete with each other, more or less as equals. But more often it is a matter of the indignities, powerlessness, and despair men suffer as they are kept in place and used by men with far greater economic and political power' (Schwalbe 1996: 231). Jennifer Somerville's review of the influential men's studies anthology by Metcalf and Humphries (1985), which included work by Eardley, Ryan and Seidler, argued that the contributors' diagnoses of men consisted of clichés about the human condition. For example, discussing Seidler's argument that men seek sexual contact in order to meet needs for intimacy which are otherwise difficult to acknowledge, she questioned the assumption that it is exclusively a male problem:

> Research evidence on the meaning of sexual contact for women suggests that it consists of the same confusion of desires, demands and needs also often unsatisfied. If this is the case, it can hardly be said to be caused by emotional ignorance and illiteracy since it is claimed that the 'relational potential' is so much more highly developed in women (Somerville 1989: 300).

Somerville quoted Seidler's remark about Freud: 'He made us aware that we are vulnerable creatures who can be deeply hurt in our personal relations, though we do everything to flee this knowledge of ourselves.' As she observed, no Freud was needed to tell us this: 'in the form presented above, it is so self-evident as to be banal'. While such accounts of the male psyche may have some descriptive validity at the level of the individual, they can hardly explain the gender order if women are subject to much the same analysis. As Segal (1990: 42) argued, the resistance of some men to involved fatherhood may be partly based upon the fact that childbirth can reactivate all the terrors and pleasures of men's early relations to their own mothers: 'Fatherhood can thus threaten men's whole perception of themselves as adults, arousing jealousy and feelings of inadequacy, leaving them feeling tired, confused, vulnerable, insecure and rejected' but, she said, many new mothers experience an identical emotional complex.

As Somerville implied, feminist object-relations theory licenses men not only to speak of the burdens of masculinity but to speak of themselves as, at least psychologically, at a disadvantage when compared with women. For example, men are said to have been denied the 'empathic qualities available to females' who experience the pleasures and rewards of 'participating in another's inner life' (Balswick 1988: 192). Segal pointed out in her discussion of the Metcalf and Humphries (1985) anthology: 'Men's power over women is not denied in these articles. But it is something *not worth having*: women, despite their relative powerlessness, are more secure in their gender identity and closer to psychic health and happiness' (1990: 80, emphasis in original).

An important aspect of the wounded man argument is the supposedly negative nature of male identity. Given the father's relative remoteness, boys lack concrete male models and so, it is said, construct their identities by rejecting the feminine rather than by embracing the masculine. This can lead to the view that masculinity is the weaker gender construct, so men encounter 'unique problems' of identity and suffer from 'emotional shallowness' (Ryan 1985: 19, 26). Such accounts implicitly or explicitly construct a female other who is not emotionally damaged: her relational potential is intact and her emotional needs are acknowledged. As Graham (1983) observed, such accounts tend to construct women's capacities for care as something women do for themselves to achieve femininity, suppressing the fact that women's relational and expressive capacities are aspects of their care for others. The strong similarity with aspects of feminist difference theory suggests that this body of work is a kind of difference theory for men.

The social theorist Giddens who, as noted earlier, relied on the object-relations model in his account of men, is another male writer who discussed women as having achieved more success in the emotional arena. He held that men have repressed their emotional dependence on women, and the need to neutralise such repressed desires, or to destroy their object, can lead to violence. Like Benjamin, Laquer and Seidler, Giddens used materialist rhetoric. He said that men have relied upon women to 'do the work of intimacy' so that women are the 'emotional under-labourers of modernity'. Indeed women are the 'emotional revolutionaries of modernity' who prepare the way for 'an expansion of the domain of intimacy' (1992: 125, 130, 200). This echoes Marxist analyses of the appropriation of labour and the historic mission of the working class, but it is the rhetoric of political economy, not the substance. As with Laquer, emotional labour is something we do for ourselves, thus he can speak of men as having made a fateful mistake: men 'misread a key trend in the the trajectory of development of modernity ... their unconscious emotional reliance upon women was the mystery they sought in women themselves ... what men wanted was something which in part women had achieved' (1992: 60–1).

By contrast, some feminist writers who stress women's care for others, and the related ability to understand others' needs, question the assumption that women are more in touch with their psychological and emotional needs. Jean Baker Miller (1976: 11) observed that a woman's ability to understand a man's emotional states does not necessarily imply an ability to understand her own: 'Subordinates, then, know much more about the dominants than vice versa. They have to. They become highly attuned to the dominants, able to predict their reactions of pleasure and displeasure ... Another important result is that the subordinates often know more about the dominants than they know about themselves.' Similarly, Orbach and Eichenbaum questioned the notion that men are particularly deficient at understanding their needs for nurturance, arguing that women too find it very difficult to acknowledge such needs. Their women clients, they concluded, strongly protected themselves against showing their dependency needs and expressed feelings of shame and self-dislike for having these needs.

> Time and time again we heard our clients assuming that they should not and could not expect care and attention from anyone else; that they should be able to take care of themselves; that needing equalled weakness and childishness. At the same time they spoke of their assumptions that they should be available to respond to the needs of others. This need to give and the difficulty with receiving was such a feature of each woman we encountered that we began to see it as central to the development of women's psychology (Orbach & Eichenbaum 1983: 13).

Rather than being in touch with their own emotional needs, women are in touch with the emotional needs of those they care for:

> Women develop emotional antennae that alert them to the needs of others. Women help those close to them process the disagreeable emotions that come up on a day-to-day basis ... *What is missing in women's lives is that they have never had the consistent experience of this being done for them* ... A woman's emotional world is strewn with neediness, both her own that she must so often repress, and that of others that she anticipates and responds to (1983: 47, emphasis in original).

About the supposed difficulty of the boy's separation from his mother, Orbach and Eichenbaum noted that at least the boy does not have to give her up, in the sense that he does not have to give up the expectation of maternal nurturance (from her and future wives): '[Boys] have the psychological task of separation (as do girls, who must separate from the same-gendered person, making it to our minds even more difficult), but they do not have to let go emotionally of their need for a woman to continue to care for and look after them' (1983: 61). In contrast, girls come to realise that they must depend on themselves, and that they must relinquish maternal care (in the life-long sense). They cannot assume that there will be someone to care for them emotionally, and thus learn that 'in the most profound sense they must rely on themselves' (Orbach & Eichenbaum 1983: 22) – and, I would add, care for others, such as their husbands.

In the object-relations model men are depicted as defensive, but neurotically so. Men may well be defensive but there actually is something to defend – thus the model turns routine politics into a psychological drama. On the way, it can say quite amazingly nasty things about men, or their psyches. Apparently this is easier for men to swallow than my straightforward political view that men are really quite unremarkable creatures, simply pursuing their interests in the situation in which they find themselves. This seems a simple enough proposition, especially when compared with the complex picture of neurotic, wounded, separated, defensive men proposed by the psychological model. But the pyschological model, unlike the materialist one, does not directly threaten the structure of men's interests.

Writing about the general feminist turn towards psychology, Delphy and Leonard (1992: 70) concluded that the resulting explanations located women's oppression 'back where patriarchal ideology has always itself located them: in anatomical differences, in motherhood, in sexuality, in childhood experiences, in the structure of the unconscious mind – and in ideologies and discourses. Anywhere but in men's material advantages.' The object-relations model is a case in point. As a critique of patriarchy it is relatively harmless.

Conclusion:
Waiting for the Man

People must work to maintain daily life; some work harder than (and work for) others, and some reap the benefits. This applies to both paid and unpaid work. I have argued that much 'progressive' thinking about men, both academic and otherwise, avoids, downplays, explains away or mystifies inequities in the organisation of domestic work at the level of description *and* at that of explanation. The principal tendency of the social conversation about men and change is, I conclude, to take care of men's interests, as women themselves care for men under the division of labour. The imperative to take care of men appears very strong.

In the discourse about men this is done by explicitly or implicitly denying men's interests and agency in the sexual division of labour and by discussing change in overly optimistic terms, with a promise of happiness through marriage. It also works through a series of significant rhetorical confusions between pleasure and performance, between emotion as feeling and emotion as doing, between gendered personality orientations and gendered jobs. Underlying all these is the inability to distinguish between consumption and production, something very characteristic of the present era.

My argument has taken the form of a critique of ideology – a critique of the way thought masks and thus protects the interests of the powerful. Critiques of ideology are as unfashionable as is the kind of materialist analysis I have relied on, but current fashions in social theory deserve ideological criticism themselves: the theoretical denial of interest suits the interested parties very well. A post-structuralist theorist once informed me over dinner that the category of capitalism was illusory – capitalists have little to fear from this kind of analysis.

Why is it so hard to acknowledge that the division of domestic work is a matter of a sexual-political economy, as we might describe the field marked out by feminist materialism? There is an extraordinary collective partial blindness. I have suggested that to some extent everyone knows that the division of labour suits men and so they resist change, yet it remains a kind of guilty collective secret, the thing we must not say – must not say, that is, 'theoretically'. By this I mean 'theory' in both its academic and its popular form. We know about men's interests but we do not follow through the consequences – we do not put them at the centre of our analysis, we do not take our knowledge too seriously.

In the division of domestic work men are not just cared for by women. Feminist materialism makes it clear that men are themselves constructed under the division of labour. The category of men as we now know them makes sense only in terms of existing gender relations: if men can act independently it is because there is someone they can depend on, if men are high achievers it is because they can rely on a highly skilled maintenance crew, and so on. The argument about men and their interests is not an argument about men in a 'state of nature', whatever that could mean; it is an argument about men as a socially constructed gender group.

Thus my critique of men is not an essentialist critique of one of the biological sexes but a critique of a social category. There is something about gender which makes people particularly inclined to a defensive essentialism. More than once a man has told me that he opposes sexual equality because 'I don't want to lose my balls.' Clearly, a great deal is at stake. Over a century ago, John Stuart Mill argued in 'The Subjection of Women' ([1869] 1984a: 271) that men's 'personal interest' in power over women, shared by 'clodhopper and nobleman alike', led to a marked degree of resistance to change. The resistance was particularly strong because it concerned the most desirable form of power – power over those to whom a man was closest. Mill argued that, to a husband, any wifely independence from his authority must 'interfere with his individual preferences'. In language recalling the feminist materialist analysis of emotional labour, Mill spoke of a crucial difference between women's oppression and economic class oppression: 'Men do not want solely the obedience of women, they want their sentiments. All men, except the most brutish, desire to have, in the woman most nearly connected with them, not a forced slave but a willing one, not a slave merely, but a favourite' (1984a: 271).

To think too clearly about men's interests in the division of labour is to risk undermining the ideological foundations of modern romantic heterosexual marriage, according to which love is freely given and all aspect of life are equitably shared. In contrast, the optimistic rhetoric of the revolving door offers reassurance: we are already 'post-feminist' and the 'traditional' man is a long way in the past; any remaining disharmony is temporary, a matter of further adjustment, a matter of 'transition'. The rhetoric of the blocked door is not very different. If change is stalled it is not because of men: every conceivable explanation is explored, except the one which is most evident to anyone familiar with the realities of life – as Delphy has said, every explanation is considered 'except men's material interests'. Discussing the persistence of the division of domestic work without acknowledging men's self-interested resistance means giving comfort to that resistance.

As Connell (1987: 215) observed, men do not care to take responsibility for their active social subordination of women. They may enjoy the benefits of male domination, while believing that these benefits are given 'by an external force, by nature or convention or even by women themselves', but such beliefs are a kind of bad faith. This bad faith appears in a variety of theoretical genres: in mainstream sociology's appeal to structures or to the 'doing' of gender, in psychology's appeal to childhood trauma, in difference theory's appeal to difference. Popular thought traverses similar terrain in somewhat less fancy garb.

Early second-wave feminist analyses stressed that 'the personal is political'. However, the division of domestic labour, an issue of personal life with enormous sexual-political significance, has not been greatly politicised. In the Introduction I raised the issue of how far the feminisation of men can proceed before precipitating a crisis in the gender order. We still don't know. While the issue of change in the division of domestic work has led to some tension about threats to masculinity, it has been largely dissipated through a slide towards masculine consumption – of both market commodities and the joys of family life – allied with a growing narcissistic interest in therapeutic remedies for social anxieties. This investigation of men and change started with the question of men and the possibility for gender convergence in domestic work; it turned out that most obvious social changes have occurred in men's incorporation by feminised therapeutic, narcissistic and consumerist modes of life, combined with a renovated masculine gender display which now includes a degree of sensitivity. A paradigm example, cited in the Introduction, was Prince Charles' public display of caring for his son.

The issue of an equitable division of domestic work is a problem that largely 'still has no name' (DeVault 1990). As Susan Moller Okin (1989) observed, even social justice theorists concerned with gender issues overlook the question of domestic labour. Early second-wave feminist calls for the overthrow of divided domestic labour were pursued only sporadically in feminist politics (Nava 1983; Franzway et al. 1989); far more attention was directed to more immediately tractable issues, such as the labour market (Lake 1986b). Left feminist theory's general abandonment of a materialist analysis of domestic work had a similar effect.

Women's struggles to alter the division of domestic labour have largely remained private, lacking the kind of collective support and legal remedies available to women faced with labour market inequalities (Luxton 1983).

Social critics are often asked for their remedies. Lynne Segal's answer (1993) was particularly clear: She pointed out that most change in men's lives occurs when '*women's power to demand change in men* has been greatest' (emphasis in original). However, the rhetoric of optimistic gradualism holds that change is a matter of waiting for men to change, thus recalling those religious teachings which counsel patience and submission. Pru Goward, head of the Australian Prime Minister's office for the Status of Women, said at a recent university graduation ceremony that the 'brave new frontier' for men was the home, and that society was 'calling men to account' for the time they spent on housework and childcare. Although 70 per cent of domestic work was still done by women, Goward was optimistic. Lifting a phrase from a recent newspaper series on men and change at the end of the 20th century, she put her hopes in 'Millennium Man'. Gender roles had become negotiable, she told her audience, and with the help of 'a glut of self-help books' men now knew they had a right to choose between work and family responsibilities. While men still clung to 'the cloak of the '50s' on their 'bad days', on their good days they were 'in a state of flux' (Melbourne *Age*, 9 May 1998).

This leaves those with an interest in change still waiting for men to change, in their own good time. Not all that much is expected, in any case. In the same week as Goward's speech, my local newspaper carried an interview with the presenter of a seminar 'How to Have a Life While Growing a Family': 'It's not just a cliché: you can have it all ... a father might resolve to spend more time with his children, starting with five minutes a week with each child' (Melbourne *Age*, 14 May 1998). After 20 or more years of being 'on the agenda', the sexual–political issue of the division of domestic labour is still largely a matter for private struggle and private despair.

Bibliography

Abbott, F. (ed.) 1987, *New Men, New Minds: Breaking Male Tradition*, The Crossing Press, Freedom.

Abercrombie, N. & A. Warde (eds) 1992, *Social Change in Contemporary Britain*, Polity, Cambridge.

Acker, K. 1989, 'Manpower', *New Statesman and Society*, 2 June, 12.

Agger, B. 1989, *Socio(onto)logy: A Disciplinary Reading*, University of Illinois Press, Urbana.

—— 1993, *Gender, Culture and Power: Towards a Feminist Postmodern Critical Theory*, Praeger, Westport CT.

Andorka, R. 1987, 'Time Budgets and Their Uses', *Annual Review of Sociology*, 13, 149–64.

Antill, J. & S. Cotton 1988, 'Factors Affecting the Division of Labor in Households', *Sex Roles*, 18(9/10), 531–53.

Apter, T. 1985, *Why Women Don't Have Wives: Professional Success and Motherhood*, Macmillan, London.

Araji, S. 1977, 'Husbands' and Wives' Attitude–Behaviour Congruence on Family Roles', *Journal of Marriage and the Family*, 39(2), 309–20.

Arber, S. & N. Gilbert 1989, 'Men: The Forgotten Carers', *Sociology*, 23(1), 111–18.

Ariès, P. 1973, *Centuries of Childhood*, Penguin, Harmondsworth.

Armengaud, F. 1993, 'Pierre Bourdieu Grand Temoin?"', *Nouvelles Questions Feministes*, 14(3), 83–8.

Ash, J. 1989, 'Tarting Up Men: Menswear and Gender Dynamics', in Attfield & Kirkham (eds), *A View from the Interior*, 29–38.

Astrachan, A. 1988, *How Men Feel*, Anchor, New York.

Atkinson, M. & S. Blackwelder 1993, 'Fathering in the 20th Century', *Journal of Marriage and the Family*, 55, 975–86.

Atkinson, R. 1993, 'Reconceptualising Family Work: The Effect of Emotion Work on Perceptions of Marital Quality', *Journal of Marriage and the Family*, 55, 888–900.

Attfield, J. & P. Kirkham (eds) 1989, *A View from the Interior: Feminism, Women and Design*, Women's Press, London.

Australian Bureau of Statistics 1993, *How Australians Use Their Time*, Commonwealth of Australia, Canberra.

Bacchi, C. 1990, *Same Difference*, Allen & Unwin, Sydney.

Backett, K. 1987, 'The Negotiation of Fatherhood', in Lewis & O'Brien, *Reassessing Fatherhood*, 74–90.

Balson, M. 1987, *Becoming Better Parents*, Australian Council for Educational Research, Melbourne.

Balswick, J. 1988, *The Inexpressive Male*, Heath, Lexington.

Barnett, R. & G. Baruch 1987, 'Determinants of Fathers' Participation in Family Work', *Journal of Marriage and the Family*, 49(1), 29–40.

Barrett, M. 1980, *Women's Oppression Today*, Virago, London.

—— 1988, *Women's Oppression Today*, revised edn, Verso, London.

—— 1992, 'Words and Things: Materialism and Method in Contemporary Feminist Analysis', in Barrett & Phillips (eds), *Destabilising Theory*, 201–19.

Barrett, M. & M. McIntosh 1979, 'Christine Delphy: Towards a Materialist Feminism?', *Feminist Review*, 1, 95–105.

Barrett, M. & A. Phillips (eds) 1992, *Destabilising Theory: Contemporary Feminist Debates*, Polity, London.

Bart, P. 1977, '"The Mermaid and the Minotaur", a Fishy Story that's Part Bull', *Contemporary Psychology*, 22, 11.

—— 1984, 'Review of Chodorow's *The Reproduction of Mothering*', in Trebilcot (ed.), *Mothering*, 147–52.

Baruch, G. & R. Barnett 1986, 'Consequences of Father's Participation in Family Work: Parents' Role Strain and Well-Being', *Journal of Personality and Social Psychology*, 51(5), 893–992.

Batten, R., W. Weeks & J. Wilson (eds) 1991, *Issues Facing Australian Families*, Longman Cheshire, Melbourne.

Bauman, Z. 1989, 'Sociological Responses to Post-modernity', *Thesis Eleven*, 23, 35–63.

Baxter, J. 1988, 'The Sexual Division of Labour in Australian Families', *Australian Journal of Sex, Marriage & Family*, 9(2), 88–93.

—— 1993, *Work at Home: The Domestic Division of Labour*, UQP, St Lucia.

Beasley, C. 1992, 'Can the Contents of a "Tool Box" Do the Housework?: Considering the Uses of Foucauldian Framework for Investigating Power and Women's Labour', Annual Conference of the Australian Sociological Association, Adelaide, December.

—— 1996, 'Charting An/other Direction? Sexual Economyths and Suggestions for a Feminist Economics', *Australian Feminist Studies*, 11(23), 99–113.

Beck, U. & E. Beck-Gernsheim 1995, *The Normal Chaos of Love* (trans. M. Ritter & J. Wiebel), Polity, Cambridge.

Becker, G. 1976, *The Economic Approach to Human Behaviour*, Chicago University Press, Chicago.

Beckett, J. & A. Smith 1981, 'Work and Family Roles: Egalitarian Marriage in Black and White Families', *Social Service Review*, 55, 314–26.

Bell, C. & H. Newby 1976, 'Husbands and Wives: The Dynamics of the Deferential Dialectic', in Leonard Barker & Allen (eds), *Dependence and Exploitation*, 153–68.

Bell, S. 1987, 'Communications Irony that is Killing off the Copywriter', *Campaign*, 24 April.

Belsky, J. & M. Lang 1986, 'Sex Typing and Division of Labor as Determinants of Marital Change Across the Transition to Parenthood', *Journal of Personality and Social Psychology*, 50(3), 517–22.

Benin, M. & J. Agostinelli 1988, 'Husbands' and Wives' Satisfaction with the Division of Labour', *Journal of Marriage and the Family*, 50, 349–61.

Benjamin, J. 1988, *The Bonds of Love*, Virago, London.

Berardo, D., C. Shehan & G. Leslie 1987, 'A Residue of Tradition: Jobs, Careers and Spouses' Time in Housework', *Journal of Marriage and the Family*, 49(2), 381–90.

Berheide, C. 1984, 'Women's Work in the Home: Seems Like Old Times', in Hess & Sussman (eds), *Women and the Family*, 37–55.

Berk, R. & S. Berk 1979, *Labor and Leisure at Home: Content and Organization of the Household Day*, Sage, Beverly Hills.

Berk, S. 1985, *The Gender Factory*, Plenum, New York.

Bernard, J. 1972, *The Future of Marriage*, Yale University Press, New Haven.

—— 1982, *The Future of Marriage*, revised edn, Yale University Press, New Haven.

Biddulph, S. 1988, *The Secret of Happy Children: A New Guide for Parents*, Bay Books, Sydney.

—— 1994, *Manhood*, Finch, Sydney.

Bielby, D. & W. Bielby 1988, 'She Works Hard for the Money: Household Responsibilities and the Allocation of Work Effort', *American Journal of Sociology*, 93(5), 1031–59.

Bittman, M. 1989, 'Division of Labour in the Household, Summer School, Changes in the Household: Implications and Future Strategies', University of Melbourne, Melbourne.

—— 1991, 'Juggling Time: How Australian Families Use Time', Office of the Status of Women, Department of the Prime Minister and Cabinet, Canberra.

—— 1993, 'Does Anything Ever Change? An Analysis of Findings on the Sexual Division of Labour from the 1992 National Study of Time Use', Annual Conference of the Australian Sociological Association, Macquarie University, Sydney, December.

—— 1996, '"All Else Confusion": What Time Use Surveys Show About Changes in Gender Equity', SPRC Discussion Paper no. 72, University of New South Wales, Sydney.

—— 1998, 'The Land of the Lost Long Weekend? Trends in Free Time Among Working Age Australians, 1974–1992', SPRC Discussion Paper no. 83, University of New South Wales, Sydney.

Bittman, M., L. Bryson & S. Donath 1992, 'Work, Family and Public Policy in Australia and Finland: A Comparative Analysis of Time Use Data', Annual Conference of the Australian Sociological Association, University of South Australia, Adelaide, December.

Bittman, M. & F. Lovejoy 1991, 'Domestic Power: Negotiating an Unequal Division of Labour within a Framework of Equality', Annual Conference of the Australian Sociological Association, Murdoch University, Perth, December.

—— 1993, 'Domestic Power: Negotiating an Unequal Division of Power within a Framework of Equality', *Australian & New Zealand Journal of Sociology*, 29(3), 302–21.

Bittman, M. & J. Pixley 1997, *The Double Life of the Family: Myth, Hope and Experience*, Allen & Unwin, Sydney.

Blackburn, R. & M. Mann 1979, *The Working Class in the Labour Market*, Macmillan, London.

Blain, J. 1994, 'Discourses of Agency and Domestic Labour: Family Discourse and Gendered Practice in Dual-Earner Families', *Journal of Family Issues*, 15(4), 515–49.

Blankenhorn, D. 1995, *Fatherless America*, Harper Collins, New York.

Blumberg, R. (ed.) 1991, *Gender, Family and Economy*, Sage, Newbury Park.

Blumstein, P. & P. Schwartz 1983, *American Couples: Money, Work, Sex*, William Morrow, New York.

Bly, R. 1990, *Iron John: A Book about Men*, Addison Wesley, Reading.

Booth, A. & J. Edwards 1980, 'Fathers: The Invisible Parent', *Sex Roles*, 6(3), 445–6.

Booth, C. 1902, *Life and Labour of the People in London*, revised edn, Macmillan, London.

Bose, C., R. Feldberg & N. Sokoloff (eds) 1989, *Hidden Aspects of Women's Work*, Praeger, New York.

Bottomore, T. & Rubel, M. 1956, *Karl Marx: Selected Writings in Sociology and Social Philosophy*, Penguin, Harmondsworth.

Boulton, M. 1983, *On Being a Mother: A Study of Women with Pre-school Children*, Tavistock, London.

Bourdieu, P. 1972, *Outline of a Theory of Practice*, CUP, Cambridge.

—— 1984, *Distinction* (trans. R. Nice), Routledge & Kegan Paul, London.

—— 1990, 'La Domination Masculine', *Actes de la Rècherche en sciences sociales*, 84, September.

Bowlby, J. 1965, *Child Care and the Growth of Love*, Penguin, Harmondsworth.

Boyle, M. & J. McKay 1995, '"You Leave Your Troubles at the Gate": A Case Study of the Exploitation of Older Women's Labor and "Leisure" in Sport', *Gender & Society*, 9(5), 556–75.

Bradman, T. 1985, *The Essential Father*, Unwin, London.

Brandon, R. 1991, *The New Women and the Old Men*, Harper Collins, London.

Brannen, J. & P. Moss 1987, 'Fathers in Dual-Earner Households – Through Mothers' Eyes', in Lewis & O'Brien (eds), *Reassessing Fatherhood*, 126–43.

Brannen, J. & G. Wilson (eds) 1987, *Give and Take in Families: Studies in Resource Distribution*, Allen & Unwin, London.

Breazedale, K. 1994, 'In Spite of Women: Esquire Magazine and the Construction of the Male Consumer', *Signs*, 20(1), 1–22.

Breines, W. 1986, 'The 1950s: Gender and Some Social Science', *Sociological Inquiry*, 56(1), 70–92.

Brines, J. 1994, 'Economic Dependency, Gender, and the Division of Labor at Home', *American Journal of Sociology*, 100(3), 652–88.

Brittan, A. 1989, *Masculinity and Power*, Blackwell, Oxford.

Brod, H. (ed.) 1987a, *The Making of Masculinities: The New Men's Studies*, Allen & Unwin, Boston.

—— 1987b, 'Introduction: Themes and Theses of Men's Studies' in Brod (ed.), *The Making of Masculinities*, 1–17.

Brod, H. & M. Kaufman (eds) 1994, *Theorizing Masculinities*, Sage, Thousand Oaks.

Broom, D. (ed.) 1984, *Unfinished Business: Social Justice for Women in Australia*, George Allen & Unwin, Sydney.

Brown, 1995, 'Review of Segal, L., *Straight Sex: The Politics of Pleasure*', *Feminism & Psychology*, 5(3), 398–400.

Bryson, L. 1983, 'Thirty Years of Research on the Division of Labour in Australian Families', *Australian Journal of Sex, Marriage & Family*, 4(3), 125–32.

Burck, C. & B. Speed (eds) 1995, *Gender, Power and Relationships*, Routledge, London.

Burns, A. & R. Homel 1989, 'Gender Division of Tasks by Parents and Their Children', *Psychology of Women Quarterly*, 13, 113–25.

Burstyn, V. 1985, 'Masculine Dominance and the State', in Burstyn & Smith, *Women, Class, Family and the State*, 45–89.

Burstyn, V. & D. Smith 1985, *Women, Class, Family and the State*, Garamond, Toronto.

Campbell, C. 1996, 'On the Concept of Motive in Sociology', *Sociology*, 30(1), 101–14.

Campos J., K. Barrett, M. Lamb, H. Goldsmith & C. Stenberg 1983, 'Socio-emotional Development', in Haith & Campos (eds), *Infancy and Developmental Psychobiology*, 783–915.

Caplow, T. & B. Chadwick 1979, 'Inequality and Life-Styles in Middletown, 1920–1978', *Social Science Quarterly*, 60(3), 367–86.

Caplow, T., H. Bahr, B. Chadwick, R. Hill & M. Williamson 1982, *Middletown Families: Fifty Years of Change and Continuity*, University of Minnesota Press, Minneapolis.

Carrigan, T., R. Connell & J. Lee 1985, 'Towards a New Sociology of Masculinity', *Theory and Society*, 14(5), 551–603.

Cartledge, S. & J. Ryan (eds) 1983, *Sex & Love: New Thoughts on Old Contradictions*, Women's Press, London.

Chambers, D. 1986, 'The Constraints of Work and Domestic Schedules on Women's Leisure', *Leisure Studies*, 5, 309–25.

Chambers-Mulholland, E. 1987, Husbands' and Wives' Housework and Child Care Allocation: A Test of Class, Economic and Resource Theories, PhD Dissertation, University of California, Irvine.

Chapman, R. 1988, 'The Great Pretender: Variations on the New Man Theme', in Chapman & Rutherford (eds), *Male Order*, 225–48.

Chapman, R. & J. Rutherford (eds) 1988, *Male Order: Unwrapping Masculinity*, Lawrence & Wishart, London.

Charles, N. & M. Kerr 1987, 'Just the Way It Is: Gender and Age Differences in Family Food Consumption', in Brannen & Wilson (eds), *Give and Take in Families*, 155–74.

Chodorow, N. 1978, *The Reproduction of Mothering*, University of California Press, Berkeley.

—— 1989, *Feminism and Psychoanalytic Theory*, Yale University Press, New Haven.

Clarke-Stewart, K. 1978, 'Popular Primers for Parents', *American Psychologist*, 33, 359–69.

Clary, M. 1982, *Daddy's Home: The Personal Story of a Modern Father Who Opted to Raise the Baby and Master the Craft of Motherhood*, Seaview, New York.

Clegg, S. 1989, *Frameworks of Power*, Sage, London.

Cline, S. & D. Spender 1988, *Reflecting Men at Twice Their Natural Size*, Collins, Glasgow.

Close, P. & R. Collins (eds) 1985, *Family and Economy in Modern Society*, Macmillan, London.

Cohen, J. 1994, 'The Earth is Round (p < .05)', *American Psychologist*, 49(12), 997–1003.

Cohen, T. 1987, 'Remaking Men: Men's Experiences Becoming and Being Husbands and Fathers', *Journal of Family Issues*, 8(1), 57–77.

Collins, R. 1985, '"Horses for Courses": Ideology and the Division of Domestic Labour', in Close & Collins (eds), *Family and Economy*, 63–82.

Colman, A. & L. Colman 1988, *The Father: Mythology and Changing Roles*, Chiron, Wilmette.

Coltrane, S. 1989, 'Household Labor and the Routine Production of Gender', *Social Problems*, 36(5), 473–91.

Connell, R. 1987, *Gender and Power*, Allen & Unwin, Sydney.
—— 1990, 'A Whole New World: Remaking Masculinity in the Context of the Environmental Movement', *Gender and Society*, 4(4), 452–78.
—— 1992, 'Drumming up the Wrong Tree', *Tikkun*, 7(1), 31–6.
—— 1993, 'The Big Picture: Masculinities in Recent World History', *Theory and Society*, 22, 597–623.
—— 1995, *Masculinities*, Polity, London.
—— 1997, 'Comment on Hawkesworth's "Confounding Gender": Re-Structuring Gender', Signs, Spring, 703–7.
Coulson, M., B. Magas & H. Wainwright 1975, '"The Housewife and Her Labour Under Capitalism" – A Critique', *New Left Review*, 89, 59–71.
Coverman, S. 1985, 'Explaining Husbands' Participation in Domestic Labor', *Sociological Quarterly*, 26(1), 81–97.
Coverman, S. & J. Sheley 1986, 'Change in Men's Housework and Child-Care Time, 1965–1975', *Journal of Marriage and the Family*, 48(May), 413–22.
Cowan, R. 1983, *More Work for Mother*, Basic Books, New York.
—— 1987, 'Women's Work, Housework and History: The Historical Roots of Inequality in Work-Force Participation', in Gerstel & Gross (eds), *Families and Work*, 164–77.
Coward, R. 1992, *Our Treacherous Hearts*, Faber and Faber, London.
Craib, I. 1987, 'Masculinity and Male Dominance', *Sociological Review*, 35(4), 721–43.
—— 1995, 'Some Comments of the Sociology of the Emotions', *Sociology*, 29(1), 1151–8.
Crisplell, D. 1992, 'The Brave New World of Men', *American Demographics*, January.
Crockett, L, D. Eggebeen & A. Hawkins 1993, 'Father's Presence and Young Children's Behavioural and Cognitive Adjustment', *Journal of Family Issues*, 14(3), 355–77.
Crompton, R. & M. Mann (eds) 1986, *Gender and Stratification*, Polity, Cambridge.
Crook, S. 1989, 'Television and Audience Activity: The Problem of the Television/Viewer Nexus in Audience Research', *Australian and New Zealand Journal of Sociology*, 25(3), 356–80.
Crouter, A., M. Perry-Jenkins, T. Huston & S. McHale 1987, 'Processes Underlying Father Involvement in Dual-Earner and Single-Earner Families', *Developmental Psychology*, 23(3), 431–40.
Curthoys, A. 1988, *For and Against Feminism*, Allen & Unwin, Sydney.
Cutler, B. 1990, 'In One Russian Day', *American Demographics*, September.
Danzig, P. 1981, 'Fatherhood and My Rebirth as a Man' in Lewis (ed.), *Men in Difficult Times*.
Darque, M. 1988, 'The Division of Labour and Decision-Making in Farming Couples: Power and Negotiation', *Sociologia Ruralis*, 28(4), 271–92.
de Beauvoir, S. 1960, *The Second Sex*, Four Square, London.
Deem, R. 1982, 'Women, Leisure and Inequality', *Leisure Studies*, 1, 29–46.
—— 1987, 'The Politics of Women's Leisure', *Sociological Review Monograph*, 33, 210–28.
Delliquadri, L. & K. Breckenridge 1980, *New Motherhood*, Macdonald Futura, London.
Delphy, C. 1979, 'A Materialist Feminism is Possible', *Feminist Review*, 4, 79–105.
—— 1984, *Close to Home: A Materialist Analysis of Women's Oppression* (trans. D. Leonard), Hutchinson, London.

—— 1993, 'Rethinking Sex and Gender', *Women's Studies International Forum*, 16(1), 1–9.

—— 1994, 'Changing Women in a Changing Europe: Is "Difference" the Future for Feminism?', *Women's Studies International Forum*, 17(2/3), 187–201.

—— 1995, 'The Invention of French Feminism: An Essential Move', *Yale French Studies*, 87, 190–221.

Delphy, C. & D. Leonard 1986, 'Class Analysis, Gender Analysis and the Family', in Crompton & Mann (eds), *Gender and Stratification*, 57–73.

—— 1992, *Familiar Exploitation: A New Analysis of Marriage in Contemporary Western Society*, Polity, Cambridge.

Dempsey, K. 1988, 'Exploitation in the Domestic Division of Labour: An Australian Case Study', *Australian and New Zealand Journal of Sociology*, 24(3), 420–36.

—— 1992, *A Man's Town: Inequality Between Women and Men in Rural Australia*, OUP, Melbourne.

—— 1995, 'Trying to Get Husbands to Do More Work at Home', Conference Paper: TASA95, Australian Sociological Association, December, Newcastle.

—— 1997, *Inequalities in Marriage*, OUP, Oxford.

Descarries, F. & C. Corbeil 1989, 'New Family Structures: The Family, Past and Present in Quebec', *Unesco Courier*, July.

DeVault, M. 1987, 'Doing Housework: Feeding and Family Life', in Gerstel & Gross (eds), *Families and Work*, 178–91.

—— 1990, 'Conflict Over Housework: A Problem That (Still) Has No Name', *Research in Social Movements, Conflicts and Change*, 12, 189–202.

Dinnerstein, D. 1976, *The Mermaid and the Minotaur*, Harper Colophon, New York.

Dobash, R. & R. Dobash 1979, *Violence Against Wives*, Free Press, New York.

Dodson, F. 1973, *How to Father*, New American Library, Bergenfield.

Donaldson, M. 1987, 'Laboring Men: Love, Sex and Strife', *Australian and New Zealand Journal of Sociology*, 23(2), 165–84.

Donzelot, J. 1980, *The Policing of Families*, Hutchinson, London.

Douthitt, R. 1989, 'The Division of Labor Within the Home: Have Gender Roles Changed?', *Sex Roles*, 20(11/12), 693–704.

Doyle, R. 1995, *The Male Experience*, Brown & Benchmark, Madison.

Duncombe, J. & D. Marsden 1993, 'Love and Intimacy: The Gender Division of Emotion and "Emotion Work"', *Sociology*, 27(2), 221–41.

—— 1995, '"Workaholics" and "Whingeing Women": Theorising Intimacy and Emotion Work – The Last Frontier of Gender Inequality?', *Sociological Review*, 43, 150–69.

Eagleton, T. 1991, *Ideology: An Introduction*, Verso, London.

Eardley, T. 1985, 'Violence and Sexuality', in Metcalf & Humphries (eds), *The Sexuality of Men*, 86–109.

Easlea, B. 1983, *Fathering the Unthinkable: Masculinity, Scientists and the Nuclear Arms Race*, Pluto, London.

Edgar, D. 1990, 'Work System Rigidity Damages Positive Family Change', Seminar on Towards a Child and Family Policy for New Zealand, Wellington, November.

Edgar, D. & H. Glezer 1992, 'A Man's Place...? Reconstructing Family Reality', *Family Matters*, 31, 36–9.

Edwards, M. 1984, 'The Distribution of Income Within Households', in Broom (ed.), *Unfinished Business*, 120–36.

Ehrenreich, B. 1983, *The Hearts of Men*, Doubleday, New York.

—— 1989, *Fear of Falling*, Pantheon, New York.

—— 1990, *The Worst Years of Our Lives*, Pantheon, New York.

Ehrenreich, B. & D. English 1979, *For Her Own Good: 150 Years of the Experts' Advice to Women*, Pluto, London.

Ehrensaft, D. 1980, 'When Women and Men Mother', *Socialist Review*, 49, 37–73.

Ellis, R. 1983, 'The Way to a Man's Heart: Food in the Violent Home', in Murcott (ed.), *The Sociology of Food and Eating*, 164–71.

Elshtain, J. 1984, 'Symmetry or Soporifics: A Critique of Feminist Accounts of Gender Development', in Richards (ed.), *Capitalism and Infancy*, 55–91.

Engels, F. 1969, *The Condition of the Working Class in England*, Panther, London.

England, P. & G. Farkas 1986, *Households, Employment and Gender: A Sociological, Economic and Demographic View*, Aldine de Gruyter, New York.

Entwisle, D. & S. Doering 1988, 'The Emergent Father Role', *Sex Roles*, 18(3/4), 119–41.

Ericksen, J., W. Yancey & E. Ericksen 1979, 'The Division of Family Roles', *Journal of Marriage and the Family*, 41, 301–13.

Erickson, R. 1993, 'Reconceptualizing Family Work: The Effect of Emotion Work on Perceptions of Marital Quality', *Journal of Marriage and the Family*, 55, 888–900.

Eshleman, J. 1985, *The Family: An Introduction*, Allyn and Bacon, Boston.

Eveline, J. 1994, '"Normalization", "Leading Ladies" and "Free Men"': Affirmative Actions in Sweden and Australia', *Women's Studies International Forum*, 17(2/3), 156–67.

Everingham, C. 1994, *Motherhood and Modernity*, Allen & Unwin, Sydney.

Evetts, J. 1988, 'Managing Childcare and Work Responsibilities: The Strategies of Married Women Primary and Infant Headteachers', *Sociological Review*, 36(3), 503–31.

Fallows, D. 1985, *A Mother's Work*, Houghton Mifflin, Boston.

Featherstone, M. 1987, 'Lifestyle and Consumer Culture', *Theory, Culture and Society*, 4, 55–70.

Fein, R. 1978, 'Research on Fathering: Social Policy and an Emergent Perspective', *Journal of Social Issues*, 34(1), 122–35.

Feminist Review (ed.) 1987a, *Sexuality: A Reader*, Virago, London.

—— 1987b, 'Femininity and Its Discontents', *Feminist Review*, 1987, 177–98.

Fenstermaker S., C. West & D. Zimmerman 1991, 'Gender Inequality: New Conceptual Terrain', in Blumberg (ed.), *Gender, Family and Economy*, 289–397.

Ferguson, A. 1984, 'On Conceiving Motherhood and Sexuality: A Feminist Materialist Approach,' in Trebilcot (ed.), *Mothering*, 153–82.

Ferguson, A. & N. Folbre 1981, 'The Unhappy Marriage of Patriarchy and Capitalism', in Sargent (ed.), *The Unhappy Marriage*, 313–38.

Ferguson, K. 1984, *The Feminist Case Against Bureaucracy*, Temple University Press, Philadelphia.

Ferree, M. 1989, 'The Struggles of Superwoman', in Bose, Feldberg & Sokoloff (eds), *Hidden Aspects*, 161–80.

Filene, P. 1987, 'The Secrets of Men's History' in Brod (ed.), *The Making of Masculinities*, 103–19.

Finch, J. 1983, *Married to the Job*, George Allen & Unwin, London.

Finch, J. & D. Groves (eds) 1983, *A Labour of Love: Women, Work and Caring*, Routledge & Kegan Paul, London.

Flax, J. 1981, 'A Materialist Theory of Women's Status', *Psychology of Women Quarterly*, 6(1), 123–36.

—— 1983, 'Political Philosophy and the Patriarchal Unconscious: A Psycho-analytic Perspective on Epistemology and Metaphysics', in Harding & Hintikka (eds), *Discovering Reality*, 245–81.

—— 1987, 'Postmodernism and Gender Relations in Feminist Theory', *Signs*, 12(4), 621–43.

Formaini, H. 1990, *Men: The Darker Continent*, Heinemann, London.

Fox, B. 1988, 'Conceptualizing "Patriarchy"', *Canadian Review of Sociology and Anthropology*, 25(2), 163–82.

Franks, H. 1984, *Goodbye Tarzan: Men After Feminism*, Allen & Unwin, London.

Franzway, S., D. Court & R. Connell 1989, *Staking a Claim: Feminism, Bureaucracy and the State*, Allen & Unwin, Sydney.

Friedan, B. 1981, *The Second Stage*, Summit Books, New York.

Funder, K., M. Harrison & R. Weston 1993, *Settling Down: Pathways of Parents after Divorce*, Australian Institute of Family Studies, Melbourne.

Furstenburg, F., S. Morgan & P. Allison 1987, 'Paternal Participation and Children's Well-Being After Marital Dissolution', *American Sociological Review*, 52, 695–701.

Gamarnikow, E., D. Morgan, J. Purvis & D. Taylorson (eds) 1983, *The Public and the Private*, Heinemann, London.

Game, A. & R. Pringle 1983, *Gender at Work*, George Allen & Unwin, Sydney.

Gamman, L. & M. Marshment (eds) 1988, *The Female Gaze: Women as Viewers of Popular Culture*, Women's Press, London.

Gardiner, J. 1975, 'Women's Domestic Labour', *New Left Review*, 89, 47–58.

Geras, N. 1987, 'Post-Marxism?', *New Left Review*, 163, 40–82.

—— 1988, 'Ex-Marxism Without Substance: Being a Real Reply to Laclau and Mouffe', *New Left Review*, 169, 34–61.

Gershuny, J. 1992, 'Change in the Domestic Division of Labour in the UK, 1975–1987: Dependent Labour versus Adaptive Partnership', in Abercrombie & Warde (eds), *Social Change*, 70–93.

Gershuny, J. & S. Jones 1987, 'The Changing Work/Leisure Balance in Britain, 1961–1984', *Sociological Review Monograph*, 33, 9–50.

Gerson, K. 1986, 'What Do Women Want From Men?: Men's Influences on Women's Work and Family Choices', *American Behavioural Scientist*, 29(5), 619–34.

Gerstel, N. & H. Gross (eds) 1987, *Families and Work*, Temple University Press, Philadelphia.

Giddens, A. 1992, *The Transformation of Intimacy: Sexuality, Love and Eroticism in Modern Societies*, Polity, Cambridge.

Gilding, M. 1994, 'Gender Roles in Contemporary Australia', in Hughes (ed.), *Contemporary Australian Feminism*, 102–27.

Gill, G. & R. Hibbins 1996, 'Wives' Encounters: Family Work Stress and Leisure in Two-Job Families', *International Journal of Sociology of the Family*, 26(2), 43–54.

Glezer, H. 1983, 'Changes in Marriage and Sex-Role Attitudes Among Young Married Women: 1971–1982', Proceedings of the Australian Family Research Conference, Melbourne, November.

Goffman, E. 1977, 'The Arrangement Between the Sexes', *Theory and Society*, 4, 301–31.

Goode, W. 1982, 'Why Men Resist', in Thorne & Yalom (eds), *Rethinking the Family*, 131–50.

Goodnow, J. 1989, 'Work in Households: An Overview and Three Studies', in Ironmonger (ed.), *Households Work*, 38–63.

Goodnow, J. & J. Bowes 1994, *Men, Women and Household Labour*, OUP, Melbourne.

Gordon, B. & R. Meth 1990, 'Men as Husbands', in Meth & Pasick (eds), *Men in Therapy*, 54–87.

Graham, H. 1983, 'Caring: A Labour of Love', in Finch & Groves (eds), *A Labour of Love*, 13–30.

—— 1986, *Caring for the Family*, Health Education Council, London.

Grant, W. 1983, *The Caring Father*, Broadman, Nashville.

Gray, J. 1993, *Men are from Mars, Women are from Venus*, Harper Collins, New York.

Graycar, R. 1985, 'Compensation for Loss of Capacity to Work in the Home', *Sydney Law Review*, 10, 528–67.

—— 1989, 'Equal Rights versus Father's Rights: The Child Custody Debate in Australia', in Smart & Sevenhuijsen (eds), *Child Custody*, 158–89.

Grbich, C. 1987, 'Primary Caregiver Fathers – A Role Study: Some Preliminary Findings', *Australian Journal of Sex, Marriage & Family*, 8(1), 17–26.

Green, C. 1988, *Babies: A Parents Guide to Surviving (and Enjoying!) Baby's First Year*, Simon & Schuster, Brookvale.

Green, M. 1976, *Fathering*, McGraw-Hill, New York.

Greenberg, M. 1985, *The Birth of a Father*, Avon, New York.

Greenberg, M. & N. Morris 1974, 'Engrossment: The Newborn's Impact Upon the Father', *American Journal of Orthopsychiatry*, 44(4), 520–31.

Greene, B. 1984, *Good Morning, Merry Sunshine: A Father's Journal of His Child's First Year*, Atheneum, New York.

Greenfield, N. & R. Teevan 1986, 'Fear of Failure in Families without Fathers', *Psychological Reports*, 59, 571–4.

Gregory, S. 1982, 'Women among Others: Another View', *Leisure Studies*, 1, 47–52.

Gregson, N. & M. Lowe 1994, 'Waged Domestic Labour and the Renegotiation of the Domestic Division of Labour within Dual Career Households', *Sociology*, 28(1), 55–78.

Groth, A. & H. Birnbaum 1979, *Men Who Rape: The Psychology of the Offender*, Plenum, New York.

Guillaumin, C. 1996, 'The Practice of Power and Belief in Nature', in Leonard & Adkins (eds), *Sex in Question*, 72–108.

Haas, L. 1993, 'Nurturing Fathers and Working Mothers: Changing Gender Roles in Sweden', in Hood (ed.), *Men, Work and Family*, 238–61.

Haith, M. & J. Campos (eds) 1983, *Infancy and Developmental Psychobiology, Handbook of Child Psychology*, vol. 2, Wiley, New York.

Hakim, C. 1995, 'Five Feminist Myths about Women's Employment', *British Journal of Sociology*, 46(3), 429–55.

—— 1996, 'The Sexual Division of Labour and Women's Heterogeneity', *British Journal of Sociology*, 47(1), 178–88.

Hall, E. 1982, *Child Psychology Today*, Random House, New York.

Hamilton, R. & M. Barrett (eds) 1988, *The Politics of Diversity*, Verso, London.

Hanisch, C. 1978, 'Men's Liberation', in Sarachild, Hanisch, Levine, Leon & Price (eds), *Feminist Revolution*, 72–6.

Hanson, S. & F. Bozett 1986, 'Fatherhood: A Library', *Marriage and Family Review*, 9(3/4), 229–53.

Harding, S. 1981, 'What is the Real Material Base of Patriarchy and Capital?', in Sargent (ed.), *The Unhappy Marriage*, 135–63.

Harding, S. & M. Hintikka (eds) 1983, *Discovering Reality: Feminist Perspectives on Epistemology, Metaphysics, Methodology and Philosophy of Science*, Reidel, Dordrecht.

Harper, J. 1980, *Fathers at Home*, Penguin, Ringwood, Vic.
Harper, J. & L. Richards 1979, *Mothers and Working Mothers*, Penguin, Ringwood, Vic.
Harris, J. & R. Liebert 1984, *The Child: Development from Birth through Adolescence*, Prentice-Hall, Englewood Cliffs NJ.
Harris, P. 1997, 'Securing Health and Happiness: A Note on Possibilities and Limits', *Australia and New Zealand Journal of Sociology*, 33(2), 153–66.
Hartmann, H. 1981a, 'The Unhappy Marriage of Marxism and Feminism: Towards a More Progressive Union', in Sargent (ed.), *The Unhappy Marriage*, 1–41.
—— 1981b, 'The Family as the Locus of Gender, Class and Political Struggle: The Example of Housework', *Signs*, 6(3), 366–94.
Hawkins, A., S. Christiansen, K. Sargent & E. Hill 1993, 'Rethinking Fathers' Involvement in Child Care: A Developmental Perspective', *Journal of Family Issues*, 14(4), 531–49.
Hearn, J. 1985, 'Men's Sexuality at Work', in Metcalf & Humphries (eds), The *Sexuality of Men*, 110–28.
Hegel, G. 1977 (1807), *The Phenomenology of Mind* (trans. A. Miller), OUP, Oxford.
Helms, D. & J. Turner 1978, *Exploring Child Behaviour: Basic Principles*, Saunders, Philadelphia.
Henriques, J., W. Hollway, C. Urwin, C. Venn & V. Walkerdine 1984, *Changing the Subject*, Methuen, London.
Henshall, C. & J. McGuire 1986, 'Gender Development', in Richards & Light (eds), *Children of Social Worlds*, 136–66.
Hertz, R. 1986, *More Equal Than Others: Women and Men in Dual-Career Marriages*, University of California Press, Berkeley.
Hess, B. & M. Sussman (eds) 1984, *Women and the Family: Two Decades of Change*, Haworth, New York.
Hess, B., E. Markson & P. Stein 1985, *Sociology*, Macmillan, New York.
Hessing, M. 1994, 'More than Clockwork: Women's Time Management in their Combined Workloads', *Sociological Perspectives*, 37(4), 611–33.
Hicks, M., S. Hansen & L. Christie 1983, 'Dual-Career/Dual-Work Families: A Systems Approach', in Macklin & Rubin (eds), *Contemporary Families*, 164–79.
Hiller, D. & W. Philliber 1986, 'The Division of Labor in Contemporary Marriage: Expectations, Perceptions and Performance', *Social Problems*, 33(3), 191–201.
Hirsch, M. & E. Keller (eds) 1990, *Conflicts in Feminism*, Routledge, New York.
Hochschild, A. 1989, *The Second Shift*, Avon, New York.
Hojgaard, L. 1997, 'Working Fathers – Caught in the Web of the Symbolic Order of Gender', *Acta Sociologica*, 40(3), 245–61.
Hollway, W. 1983, 'Heterosexual Sex: Power and Desire for the Other', in Cartledge & Ryan (eds), *Sex and Love*, 124–40.
—— 1984, 'Gender Difference and the Production of Subjectivity', in Henriques, Hollway, Urwin, Venn & Walkerdine (eds), *Changing the Subject*, 227–63.
Hondagneu-Sotelo, P. & M. Messner 1994, 'Gender Displays and Men's Power', in Brod & Kaufman (eds), *Theorising Masculinities*, 200–18.
Hood, J. (ed.) 1993, *Men, Work and Family*, Sage, Newbury Park.
Horkheimer, M. 1972a, *Critical Theory* (trans. J. Cummings), Herder & Herder, New York.

—— 1972b, 'Authority and the Family', in Horkheimer, *Critical Theory*, 47–131.

Hughes, K. (ed.) 1994, *Contemporary Australian Feminism*, Longman Cheshire, Melbourne.

Hwang, C. 1987, 'The Changing Role of Swedish Fathers', in Lamb (ed.), *The Father's Role*, 115–38.

Ilg, F. & L. Ames 1962, *Parents Ask*, Harper & Row, New York.

Ingham, M. 1984, *Men*, Century, London.

Ironmonger, D. (ed.) 1989a, *Households Work*, Allen & Unwin, Sydney.

—— 1989b, *Australian Households: A $90 Billion Industry*, Centre for Applied Research on the Future, University of Melbourne, Melbourne.

Jackson, B. 1983, *Fatherhood*, George Allen & Unwin, London.

Jackson, S. 1996, *Christine Delphy*, Sage, London.

Jackson, S. & S. Scott 1997, 'Gut Reactions to Matters of the Heart: Reflections on Rationality, Irrationality and Sexuality', *Sociological Review*, 45(4), 551–75.

James, D. 1988, 'Fatherhood: An Emerging Frontier for Social Workers', *Australian Social Work*, 41(2), 5–8.

James, D. & G. Russell 1987, 'Reproduction and the New Man', *Australian Journal of Sex, Marriage & Family*, 8(3), 124–33.

James, N. 1989, 'Emotional Labour: Skill and Work in the Social Regulation of Feelings', *Sociological Review*, 37(1), 16–42.

John, D. & B. Shelton 1997, 'The Production of Gender among Black and White Women: The Case of Household Labor', *Sex Roles*, 36(3/4), 171–93.

Jonasdottir, A. 1988a, 'Sex/Gender, Power and Politics: Towards a Theory of the Foundations of Male Authority in the Formally Equal Society', *Acta Sociologica*, 31(2), 157–74.

—— 1988b, 'On the Concept of Interest, Women's Interests and the Limitations of Interest Theory', in Jones & Jonasdottir (eds), *The Political Interests of Gender*, 33–65.

Jones, K. & A. Jonasdottir (eds) 1988, *The Political Interests of Gender*, Sage, London.

Jump, T. & L. Haas 1987, 'Fathers in Transition: Dual-Career Fathers Participating in Child Care', in Kimmel (ed.), *Changing Men*, 98–114.

Kallstrom, G. 1995, 'Domestic Help: Class Oppression or a Necessity?', *Nord Nytt*, 57(March), 87–95.

Kamo, Y. 1988, 'Determinants of the Household Division of Labor', *Journal of Family Issues*, 9(2), 177–200.

Kaufman, M. (ed.) 1987a, *Beyond Patriarchy*, OUP, Toronto.

—— 1987b, 'The Construction of Masculinity and the Triad of Men's Violence', in Kaufman (ed.), *Beyond Patriarchy*, 1–29.

—— 1994, 'Men, Feminism and Men's Contradictory Experiences of Power', in Brod & Kaufman (eds), *Theorising Masculinities*, 142–63.

Kimmel, M. (ed.) 1987, *Changing Men: New Directions in Research on Men and Masculinity*, Sage, Newbury Park.

Kimmel, M. & M. Kaufman 1997, 'Weekend Warriors: The New Men's Movement', in Walsh (ed.), *Women, Men and Gender*, 406–20.

Kimmel, M. & M. Messner (eds) 1989, *Men's Lives*, Macmillan, New York.

Koedt, A., E. Levine & A. Rapne (eds) 1973, *Radical Feminism*, Quadrangle, New York.

Komarovsky, M. 1976, *Dilemmas of Masculinity: A Study of College Youth*, Norton, New York.

Komter, A. 1989, 'Hidden Power in Marriage', *Gender and Society*, 3(2), 187–216.

Kraemer, S. 1995, 'What are Fathers for?', in Burck & Speed (eds), *Gender, Power and Relationships*, 202–17.

Kroker, A. & M. Kroker 1991, *The Hysterical Male: New Feminist Theory*, St Martin's Press, New York.

Kunzler, J. 1994, 'Why Men Do (No) Housework? Explaining Male Participation in Domestic Labor: A Meta-Analysis', Conference Paper, International Sociological Association, Madrid.

Laclau, E. & C. Mouffe 1985, *Hegemony and Socialist Strategy: Towards a Radical Democratic Politics*, Verso, London.

—— 1987, 'Post-Marxism without Apologies', *New Left Review*, 166, 79–106.

Lake, M. 1986a, 'The Politics of Respectability: Identifying the Masculinist Context', *Historical Studies*, 22(86), 116–31.

—— 1986b, 'A Question of Time', in McKnight (ed.), *Moving Left*, 135–48.

—— 1989, 'Sidelines', *The Age Monthly Review*, October, 11.

Lamb, M. (ed.) 1986, *The Father's Role: Applied Perspectives*, Wiley, New York.

—— 1987, *The Father's Role: Cross-Cultural Perspectives*, Lawrence Erlbaum, Hillsdale.

Lamb, M. & J. Levine 1983, 'The Swedish Parental Insurance Policy: An Experiment in Social Engineering', in Lamb & Sagi (eds), *Fatherhood and Family Policy*, 39–51.

Lamb, M. & A. Sagi (eds) 1983, *Fatherhood and Family Policy*, Lawrence Erlbaum, Hillsdale.

Laquer, T. 1990, 'The Facts of Fatherhood', in Hirsch & Keller (eds), *Conflicts in Feminism*, 205–21.

LaRossa, R. 1988, 'Fatherhood and Social Change', *Family Relations*, 37, 451–7.

—— 1997, *The Modernization of Fatherhood: A Social and Political History*, University of Chicago Press, Urbana.

Leahy, T. 1990, Lectures on Feminism, no. 2, unpublished manuscript, Sydney.

Lee, J. 1988, 'Care to Join Me in an Upwardly Mobile Tango?: Postmodernism and the "New Woman"', in Gamman & Marshment (eds), *The Female Gaze*, 166–72.

Lengermann, P. & J. Niebrugge-Brantley 1990, 'Feminist Sociological Theory: The Near-Future Prospects', in Ritzer (ed.), *Frontiers of Social Theory*, 316–44.

Leonard, D. 1987, 'Review of R. Hertz, *More Equal than Others*', *Work, Employment and Society*, 1, 410–11.

Leonard, D. & L. Adkins (eds) 1996, *Sex in Question: French Materialist Feminism*, Taylor & Francis, London.

Leonard, D. Barker & S. Allen (eds) 1976, *Dependence and Exploitation in Work and Marriage*, Longman, London.

Leonard, P. 1984, *Personality and Ideology*, Macmillan, London.

Lewis, C. 1986, *Becoming a Father*, Open University Press, Milton Keynes.

Lewis, C. & M. O'Brien (eds) 1987, *Reassessing Fatherhood*, Sage, London.

Lewis, G. 1983, *Real Men Like Violence*, Kangaroo, Sydney.

Lewis, R. (ed.) 1981, *Men in Difficult Times*, Prentice-Hall, Englewood Cliffs NJ.

Lewis, R. 1986, 'Introduction; What Men Get Out of Marriage and Parenthood', in Lewis & Salt (eds), *Men in Families*, 11–25.

Lewis, R. & R. Salt (eds) 1986, *Men in Families*, Sage, Newbury Park.

Light, D. & S. Keller 1985, *Sociology*, 4th edn, Knopf, New York.

Lindsey, L. 1997, *Gender Roles: A Sociological Perspective*, Prentice-Hall, Upper Saddle River NJ.

Link, A. (ed.) 1967, *The Papers of Woodrow Wilson, vol. 2: 1881–1884*, Princeton University Press, Princeton.

Lisak, D. 1991, 'Sexual Aggression, Masculinity and Fathers', *Signs*, 16(2), 238–62.

Livingstone, D. & M. Luxton 1989, 'Gender Consciousness at Work: Modification of the Male Breadwinner Norm Among Steelworkers and their Spouses', *Canadian Review of Sociology and Anthropology*, 26(2), 240–75.

Locker, B. 1984, 'Multiple Role Women', *Australian Journal of Sex, Marriage & Family*, 5(1), 6–15.

Lummis, T. 1982, 'The Historical Dimension of Fatherhood: A Case Study 1890–1914', in McKee & O'Brien (eds), *The Father Figure*, 43–56.

Lupri, E. & G. Symons 1982, 'The Emerging Symmetrical Family: Fact or Fiction?', *International Journal of Comparative Sociology*, 23(3/4), 166–89.

Luxton, M. 1983, 'Two Hands for the Clock: Changing Patterns in the Gendered Division of Labour in the Home', *Studies in Political Economy*, 12, 27–44.

Lynch, K. 1989, 'Solidary Labour: Its Nature and Marginalization', *Sociological Review*, 37(1), 1–14.

Lynd, R. & H. Lynd 1929, *Middletown: A Study in American Culture*, Harcourt & Brace, New York.

MacDonald, K. & R. Parke 1984, 'Bridging the Gap: Parent–child Play Interaction and Peer Interactive Competence', *Child Development*, 55, 1265–77.

Machung, A. 1989, 'Talking Career, Thinking Job: Gender Differences in Career and Family Expectations of Berkeley Seniors', *Feminist Studies*, 15(1), 35–58.

Mackay, H. 1989, *The Mackay Report: Men and Women*, Mackay Research, Sydney.

—— 1991, *The Family: '90s Style*, Mackay Research, Sydney.

Macklin, E. & R. Rubin (eds) 1983, *Contemporary Families and Alternative Lifestyles*, Sage, Beverly Hills.

Manke, B., B. Seery, A. Crouter & S. McHale 1994, 'The Three Corners of Domestic Labor: Mother's, Father's and Children's Weekday and Weekend Housework', *Journal of Marriage and the Family*, 56, 657–68.

Mansfield, P. & J. Collard 1988, *The Beginning of the Rest of Your Life?*, Macmillan, London.

Margolis, M. 1984, *Mothers and Such*, University of California Press, Berkeley.

Marsiglio, W. (ed.) 1995, *Fatherhood: Contemporary Theory, Research and Social Policy*, Sage, Thousand Oaks.

Martin, J. & C. Roberts 1984, *Women and Employment: A Lifetime Perspective*, Her Majesty's Stationery Office, London.

Massey, G., K. Hahn & D. Sekulic 1995, 'Women, Men and the "Second Shift" in Socialist Yugoslavia', *Gender and Society*, 9(3), 359–79.

Maynard, M. 1990, 'The Re-Shaping of Sociology? Trends in the Study of Gender', *Sociology*, 24(2), 269–90.

McKee, L. 1982, 'Fathers' Participation in Infant Care: A Critique', in McKee & O'Brien (eds), *The Father Figure*, 120–38.

McKee, L. & M. O'Brien (eds) 1982, *The Father Figure*, Tavistock, London.

McKnight, D. (ed.) 1986, *Moving Left: The Future of Socialism in Australia*, Pluto Press, Sydney.

Meissner, M., E. Humphreys, S. Meis & W. Scheu 1975, 'No Exit for Wives: Sexual Division of Labour and the Cumulation of Household Demands', *Canadian Review of Sociology and Anthropology*, 12(4), 424–39.

Messner, M. 1993, '"Changing Men" and Feminist Politics in the United States', *Theory and Society*, 22, 723–37.

Metcalf, A. & M. Humphries (eds) 1985, *The Sexuality of Men*, Pluto, London.

Meth, R. & R. Pasick (eds) 1990, *Men in Therapy*, Guilford, New York.

Miles, A. 1991, 'Confessions of a Harlequin Reader: Romance and the Myth of Male Mothers', in Kroker & Kroker (eds), *The Hysterical Male*, 92–131.

Mill, J. S. 1984a (1869), 'The Subjection of Women', in Mill, *Essays on Equality*, 261–82.

——— 1984b (1869), *Essays on Equality, Law and Education* (ed. J. Robson), University of Toronto Press, Toronto.

Miller, J. & H. Garrison 1982, 'Sex Roles: The Division of Labor at Home and in the Workplace', *Annual Review of Sociology*, 8, 237–62.

Miller, J. Baker 1976, *Toward a New Psychology of Women*, Beacon, Boston.

Minkowitz, D. 1995, 'In the Name of the Father', *Ms*, 6(3), 64–71.

Mintz, S. & S. Kellogg 1988, *Domestic Revolutions: A Social History of American Family Life*, Macmillan, New York.

Mitscherlich, A. 1969, *Society Without the Father*, Tavistock, London.

Molyneux, M. 1979, 'Beyond the Domestic Labour Debate', *New Left Review*, 116, 3–27.

Montaigne, M. 1958, *Essays* (trans. J. Cohen), Penguin, Harmondsworth.

Moorcock, M. 1988, 'Manwatching', *New Statesman and Society*, 5(August), 34–5.

Moore, S. 1988, 'Getting a Bit of the Other: The Pimps of Post-Modernism', in Chapman & Rutherford (eds), *Male Order*, 165–92.

——— 1989, 'The Year of the Post-Man', *New Statesman and Society*, 6 (January), 47.

——— 1990, 'Fathers in Waiting', *New Statesman and Society*, 2(March), 41–2.

Morgan, D. 1992, *Discovering Men*, Routledge, London.

Morrison, P. 1991, 'Pregnant Fatherhood: 2 Years On', in Seidler (ed.), *The Achilles Heel Reader*, 103–24.

Morrow, V. 1996, 'Rethinking Childhood Dependency', *Sociological Review*, 44(1), 58–77.

Mort, F. 1996, *Cultures of Consumption: Masculinities and Social Space in Late Twentieth-Century Britain*, Routledge, London.

Mott, F. 1993, *Absent Fathers and Child Development: Emotional and Cognitive Effects at Ages Five to Nine*, Centre for Human Resource Research, Ohio State University, Columbus.

Murcott, A. 1983a, '"It's a Pleasure to Cook for Him": Food, Mealtimes and Gender in some South Wales Households', in Gamarnikow, Morgan, Purvis & Taylorson (eds), *The Public and the Private*, 78–90.

——— (ed.) 1983b, *The Sociology of Food and Eating*, Gower, Aldershot.

Nakhaie, M. 1995, 'Housework in Canada: The National Picture', *Journal of Comparative Family Studies*, 26(3), 409–25.

Nava, M. 1983, 'From Utopian to Scientific Feminism? Early Feminist Critiques of the Family', in Segal (ed.), *What is to be Done about the Family?*, 65–105.

Neveu, E. 1990, '"Sociostyles": Un Fin de Siècle sans Classes', *Sociologie du Travail*, 32(2), 137–54.

Newson, J. & E. Newson 1963, *Patterns of Infant Care in an Urban Community*, Penguin, Harmondsworth.

Nock, S. & P. Kingston 1988, 'Time with Children: The Impact of Couples' Work-Time Commitments', *Social Forces*, 67(1), 59–85.

Oakley, A. 1974, *The Sociology of Housework*, Robertson, Bath.

——— 1986, 'Feminism and Motherhood', in Richards & Light (eds), *Children of Social Worlds*, 74–94.

Okin, S. 1989, *Justice, Gender and the Family*, Basic Books, New York.

Orbach, S. & L. Eichenbaum 1983, *What Do Women Want?*, Michael Joseph, London.

Osherson, S. 1986, *Finding Our Fathers*, Fawcett Columbine, New York.

Owen, D. 1984, 'Bringing Up Baby', *New Republic*, 1 October, 38–40.

Pahl, J. 1989, *Money and Marriage*, Macmillan, London.

Parke, R. & D. Sawin 1975, 'Infant Characteristics and Behaviour as Elicitors of Maternal and Paternal Responsibility in the Newborn Period', Conference, Society for Research in Child Development, Denver, April.

—— 1980, 'The Family in Early Infancy: Social Interactional and Attitudinal Analyses', in Pedersen (ed.), *The Father–Infant Relationship*.

Parke, R., K. MacDonald, A. Beitel & N. Bhavnagri 1988, 'The Role of the Family in the Development of Peer Relationships', in Peters & McMahon (eds), *Social Learning and Systems Approaches*, 17–44.

Parke R., S. O'Leary & S. West 1972, 'Mother–Father–Newborn Interaction: Effects of Maternal Medication, Labor and Sex of Infant', Proceedings of the 80th Annual Convention of the American Psychological Association, 7, 85–6.

Pateman, C. 1988, *The Sexual Contract*, Polity, Cambridge.

Pease, B. 1992, 'Teaching Anti-Patriarchal Men's Studies in Social Work', 26th International Congress of Schools of Social Work, Washington, 15–19 July.

Pedersen, F. (ed.) 1980, *The Father–Infant Relationship: Observational Studies in a Family Context*, Preager, New York.

Peters, R. & R. McMahon (eds) 1988, *Social Learning and Systems Approaches to Marriage and the Family*, Brunner/Mazel, New York.

Peterson, S. 1984, 'Against "Parenting"', in Trebilcot (ed.), *Mothering*, 62–9.

Phillips, G. 1986, 'Men Talking to Men About Their Relationships', *American Behavioural Scientist*, 29(3), 321–41.

Pleck, J. 1985, *Working Wives, Working Husbands*, Sage, Beverly Hills.

—— 1987, 'Employment and Fatherhood: Issues and Innovative Policies', in Lamb (ed.), *The Father's Role*, 385–412.

Pollitt, K. 1992, 'Are Women Morally Superior to Men?', *Nation*, 28 December.

Pollock, L. 1984, *Forgotten Children*, CUP, Cambridge.

Popenoe, D. 1996, *Life without Father*, Simon & Schuster, New York.

Prescott, E. 1983, 'New Men', *American Demographics*, 5(August), 16–21, 45.

Presser, H. 1988, 'Shift Work and Child Care among Young Dual-Earner American Parents', *Journal of Marriage and the Family*, 50, 133–48.

Promise Keepers 1994, *Seven Promises of a Promise Keeper*, Focus on the Family, Colorado Springs.

Ptacek, J. 1988, 'Why Do Men Batter Their Wives?', in Yllo & Bograd (eds), *Feminist Perspectives on Wife Abuse*, 133–57.

Quinn, R. & G. Staines 1979, *Quality of Employment Survey, 1977*, Inter-University Consortium for Political and Social Research, Ann Arbor.

Reed, P. 1990, 'Beyond Bondage', *New Statesman and Society*, 20 (July), 31–2.

Reiger, K. 1985, *The Disenchantment of the Home: Modernizing the Australian Family 1880–1940*, OUP, Melbourne.

Ribble, M. 1943, *The Rights of Infants*, Columbia University Press, New York.

Rich-Shea, L. 1987, 'The Co-Parenting Father', in Abbott (ed.), *New Men, New Minds*, 26–30.

Richards, B. (ed.) 1984, *Capitalism and Infancy*, Free Association Books, London.

Richards, M. 1982, 'How Should We Approach the Study of Fathers?', in McKee & O'Brien (eds), *The Father Figure*, 57–71.

Richards, M. & P. Light (eds) 1986, *Children of Social Worlds: Development in a Social Context*, Polity, Cambridge.

Richman, J. 1982, 'Men's Experiences of Pregnancy and Childbirth', in McKee & O'Brien (eds), *The Father Figure*, 89–103.

Ritzer, G. (ed.) 1990, *Frontiers of Social Theory: The New Synthesis*, Columbia University Press, New York.

Robinson, B. & R. Barret 1986, *The Developing Father: Emerging Roles in Contemporary Society*, Guilford, New York.

Robinson, J. 1988, 'Who's Doing the Housework?', *American Demographics*, 10(12), 24ff.

Robinson, J. & G. Godby 1997, *Time for Life: The Surprising Ways Americans Use Their Time*, Pennsylvania University Press, University Park, PA.

Roeber, J. 1987, *Shared Parenthood: A Handbook for Fathers*, Century, London.

Ross, C. 1987, 'The Division of Labor at Home', *Social Forces*, 65(3), 816–33.

Ross, C., J. Mirowsky & J. Huber 1983, 'Dividing Work, Sharing Work and In-Between: Marriage Patterns and Depression', *American Sociological Review*, 48, 809–23.

Ross, J. 1979, 'Fathering: A Review of Some Psychoanalytic Contributions on Paternity', *International Journal of Psychoanalysis*, 60, 317–27.

Rubin, L. 1985, *Intimate Strangers*, Fontana, London.

Ruddick, S. 1990, 'Thinking about Fathers', in Hirsch & Keller (eds), *Conflicts in Feminism*, 222–33.

Russell, G. 1978, 'The Father Role and Its Relation to Masculinity, Femininity and Androgyny', *Child Development*, 49, 1174–81.

—— 1983a, *The Changing Role of Fathers?*, UQP, St Lucia.

—— 1983b, *A Practical Guide for Fathers*, Nelson, Melbourne.

—— 1986, 'Primary Caretaking and Role-Sharing Fathers', in Lamb (ed.), *The Father's Role*, 29–57.

—— 1987, 'Problems in Role-Reversed Families', in Lewis & O'Brien (eds), *Reassessing Fatherhood*, 161–79.

Russell, G., D. James & J. Watson 1988, 'Work/Family Policies: The Changing Role of Fathers and the Presumption of Shared Responsibility for Parenting', *Australian Journal of Social Issues*, 23(4), 249–67.

Russell, G. & A. Russell 1987, 'Mother–Child and Father–Child Relationships in Middle Childhood', *Child Development*, 58, 1573–85.

Rutherford, J. 1988, 'Who's That Man?', in Chapman & Rutherford (eds), *Male Order*, 21–67.

Ryan, T. 1985, 'Roots of Masculinity', in Metcalf & Humphries (eds), *The Sexuality of Men*, 15–27.

Salk, L. 1972, *What Every Child Would Like His Parents to Know*, McKay, New York.

Sanchez, L. 1993, 'Women's Power and the Gendered Division of Labor in the Third World', *Gender and Society*, 7(3), 434–59.

—— 1994, 'Material Resources, Family Structure Resources and Husbands' Housework Participation: A Cross-National Comparison', *Journal of Family Issues*, 15(3), 379–402.

Saraceno, C. 1987, 'Division of Family Labour and Gender Identity', in Sassoon (ed.), *Women and the State*, 191–206.

Sarachild, K., C. Hanisch, F. Levine, B. Leon & C. Price (eds) 1978, *Feminist Revolution: An Abridged Edition with Additional Writings*, Random House, New York.

Sargent, L. (ed.) 1981, *The Unhappy Marriage of Marxism and Feminism*, Pluto, London.

Sassoon, A. (ed.) 1987, *Women and the State*, Hutchinson, London.

Sattel, J. 1989, 'The Inexpressive Male: Tragedy or Sexual Politics', in Kimmel & Messner (eds), *Men's Lives*, 374–82.

Schumm, W. 1987, 'Feminism and Family Studies: Another Viewpoint', *Journal of Family Issues*, 8(2), 253–6.

Schwalbe, M. 1996, *Unlocking the Iron Cage: The Men's Movement, Gender Politics and American Culture*, OUP, New York.

Scutt, J. 1983, *Even in the Best of Homes: Violence in the Family*, Penguin, Ringwood, Vic.

Sears, W. 1988, *Becoming a Father: How to Nurture and Enjoy Your Baby*, Collins Dove, Melbourne.

Seccombe, W. 1974, 'The Housewife and Her Labour under Capitalism', *New Left Review*, 83, 3–24.

—— 1986, 'Reflections on the Domestic Labour Debate', in Hamilton & Barrett (eds), *The Politics of Diversity*, 190–207.

Segal, L. (ed.) 1983, *What Is to Be Done about the Family?*, Penguin, Harmondsworth.

Segal, L. 1990, *Slow Motion: Changing Masculinities, Changing Men*, Virago, London.

—— 1993, 'Changing Men: Masculinities in Context', *Theory and Society*, 22, 625–41.

—— 1994, *Straight Sex: The Politics of Pleasure*, Virago, London.

Seidler, V. 1985, 'Fear and Intimacy', in Metcalf & Humphries (eds), *The Sexuality of Men*, 150–80.

—— 1989, *Rediscovering Masculinity: Reason, Language and Sexuality*, Routledge, London.

—— (ed.) 1991, *The Achilles Heel Reader: Men, Sexual Politics and Socialism*, Routledge, London.

Shamir, B. 1986, 'Unemployment and the Household Division of Labor', *Journal of Marriage and the Family*, 48(1), 195–206.

Shapiro, S. 1987, 'Sex, Gender and Fashion in Medieval and Early Modern Britain', *Journal of Popular Culture*, 20(4), 113–28.

Shelton, B. 1990, 'The Distribution of Household Tasks: Does Wife's Employment Status Make a Difference?', *Journal of Family Issues*, 11(2), 115–35.

Shelton, B. & D. John 1993, 'Does Marital Status Make a Difference?: Housework Among Married and Cohabiting Men and Women', *Journal of Family Issues*, 14(3), 401–20.

—— 1996, 'The Division of Household Labor', *Annual Review of Sociology*, 22, 299–322.

Sherrod, D. 1987, 'The Bonds of Men: Problems and Possibilities in Close Male Relationships', in Brod (ed.), *The Making of Masculinities*, 213–39.

Shorter, E. 1976, *The Making of the Modern Family*, Collins, Glasgow.

Skynner, R. & J. Cleese 1983, *Families and How To Survive Them*, Methuen, London.

Smart, C. & S. Sevenhuijsen (eds) 1989, *Child Custody and the Politics of Gender*, Routledge, London.

Smith, A. & W. Reid 1986, 'Role Expectations and Attitudes in Dual-Earner Families', *Social Casework*, 67, 394–403.

Smith, D. 1987, *The Everyday World as Problematic*, Open University Press, Milton Keynes.

Somerville, J. 1989, 'The Sexuality of Men and the Sociology of Gender', *Sociological Review*, 37(2), 277–307.

South, S. & G. Spitze 1994, 'Housework in Marital and Nonmarital Households', *American Sociological Review*, 59, 327–47.

Spock, B. 1968, *Baby and Child Care*, Hawthorn, New York.

Stanley, S., J. Hunt & L. Hunt 1986, 'The Relative Deprivation of Husbands in Dual-Earner Households', *Journal of Family Issues*, 7(1), 3–20.

Stevens, J. & M. Mathews (eds) 1978, *Mother/Child Father/Child Relationships*, National Association for the Education of Young Children, Washington.

Stockman, N, N. Bonney & Sheng Xuewen 1995, *Women's Work in East and West: The Dual Burden of Employment and Family Life*, UCL Press, London.

Stoller, R. 1975, *The Transsexual Experiment*, Hogarth Press, London.

Sullivan, O. 1997, 'Time Waits for No (Wo)man: An Investigation of the Gendered Experience of Domestic Time', *Sociology*, 31(2), 221–39.

Syfers, J. 1973, 'Why I Want a Wife', in Koedt, Levine & Rapne (eds), *Radical Feminism*, 60–3.

Szirom, T. 1988, *Teaching Gender?: Sex Education and Sexual Stereotypes*, Allen & Unwin, Sydney.

Tavris, C. 1992, *The Mismeasure of Woman*, Simon & Schuster, New York.

Thagaard, T. 1997, 'Gender, Power and Love: A Study of Interaction between Spouses', *Acta Sociologica*, 40(4), 357–76.

Thomas, C. 1995, 'Domestic Labour and Health: Bringing It All Back Home', *Sociology of Health and Illness*, 17(3), 328–52.

Thompson, L. & A. Walker 1989, 'Gender in Families: Women and Men in Marriage, Work and Parenthood', *Journal of Marriage and the Family*, 51, 845–71.

Thorne, B. & M. Yalom (eds) 1982, *Rethinking the Family: Some Feminist Questions*, Longman, New York.

Thornton, A. 1989, 'Changing Attitudes Towards Family Issues in the United States', *Journal of Marriage and the Family*, 51, 873–93.

Throssell, K. 1991, 'Farewell the Corporate Man', *Australian Left Review*, May, 22–7.

Tichenor, V. 1997, 'Marital Power Dynamics as a By-Product of Doing Gender: The Case of Cross-Class Families', Conference Paper, Conference of the American Sociological Association, Toronto.

Titmuss, R. 1958, *Essays on 'The Welfare State'*, Unwin University Books, London.

Townsend, B. & K. O'Neill 1990, 'American Women Get Mad', *American Demographics*, August.

Travers, P. & S. Richardson 1993, *Living Decently: Material Well-being in Australia*, OUP, Melbourne.

Trebilcot, J. (ed.) 1984, *Mothering: Essays in Feminist Theory*, Rowman & Allenhead, Totowa.

Ungerson, C. 1983, 'Why Do Women Care?', in Finch & Groves (eds), *A Labour of Love*, 31–49.

Vallender, I. 1988, *The Father's Role in the Family*, National Children's Bureau, London.

Van Leeuwen, M. 1997, 'Servanthood or Soft Patriarchy? A Christian Feminist Looks at the Promise Keepers Movement', *Journal of Men's Studies*, 5(3), 233–61.

VanEvery J. 1995, 'De/Reconstructing Gender: Women in Antisexist Living Arrangements', *Women's Studies International Forum*, 18(3), 256–69.

Wajcman, J. 1996, 'The Domestic Basis for the Managerial Career', *Sociological Review*, 44(4), 609–79.

Walby, S. 1989, 'Theorizing Patriarchy', *Sociology*, 23(2), 213–34.

—— 1990, *Theorizing Patriarchy*, Blackwell, Oxford.

Walkerdine, V. & H. Lucey 1989, *Democracy in the Kitchen: Regulating Mothers and Socializing Daughters*, Virago, London.

Walsh, M. (ed.) 1997, *Women, Men and Gender*, Yale University Press, New Haven.

Wandor, M. (ed.) 1972, *The Body Politic: Writings from the Women's Liberation Movement in Britain 1969–1972*, stage 1, London.

Ward, R. 1993, 'Marital Happiness and Household Equity in Later Life', *Journal of Marriage and the Family*, 55, 427–38 .

Warde, A. 1990, 'Household Work Strategies and Forms of Labour: Conceptual and Empirical Issues', *Work, Employment and Society*, 4(4), 495–515.

Wearing, B. 1984, *The Ideology of Motherhood*, George Allen & Unwin, Sydney.

—— 1994, *Gender: The Pain and Pleasure of Difference*, Longman Cheshire, Melbourne.

Wearing, B. & S. Wearing 1988, '"All in a Day's Leisure": Gender and the Concept of Leisure', *Leisure Studies*, 7, 111–23.

Weber, M. 1968, *Max Weber, Economy and Society* (ed. G. Roth & C. Wittich), Bedminster, New York.

Weeks, W. & R. Batten 1991, 'Women's Work and the Gendered Division of Labour', in Batten, Weeks & Wilson (eds), *Issues Facing Australian Families*, 32–45.

Weinraub, M. 1978, 'Fatherhood: The Myth of the Second-Class Parent', in Stevens & Mathews, *Mother/Child Father/Child Relationships*, 109–33.

Weiss, R. 1985, 'Men and the Family', *Family Process*, 24, 49–58.

West, C. & D. Zimmerman 1987, 'Doing Gender', *Gender and Society*, 1, 125–51.

West, C. & S. Fenstermaker 1995, 'Doing Difference,' *Gender and Society*, 9(1), 8–37.

Wheelock, J. 1990, *Husbands at Home*, Routledge, London.

White, N. 1984, 'On Being One of the Boys: An Exploratory Study of Women's Professional and Domestic Role Definitions', *Women's Studies International Forum*, 7(6), 433–40.

Williamson, J. 1988, 'Having Your Baby and Eating It', *New Statesman*, 15 April, 44–5.

Wilson, J. 1990, *Single Fathers*, Sun, Melbourne.

Wittig, M. 1996, 'The Category of Sex', in Leonard & Adkins (eds), *Sex in Question*, 24–9.

Wolcott, I. 1990, 'Between Tradition and Transition: Workers with Family Responsibilities', *Australian Journal of Social Issues*, 25(4), 290–300.

Wortis, R. 1972, 'Child-Rearing and Women's Liberation', in Wandor (ed.), *The Body Politic*, 124–30.

Wright, E., K. Shire, S. Hwang, M. Dolan & J. Baxter 1992, 'The Non-Effects of Class on the Gender Division of Labor in the Home', *Gender and Society*, 6(2), 252–82.

Yllo, K. & M. Bograd (eds) 1988, *Feminist Perspectives on Wife Abuse*, Sage, Newbury Park.

Young, I. 1981, 'Beyond the Unhappy Marriage: Critique of the Dual Systems Theory', in Sargent (ed.), *The Unhappy Marriage*, 43–69.

—— 1984, 'Is Male Gender Identity the Cause of Male Domination?', in Trebilcot (ed.), *Mothering*, 129–46.

Young, M. & P. Willmott 1957, *Family and Kinship in East London*, Routledge & Kegan Paul, London.

—— 1973, *The Symmetrical Family: A Study of Work and Leisure in the London Region*, Routledge & Kegan Paul, London.

Zhang, C. & J. Farley 1995, 'Gender and the Distribution of Household Work', *Journal of Comparative Family Studies*, 26(2), 195–205.

Zigler, E., M. Lamb & I. Child (eds) 1982, *Socialization and Personality Development*, OUP, New York.

Index